COLLEGE

IT HAPPENED TO ME

Series Editor: Arlene Hirschfelder

Books in the It Happened to Me series are designed for inquisitive teens digging for answers about social issues, certain illnesses, or lifestyle interests. These books feature up-to-date information, relatable teen views, and thoughtful suggestions to help you figure out stuff. Besides special boxes that highlight singular facts, each book is enhanced with the latest reading lists, websites, and other recommendations.

The following titles may also be of interest:

Activism: The Ultimate Teen Guide, by Kathlyn Gay
ADHD: The Ultimate Teen Guide, by John Aspromonte
Autism Spectrum Disorder: The Ultimate Teen Guide, by Francis Tabone
Bigotry and Intolerance: The Ultimate Teen Guide, by Kathlyn Gay
Bullying: The Ultimate Teen Guide, by Mathangi Subramanian
Chronic Illnesses, Syndromes, and Rare Disorders: The Ultimate Teen Guide,
    by Marlene Targ Brill
Creativity: The Ultimate Teen Guide, by Aryna M. Ryan
Depression: The Ultimate Teen Guide, by Tina P. Schwartz
Eating Disorders: The Ultimate Teen Guide, by Jessica R. Greene
Epilepsy: The Ultimate Teen Guide, 2nd Edition, by Kathlyn Gay
Food Allergies: The Ultimate Teen Guide, by Jessica Reino
Self-Injury: The Ultimate Teen Guide, by Judy Dodge Cummings
Sexual Decisions: The Ultimate Teen Guide, 2nd Edition, by L. Kris Gowen
Shyness: The Ultimate Teen Guide, by Bernardo J. Carducci, PhD, and Lisa Kaiser
Social Networking: The Ultimate Teen Guide, by Jenna Obee
Speech and Language Challenges: The Ultimate Teen Guide, by Marlene Targ Brill
Substance Abuse: The Ultimate Teen Guide, by Sheri Bestor

COLLEGE

THE ULTIMATE TEEN GUIDE

LISA MAXWELL ARTER

ROWMAN & LITTLEFIELD
Lanham • Boulder • New York • London

Published by Rowman & Littlefield
An imprint of The Rowman & Littlefield Publishing Group, Inc.
4501 Forbes Boulevard, Suite 200, Lanham, Maryland 20706
www.rowman.com

Unit A, Whitacre Mews, 26-34 Stannary Street, London SE11 4AB

British Library Cataloguing in Publication Information Available

Library of Congress Cataloging-in-Publication Data

Names: Arter, Lisa Maxwell, 1974– author.
Title: College : the ultimate teen guide / Lisa Arter.
Description: Lanham : Rowman & Littlefield, [2019] | Series: It happened to
  me | Includes bibliographical references.
Identifiers: LCCN 2018022683 (print) | LCCN 2018031045 (ebook) | ISBN
  9781538104132 (electronic) | ISBN 9781538104125 (cloth : alk. paper)
Subjects: LCSH: College student orientation—United States—Handbooks,
  manuals, etc. | Universities and colleges—Admission—Handbooks, manuals,
  etc.
Classification: LCC LB2343.32 (ebook) | LCC LB2343.32 .A77 2019 (print) | DDC
  378.1/98—dc23
LC record available at https://lccn.loc.gov/2018022683

♾™ The paper used in this publication meets the minimum requirements of American
National Standard for Information Sciences—Permanence of Paper for Printed Library
Materials, ANSI/NISO Z39.48-1992.

Printed in the United States of America

To _____,
[*write your name on the preceding line*]

without whom this monumental addition to quality literature
could not have been accomplished.
Bless you.
Special recognition goes to my mother, who taught me to write;
my husband, who encouraged me to write;
and my children, who let me write.
Abundant gratitude to Ken Ayers, Mandy Jones,
and all of the high school and college students, faculty, and staff
who shared questions, comments, and insights.
And to Kim—because shoes.

Contents

How to Use This Book   ix

Introduction   xi

Part I: Getting into College

1 Choosing a College   3

2 Applying to College   19

3 The College Visit   23

4 Financial Aid   27

5 The Acceptance   33

Part II: Staying in College

6 Housing   43

7 Classes   49

8 Who's Who   81

9 Your Health   91

10 Risky Behaviors   109

11 Relationships   127

12 Finances   141

13 Extracurricular Activities   169

14 Changes   181

Appendix A: Q&A Tour Form   187

Appendix B: Campus Tour Record   191

Appendix C: Moving List   195

Notes   205

Resources for Teens   215

Index   217

About the Author   221

How to Use This Book

Dear Book Owner (if you are a book borrower, jump to the second paragraph),
Don't just read this book—*use it*. Carry it around with you and write in it, dog-ear pages, highlight and underline important text (OK, I know that would mean *all* of it would be underlined, but you can use personal preference). It isn't a novel, so you don't need to read it in order. Jump around. Show it to your friends and roommates and encourage them to buy their own copy (seriously, I have student loans I'm still repaying. And don't judge—likely, you will, too). I want this book to look like it's survived a battle by the end of your freshman year—just like you.

Because getting into college is only the first part of the adventure, I've divided this book into two parts: (1) getting into college and (2) staying in college. Both halves are full of valuable information as well as sources that will help you deepen your understanding. To decide what I should include in this book, I spoke with current and former high school and college students, counselors, faculty, staff, administrators, residence assistants, learning support personnel, campus security, and parents. While some of the information, especially in part 2, may seem tangential to the college experience, each of those areas is a reason students have reported contributed to their decision to drop out of college. For example, not knowing how to do laundry, effectively grocery shop, or create and stick to a personal budget are stressors that contribute to a student's feeling overwhelmed. This feeling of being overwhelmed causes anxiety and/or depression to the extent that students, who are otherwise progressing in their college experience, quit. Health concerns (physical, mental, and sexual) are also frequent contributors to a student's decision to drop out. Hopefully, you will never grapple with these issues personally but it is likely that you will know a college peer who does. Having this information will better prepare you for success. As the proverb says: forewarned is forearmed.

Best of luck.

Introduction

In 1974 (ironically, the year I was born), Richard Armour published *The Academic Bestiary*, a satirical dictionary of colleges and universities. More than thirty years later, while digging through my favorite used bookstore during a brief break between doctoral classes, I came across a first-edition copy of this book (first editions make English teachers weak in the knees). Despite his having published more than sixty-five books, I had never heard of Dr. Armour. I read the back cover, giggled, and paid the six dollars for the book.

Ten years later, I still enjoy Armour's anthropomorphic descriptions of various elements of higher education, or "Academe," where life "is different from . . . the Real World in many ways, some of them incredible to the inexperienced."[1] The typical eighteen-year-old has spent two-thirds of his or her life in school, but many aspects of the Academe resemble school in only the vaguest disguise. Therefore, while some may warn that the ivory arches of a campus should quote Dante's version of *The Inferno* ("Abandon all hope, ye who enter here"), the truth is the motto of Apollo's temple in Delphi ("Know thyself") is more apt to college life (perhaps with a bit of "Remember thou art mortal" thrown in for good measure).

You may have several reasons for choosing to attend college. Common ones I hear from freshmen include an influential teacher, an occupational goal that requires a degree, wanting to leave home, and "my parents went and are making me go." If you are truly a first-generation higher education perspective student (whew—that's a long title; let's shorten it to *first-gen*), the last reason isn't pertinent to you. Although, perhaps your parents are "making" you go *because* they didn't and they want a different life for you. If you aren't a first-gen, we'll allow you to share the information as we believe in "the more the merrier" in higher education.

Whatever reason(s) you have for choosing (or even considering) to attend college, *congratulations on making the biggest decision of your life!* I'm not kidding. Attending college (followed by *where* you decide to attend college) is *the biggest decision of your life.*

Breathe.

OK, I hear you. "What about where I work?" "What about where I live?" "What about the kind of car I buy?" "What about who I marry?" "What about how many kids I have?" "What about when and where I retire?"

All important decisions. But you need to know that every single one of those will be influenced by your higher education decision.

Honestly. Stick with me for a minute.

The first should be kinda easy to realize: When you choose a college, you'll need to choose a major (more on that later). Your college and major will determine where you work. After all, isn't that one of the reasons you are considering college?

Where you live? Because of the relationships (personal and professional) you make in college, you are likely to remain in that area. If you do move, it will likely be because of a job opportunity you got because of your degree and experience (which you received from your college).

Your car? Better job = more money = more car-buying options.

Your spouse? In 2013, *USA Today* reported that 28 percent of married graduates attended the same college as their spouse.[2] The following year, the *Wall Street Journal* reported that nearly 30 percent met their spouses through friends (likely ones they made in college), and about 10 percent met their spouse through work.[3]

Kids? The *Atlantic* claims that the higher the woman's educational level, the fewer kids.[4] Not a female? You'll still need one if you want a baby and her education is quite likely to affect the number of children she gives birth to.

The CDC (Centers for Disease Control and Prevention—don't ask me why it isn't called the CDCP), reports that people with higher levels of education (and higher incomes) have lower rates of chronic diseases such as obesity (and lower obesity rates for their children), are less likely to smoke, are more likely to have health insurance, and live, on average, two to three years longer than those with only a high school diploma and almost ten years longer than those who didn't complete high school.[5]

Retirement? Both public and private retirement income is based largely on the amount of money you make during your life. Want more money in retirement? You'll need to make more money during your working years. Each year, the Bureau of Labor Statistics publishes a report explaining the national earnings and unemployment rates by educational levels. The report for 2013 showed that a person with a high school diploma made an average of $668/week.[6] A person with a bachelor's degree earned $1,101/week—almost twice as much. Additionally, a person with only a high school diploma had a 6 percent chance of being unemployed while a person with a bachelor's degree had only a 3.5 percent chance of being unemployed.

Vocabulary Moment

The term *bachelor* in *bachelor's degree* is from the medieval Latin term *baccalaureate*, which is a play on the Latin words *bacca lauri* or *laurel berries*.

When I was in high school, a teacher told our class that an education is the only thing worth going into debt for. Cars lose value as soon as you drive them off the lot. Technology is old before it hits store shelves. Real estate is a gamble. But education? No one can take it from you, and even after you make your monthly student loan payment, you still have more take-home money than you would without the degree.

Recently, the increasing cost of college and horror stories of graduates not being able to make their payments have filled the news and left many questioning whether college still pays for itself. I believe it does but please understand that when I talk about "college" I am including two-year associate degrees and vocational/technical school certificates as well as four-year bachelor's degrees. While an associate degree doesn't provide as much income as a bachelor's degree (average of $792/week and a 4.5 percent unemployment rate),[7] it is better than stopping your education after high school.

Vocational/technical schools (occasionally, they are still called trade or career schools) provide training for a specific job's necessary skill set such as mechanic, chef, and allied health care provider. Salary ranges widely depending on certification but is more (to considerably more) than minimum wage.

Does the thought of student loans still worry you? We'll discuss options such as a certificate program to help you work your way through college, grants, scholarships, completing your general education classes at a community college, military service, or a combination of options. The extra good news? There are financial aid options saved especially for first-gen students!

Full confession—I wasn't a first-gen student. But I wasn't a second-gen student either. My paternal grandparents graduated from college but my father didn't, nor did anyone on my mother's side. As such, I didn't get financial aid benefits for being a first-gen student but neither did I get instruction from parents who had gone through the college process (my grandparents had passed away by then). Fortunately, my two older sisters had gone to college so I got a little help, but most of my information came from bull-headedly and blindly bumbling through the process and asking high school friends who were first-year college students for help. It worked, but I would've *loved* a guidebook.

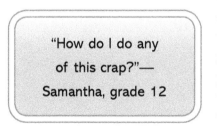

"How do I do any of this crap?"—Samantha, grade 12

The night before I left for college, my sister told me that I would change more in the next four years than I had in the previous four years. I thought back to who I was my freshman year of high school and thought, "No way! Fourteen-year-old me was *very* different than eighteen-year-old me." But she was right. Four years later, twenty-two-year-old me would be hard-pressed to even recognize eighteen-year-old me. Know thyself, indeed.

Freaked out yet? Don't be! Let me leave you with the advice my mother gave me: be on time to class; sit up front; give the teacher what she wants, when she wants it; and be yourself. Do this and you'll be just fine.

I did and I was. I promise, you will be, too.

GETTING INTO COLLEGE

CHOOSING A COLLEGE

···

In the introduction, I mentioned several different options for higher education. In the first part of this chapter, we'll discuss those different options in detail (pros and cons). My goal is not to convince you that any one option or degree is better than another. Instead, in the tradition of good teachers, I simply want to provide you with the information and skills you'll need to make the best decision for you.

Before you begin researching colleges, make a list (copy the one in table 1.1 or make your own) of ten things you want in a college and ten things you don't. For

Table 1.1 Top Ten College Wants and Don't Wants

What I Want	What I Don't Want
1.	1.
2.	2.
3.	3.
4.	4.
5.	5.
6.	6.
7.	7.
8.	8.
9.	9.
10.	10.

example, you may want a school that has a highly ranked soccer team, an award-winning music program, an active theater program, or a pre-nursing program that has 99 percent of their graduates accepted into a BSN (bachelor of science in nursing) program.

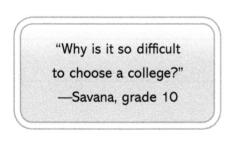

"How do you decide what college to go to?"—Ike, grade 10

Do you want a small school (fewer than five thousand students) or a large school (more than thirty thousand students)? Do you want to stay close to home or move as far away as possible? Do you want a liberal arts experience or are you looking to earn qualifications for a specific technical career? Make your lists and then begin researching colleges that fit those desires. You will be spending several years there so be honest with yourself about what you are looking for.

The three most populous states are California, Florida, and Texas, while the three least populous states are Alaska, Vermont, and Wyoming. Each populous state has small communities (Arcata, California, home to Humboldt State University, has fewer than eighteen thousand residents), while the least populous states contain big cities (the metro region of Anchorage, Alaska, is home to more than four hundred thousand people and four higher education facilities). If you are looking for a school in a metropolitan area, explore some of the cities listed in table 1.2.

Many small towns are home to colleges and universities and *size doesn't matter when it comes to quality*. Each year, the *Princeton Review* highlights the best college towns in America. These towns vary in population but all have a college feel to them with much of the area focused on the school and students. Typically, college towns have fine arts options (e.g., museums, live theater, and concerts) and sports venues (at least NCAA) you would find in larger cities. Additionally, local businesses and apartment complexes usually work closely with the school to provide part-time jobs and housing options, so don't assume that there will be fewer opportunities simply because there are fewer people.

"Why is it so difficult to choose a college?" —Savana, grade 10

With over 3,500 higher education choices in America, you can find any combination you want. For example, I earned my BA and MA from a very small (fewer than 1,500 undergraduates) religious institution in a large city (over

Table 1.2 The Ten Most Populous Cities with at Least One Institution of Higher Education

City	Population
New York, NY	8.5 million
Los Angeles, CA	4 million
Chicago, IL	2.7 million
Houston, TX	2.3 million
Philadelphia, PA	1.5 million
Phoenix, AZ	1.5 million
San Antonio, TX	1.4 million
San Diego, CA	1.4 million
Dallas, TX	1.3 million
San Jose, CA	1 million

"What types of colleges are there?"
—Dakota, grade 10

300,000 people) with ten colleges in the city (including a community college, two trade schools, two religious schools, and a state university). The school was on the West Coast and we were within an hour of the Pacific Ocean, snow skiing, the desert, and Disneyland. My doctorate was at a very large university (over 70,000 students) in a metropolis (over 1.5 million) in the Southwest where I was within one hour of the desert and—well, only the desert. *So much desert.* I now teach at a large(ish) school (over 10,000 undergraduates) in a small(ish) city (about 30,000 residents) in the Rocky Mountains surrounded by state and national parks.

With so much to consider, the first thing you should understand is the types of colleges available.

The "best" college for a student is the college that offers a student the most opportunities to develop a student's interests and career goals. © *iStock / cacaroot*

Types of Colleges

Vocational/Technical/Trade/Career School

A vocational school provides you with the knowledge and skills for a specific job. In contrast, a bachelor's degree gives you a wider range of knowledge and skills to prepare you for a choice of various jobs you'll be qualified for. While bachelor's degree programs take four to five years to complete, many vocational programs can be completed in two years or less.

If you want a hands-on career and already know what you are interested in doing (versus taking a few years of general education classes and trying to "find" yourself), a vocational school may be the perfect fit for you.

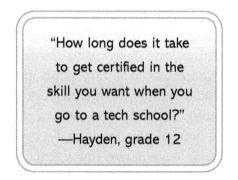

"How long does it take to get certified in the skill you want when you go to a tech school?"
—Hayden, grade 12

Have you ever wondered why you couldn't take a class at school that truly interests you, such as learning about the culinary arts or discovering the ins and outs of being an emergency medical technician? Vocational education is an option that is becoming increasingly popular for students seeking a wider variety of class choices. Sometimes, when people hear the words *vocational education*, a negative image pops into their minds. Many people believe that vocational education is primarily offered to non–college-bound students, dropouts, or students with special needs. What people don't realize is that vocational education can give students the opportunity to improve their employability skills, become informed about different career options, and learn helpful skills they can use throughout the rest of their lives even before going to college and being released into the real world.[1]

"What kind of classes are there? Do we just sit there for 2 hours?"
—Rudy, grade 8

Before you discount vocational schools or professions, consider that *Forbes* reports the hardest positions to fill are those in the trade professions such as welders, truck drivers, and machinists.[2] Additionally, much of the labor force that is trained in vocational trades is aging out. This combination means that there will be many job positions for skilled laborers. *CNN Money* reports that millions of jobs are available but there aren't skilled vocational workers to fill them.[3] There are dozens of careers that pay twenty-five to fifty dollars an hour that you can train for at a vocational college.

Thinking of vocational school but still worried about affording the tuition? The Mike Rowe Works Foundation offers scholarships for students wanting to train for vocational positions. For more information on employment and scholarship opportunities, visit ProfoundlyDisconnected.com.

Just as different colleges don't offer the exact same degree options, vocational schools don't always offer the same programs as other vocational schools. However, the typical vocational school offers certificates, licenses, or associate degrees in hands-on, skills-based career areas.

Do you like working with your hands? Do you enjoy the satisfaction of building and fixing things? Vocational schools specialize in hands-on training in many areas of mechanics. If you like working with vehicles, you can certify as a mechanic on everything from motorcycles to small engines to diesel/heavy truck maintenance.

Is woodworking your thing? Certified carpenters—including cabinet and/or furniture makers and those specializing in home repairs or full remodels—are in demand. I have a friend who is a certified carpenter who builds movie sets in Hollywood.

Wood isn't the only part of a house that needs repairs. Plumbing and HVACR (heating, ventilation, air conditioning, and refrigeration) technicians are kept quite busy and often work emergency hours (which is code for overtime pay). Each time a house is sold, a certified home inspector must examine the house for needed repairs. For each of these positions, you can work for a company or as an independent contractor (own your own business) or build your own business with people working for you! The average annual salary for each of these is $46,000 to $50,000 and many technicians also receive a benefits package (health insurance and retirement).

If fixing things isn't your dream job, what about working with patients? Specifically, do you enjoy working to make sick people well and helping healthy people stay that way? You don't have to be a doctor or a nurse to be a health-care worker. A vocational school can train you for many positions in the medical and dental industries including: dental assistant, LPN/LVN (licensed practical nurse/

Did You Know?

Harrison Ford was a full-time carpenter who worked small acting jobs for money to remodel his house when George Lucas asked him to help read with other actors auditioning for *Star Wars*.

licensed vocational nurse), pharmacy technician, phlebotomist, radiology technician, massage therapist, or as a physical therapy or occupational therapy aide. Are you interested in the medical field but not excited about working directly with people? Consider medical billing and coding, an office occupation that some companies are willing to let you do from home. Are you interested in medical but think these jobs sound boring? Consider becoming an EMT (emergency medical technician)—yes, the people who drive the ambulances!

Are you an animal person but not sure that an extra four years of college beyond your bachelor's degree (and at least one additional year of internship) is worth it? A vocational school can train you as a veterinary assistant in as little as two years.

Do you like animals but prefer to avoid the medical side? You can become a certified dog obedience trainer or a pet groomer. Or, you could earn certifications in both to give yourself career options. These positions are filled with people working for companies (even big ones such as PetCo and PetSmart) or for themselves as independent business owners.

Are you a health nut who loves to work out in a gym but you realize that being a customer doesn't pay well? Consider becoming a personal trainer and working with other people who share your passion for physical fitness.

What about computers? Jobs for certified computer/technology technicians are varied and available. Web page designers, technical writers, coders, IT professionals, network associates, PC maintenance and repair, AutoCAD drafters . . . the list goes on.

Does the thought of being at a desk for forty hours/week make you cringe? Do you want a job where you can spend time outdoors? Vocational programs can prepare you for stepping outside of your house with landscape design and management or stepping into state and national park service through wildlife and forestry conservation.

Are you creative and can see yourself helping others to achieve their creative dreams? Do your friends and family members ask for your opinion on what to wear, what to eat, or how to decorate? You can become certified in floral design, jewelry design and repair, dressmaking and design, catering, or do it all as an events planner. You could focus specifically on weddings or open up to all kinds of parties. Do you prefer to help people redecorate their homes? Become an interior decorator.

As I've mentioned, several of these programs would allow you to work for others (big or small companies) or to run your own business. If you choose the latter, I encourage you to return to vocational school to earn certifications in bookkeeping (basic accounting) and business management.

This is nowhere near an exhaustive list of vocational options. You can specialize in travel and tourism, hotel and restaurant management, child day care, or become a legal transcriptionist. Keep in mind that one of the biggest draws for a vocational certification is as a step toward a degree. A radiologist friend of mine worked his way through medical school as a phlebotomist (his business card said "professional blood sucker"). More than one lawyer started out as a legal transcriptionist or court reporter. Many people earn multiple certifications so they can open their own businesses and provide a range of services. Not only does this keep them in high demand, they are less likely to get bored doing the same thing each day.

Two-Year Community or Junior College

Community, or junior, colleges typically act as a less-expensive way to take your general education courses such as English and math. Most community colleges don't have on-campus housing and many partner with high schools to allow you to take some college courses while you are still living at home. As long as the college is accredited, you can transfer the credits from those classes to whatever four-year college or university you choose to attend. Some community colleges offer two-year associate degrees and a few are beginning to offer four-year bachelor's degrees.

If you are considering a two-year college, it is likely because there is one in your area so make an appointment with the recruiting department and talk to it about available courses, programs, tuition, and scholarships.

Vocabulary Moment

Accreditation is the process that acknowledges a school is qualified. Every aspect of the school—including faculty qualifications, program quality, even the safety, cleanliness, and attractiveness of the facilities—is inspected to determine the pros and cons of the school. A certain amount of quality must be shown for a school to be accredited.

Four-Year Liberal Arts College

First of all, *liberal arts* has nothing to do with political inclination. *Liberal arts* refers to a "liberality," or "the quality of being open to new ideas" on a range of subjects. A bachelor's degree from a liberal arts college will require you to take classes in a range of subjects and not just those that specifically apply to your major.

The focus of a liberal arts college is undergraduate education. As such, faculty prioritize teaching over research and publications and you are more likely to

> "Why do you have to take history and English when you don't need some of those things for what you want to go into?"—Melody, grade 10

have professors teach your classes instead of graduate students. Additionally, the student-to-teacher ratio is lower (to much lower) at a liberal arts college.

Liberal arts colleges aim to educate the whole student in breadth, as well as depth, of knowledge while helping students develop important intellectual skills that are vital in all areas of life. These skills include communication, critical thinking, and looking at a problem from an interdisciplinary angle to see the value of many different points of view.

During your first year or two at a liberal arts college, you will take a series of general education (gen ed) courses in literature, math, anthropology, sociology, philosophy, psychology, physical education, and history, among others. If you are earning a BA (bachelor of arts) instead of a BS (bachelor of science), you will also be required to take classes in a foreign language. The remainder of your degree will focus on classes specific to your major. Liberal arts colleges offer STEM-related (math, biology, computing, etc.) degrees in addition to humanities or social science degrees (history, English, psychology). Graduate schools recruit heavily from liberal arts programs as do employers.[4]

In the recent STEM-focused world, humanities and liberal arts have taken a hit but if you look at the skills employers are recruiting, you'll quickly see that a degree in liberal arts is in demand. STEM careers *may* provide higher salaries,[5] but job satisfaction ratings and better life-work balance reports are higher in non-STEM fields. Most work-life balance research focuses on gender, and because men make up a higher percentage of STEM workers, getting a clear cause-and-effect answer isn't easy. However, looking at job ranking for best work-life balance shows more non-STEM careers.

Research Universities

Research universities are large schools dedicated to the knowledge that professors produce through their professional inquiries and publications. While there are undergraduate programs, the majority of these classes are quite large and taught by graduate students. If a professor is teaching the class, it may be a lecture in a room with hundreds of students and you will still have more contact with a graduate student TA (teaching assistant), at least until you get to upper-division courses, which are often called seminars.

! Did You Know?

- The Ivy League colleges are Brown (Providence, Rhode Island), Columbia (New York City), Cornell (Ithaca, New York), Dartmouth (Hanover, New Hampshire), Harvard (Cambridge, Massachusetts), University of Pennsylvania (Philadelphia), Princeton (Princeton, New Jersey), and Yale (New Haven, Connecticut). However, less than 0.4 percent of college students attend an Ivy school.

! Vocabulary Moment

- An *undergraduate course* is one you take for a bachelor's degree; a *graduate course* is one you take for a master's or doctorate degree.

Research universities typically offer a wider range of degree programs including pre-professional degrees (pre-medicine, pre-law, etc.). They also offer more graduate school degrees for masters and doctorates. In addition to producing their own research, professors mentor graduate students and teach some undergraduate courses. Some research universities will allow you to take graduate classes as an undergraduate and participate in professor-led research. These things look great on a resume or graduate school application.

! Vocabulary Moment

- A *university* is a college that offers at least one graduate program.

A university is broken into smaller colleges or schools such as the School of Business or College of Education. This structure exists at all universities (including liberal arts colleges that have grown enough to offer graduate courses).

Specialty Colleges

Certain colleges have particular focuses in addition to research or liberal arts or technical programs. Here are the most common specialty colleges:

- *Religious schools:* Some private colleges are affiliated with a particular religion or are nondenominational but still religiously focused. This relationship may be historic (it was founded as a religious school but doesn't affect your day-to-day education) or still highly involved in the religious goals of the

---

Did You Know?

The first college to grant degrees to women was Oberlin College in 1841. In 1862, it became the first college to grant a bachelor's degree to an African American woman.[a]

---

college. These schools may require you to attend weekly chapel services, have stricter dress codes, and include a morality clause against drinking, smoking, and swearing. Most of these schools do not require you to be a member of the affiliated religion as long as you abide by the principles. In addition to typical application material, it is likely that you will need to include a statement of faith and recommendation from a member of the clergy.

- *Same-sex schools:* Most higher education institutes are coed (girls and boys), but a few private schools are still dedicated to only men or only women attending. There are only four male-only public colleges left in the United States, while thirty-seven female-only colleges remain. These schools may also be religiously affiliated (usually seminaries) but some are simply historically same-sex schools, such as Barnard College in New York City; Mills College in Oakland, California (both all female); and Hampden-Sydney College in Hampden Sydney, Virginia (all male). Many of these schools were founded originally to give females an opportunity to attend college and have decided to remain same-sex (at least their undergraduate programs) for a variety of reasons.

- *Arts schools:* Similarly to the way technical schools focus on teaching a specific trade, arts schools focus on teaching a fine arts skill such as photography, theater, fashion, or music. These can be public or private schools and are sometimes called conservatories. In addition to typical application material, you will likely need to provide a portfolio of your work such as several photographs or a video of your performances.

- *Specialized-mission colleges:* The mission of these colleges is to make higher education more available to historically underrepresented minorities. An HBCU (historically black college or university) or HSI (Hispanic-serving institution) focuses on educating African American and Hispanic/Latino/a students, respectively. Most will allow members of any ethnicity to attend, but the emphasis is on minority students and will likely have minimum quotas regarding the percentage of minority students. In 1968, the Navajo Nation founded the first tribal college in Arizona. TCUs (tribal colleges and universities) allow Native students to begin their higher education degrees near or on their home reservation communities. There are more than thirty fully accredited TCUs in the United States.

> ### Did You Know?
>
> • Named after Jehudi Ashmun (1794–1828), an American minister who helped establish Liberia, Ashmun Institute was the first college established for African American students (April 29, 1854). In 1866, Ashmun Institute was renamed Lincoln University—yep, the same Lincoln University that requires a health class for everyone with a body mass index of 30+.[b]

Location, Location, Location

Where matters! You are going to be living at the school for years. It is also possible that you will take a job close to your alma mater so you may live in that area forever. Even if you only spend a few years at that location, it will make a difference to you. Perhaps you want long, snowy winters so you can ski every weekend (of course you'll do your homework first). Maybe you are sick of snow and don't want to see another flake as long as you live.

Remember that want and don't want list you made earlier? (I told people you made it, so don't make me a liar.) If location, size of area, and weather issues weren't on those lists, make a separate list now just for those things. Go ahead. I'll wait.

OK. Once you have honestly made a list of location dos and don'ts, you can further narrow your college search. And you *must* be honest with yourself. If you don't like heat, stay out of the South. If you start to shiver once the thermometer dips below eighty degrees, avoid the North. If you need mountains to survive, the Midwest might not be the place for you. If you have severe hydrophobia (the fear of water, not rabies—although, if you do have rabies, please stop reading right now and get to the nearest hospital), you may want to stay away from the coasts and Michigan. Seriously. Michigan has the second largest total area of water (Alaska is first) with over 100,000 square miles of the wet stuff. However, percentagewise, Michigan is ranked first with its water area taking up a higher percentage of its total size than Hawaii. (Alaska is *huge* and its more than 240,000 square miles of water is only 14 percent of its total size.)

Population size also matters in regard to location. Does the hustle and bustle of millions of commuters make you feel alive? Google "most populous cities" and start looking for colleges in those areas. (Those of you who are paying attention know that I already did this for you.)

Do you prefer the only other living creature in a fifty-mile radius to be a ground squirrel? Look for colleges in small and/or rural towns. For example, the University of Idaho in Moscow is a research university with more than nine thousand undergraduates but is in a city of fewer than twenty-five thousand residents. Not rural enough? Western Carolina University serves over ten thousand students in Cullo-whee, North Carolina—a town of fewer than ten thousand residents.

Do you have health problems that are exacerbated by high altitude, excessive humidity, or particular allergies? Do your research and don't live there! Sites such as City-Data.com and WeatherSpark.com will give you all the info you need on population, altitude, average and extreme weather, and cost of living averages (you'll want to pay particular attention to this if you aren't planning on living in on-campus housing).

As you search, remember that if you go to a school outside of the state in which you currently reside, you will be considered "out of state" and will, most likely, have a significant tuition increase. When you get onto a particular school's web page and look up the cost of attendance, look at in-state and out-of-state costs.

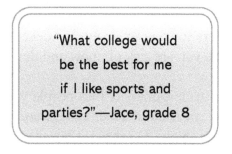

"What college would be the best for me if I like sports and parties?"—Jace, grade 8

The reason in-state is cheaper is because each state collects taxes from its citizens and gives a portion of those dollars to schools, including state colleges. (States do not fund private colleges so most private schools have the same tuition no matter where you are from.) State schools use this money to support citizen students. Instead of thinking of out-of-state tuition costing "more," realize that is the amount all students pay, and you get some tuition (the difference for in-state) paid for by the taxpayers of your fair community. It is possible to become a citizen of the state in which you are attending college but it takes at least a year and may cause problems if you are on your parents' drivers or health insurance or if they still want to claim you as a dependent on their taxes. Look into all the pros and cons before changing state citizenship.

If you are having trouble wrapping your head around all these options (and there are more than 3,500 American colleges to choose from), check out the College Search tool at College Board (bigfuture.collegeboard.org/college-search), which will help you find those schools that best fit your preference. Additionally, *US News and World Report* offers an online "College Personality Quiz" for you to take. The quiz asks you multiple-choice questions about various aspects of your life and makes suggestions for different types of colleges based on your answers.[6]

Choosing a Major or "What Do You Want to Be When You Grow Up?"

Choosing a major (and any minor, endorsement, certification, or double-major) is one of the most important decisions you can make. And, like all major decisions—except whether or not to jump out of the way of oncoming traffic—shouldn't be rushed. Personally, I believe that you should wait until your second year to declare a major.

Think of your first year as dating around with various potential professions. Don't rush into a lifelong career commitment. Your first year of college will be filled with new experiences, a broad range of general education classes, and dozens of extracurricular activities all designed to expose you to worlds, ideas, and people you had no idea existed. Don't be in a hurry to declare a major. Many people will tell you that you need to select a major, plan your career path, and so on, but don't panic if you haven't figured out your life—*very* few eighteen-year-olds have. Take the time to explore your options and be OK if you begin college as a general studies or undeclared student—that's why those options exist.

Half of all students entering college have yet to decide on their major; between 50 and 70 percent will change their major at least once (most will change their major three times before graduating). © *iStock / RyanKing999*

When you are deciding on a major, think about what you want to do with your professional life. Imagine your dream job and then talk to advisors, professors, and your career services department to find out what degree(s), internships, honors societies, and so on you should get involved with.

Still don't know what you want to be when you grow up? Colleges have departments specifically designed to help you figure this out. Career services (or career center or career placement or career office) can help you decide what career is a good fit for your interests, goals, values, abilities, and personality. Your ideal career might be something you don't even know exists! Once your career counselor goes through your interest inventory, skills assessments, job requirements, earnings, and job outlook, she or he can guide you toward the major that would best prepare you for that career.

> "What do you have to do to pick your major? How do you know what you want to major in?"
> —Maddison, grade 10

Remember to revisit career services to get help writing résumés and cover letters, role-playing job interviews, reviewing job listings for postgraduate careers as well as part-time jobs during college, and even finding appropriate professional clothing if needed. If you decide that four to five years of college has been such an awesome experience that you want to attend graduate school, career services can help with exploring those options.

Once you declare a major, remember you aren't married to it—*you can change your major*. The process itself is simple; visit your advisor and explain that you want to change your major and what your new choice is. He will go through the degree requirements for the new major, check to see which classes you've already taken that will count toward your new program (this is another bonus of taking general education classes your first year as these count toward all majors), and creating a new graduation map. The further you are into your program when you change your major, the more time you will likely spend in college but it is still less time than starting over after five or ten years of being miserable in the wrong profession. General education

> "Can you change your major after you have already started working towards it?"
> —Jacelin, grade 10

classes count toward all majors but degree-specific classes may not count toward your new choice. However, it is possible that you have taken enough classes in your old major to have earned a minor so ask your advisor about that option.

When you declare a major, you are not vowing 'til death do you part—though the struggle many students undertake when determining whether to stick with their major or change it is often compared to the decision to remain in a dysfunctional relationship. But you don't have to stay in any relationship—personal or professional—that isn't right for you.

The idea that at seventeen or eighteen you so absolutely and confidently know what you want to do with the rest of your life is not a realistic one. It is unlikely that you will have enough life experience to support your career view when you graduate from high school. Even if you have "always known" what you want to be and do, once you start taking classes in that area, you may realize that reality is nothing like your ideals. You may like the idea of working only three to four days each week and saving the lives of accident victims in an emergency room but realize in your first rotation that you don't like sick people. You may have loved school and never wanted to leave but realize in your first practicum that you don't like kids. You may have visions of designing and building grand structures but getting through basic geometry is far more of a struggle than you imagined. You may enjoy writing and can't wait to see your name at the top of the *New York Times* best-selling authors list, but realize that, at eighteen, you haven't experienced enough life to write about it.

There are a million reasons to change your major. In fact, most students change their major at least once. I did. This confession comes as a surprise to my students. Apparently, I am "such an English teacher" (whatever that means), that they can't imagine my ever wanting to be anything else. Like many people, throughout my life I wanted to be many things: Pegasus jockey, professional ice cream taster, *National Geographic* photojournalist, mega-millions lottery winner, iceberg mover, professional sleeper, fortune cookie writer, elephant dresser, water slide tester, voice-over artist, talk show hostess, *oshiya* (in Japan, *oshiya* are paid to shove people onto trains), and a *toques* (in Mexico, *toques* shock drunk people with batteries to sober them up). *Note: only the first one of these is* not *a real profession! At least, not anymore.* (FYI: I am still interested in some of these jobs so if you know a talk show producer looking for a hostess or you just need being shoved into a train, please contact me ASAP.)

In the section on general education classes, I mentioned that the purpose is twofold:

1. To give each student a breadth of information useful to functioning in a variety of situations throughout one's life as a useful citizen
2. To expose you to a variety of content areas and careers

Institutions of higher education understand that students are likely to question their career choices and decide to try something else. If the classes you take in your area aren't thrilling you, change your major. Graduation isn't a race; we don't give diplomas only to the first hundred who cross the finish line. Better to spend an extra year in school training for something you love than fifty years in a job you hate.

Once you've decided to change your major, visit your academic advisor for the correct forms (yes, there are *always* forms). Most schools have the forms online and there is no fee to change your major.

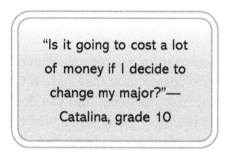

"Is it going to cost a lot of money if I decide to change my major?"— Catalina, grade 10

Worried about how far a change in major may set you back? If you have an online program manager such as DegreeWorks, there is an option to see what classes your new major would require, which classes you've already taken that will still count toward your new major, and how much extra time you may have to spend in school. If your school doesn't have a program available, your academic advisor can help you map out your new academic path.

Not sure what you want your new major to be? Visit career services. Remember them? They have advisors specifically trained to counsel you on potential careers based on your interests, personality, skills, and life goals.

OK—I know that most of this section encourages you to wait to declare a major but it is possible that you already know your dream career—or at least the general area such as business or theater. If that's the case, you'll want to add this to your choose-a-college list. The *Princeton Review* lists the best colleges for a variety of different areas: academics, demographics, extracurriculars, politics, quality of life, types of schools, social scene, and town life.

Once you've refined your list of want and don't want for college, explored your options, decided on your application fee budget, and narrowed down your list of ideal colleges, it's time to apply!

APPLYING TO COLLEGE

To apply or not to apply? Depending on where you are in your education, there's a good chance that you are already fielding questions about where you are applying. Whether or not you are applying to any particular school really isn't the most stressful part. *How* you apply to college is what will cause you stress. The process of applying to a college will take an average of three to six months, so start early!

Every college has its own application process. Fortunately, there are several key elements that most colleges require and—bless you, twenty-first century—applications are

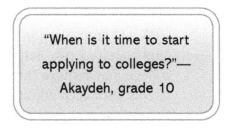

"When is it time to start applying to colleges?"— Akaydeh, grade 10

now online, which allows for quite a bit of cut and paste. (Seriously, whenever you feel frustrated with the process, just remind yourself that former generations had to fill this stuff out by hand!) So, what are these key elements?

- *Biographical information:* name, birth date, social security number, address, and parent information.
- *Educational information:* graduating high school, GPA (grade point average), and test scores. Don't lie about any of this as you'll have to send official copies of transcripts and test scores. Schools may also want you to list extracurricular activities and any awards you have won.

Vocabulary Moment

Official transcripts are copies you pay for that are often sent directly from your high school to the college. *Unofficial* transcripts are copies of copies you can send to your application schools. Some colleges require official copies with applications and others will accept unofficial copies with the application but want official copies if you are accepted. This system often can save you money in the application process.

Other things that colleges require with the application form include

- *Application fee:* Yes—you have to pay them to look at your application. Fees vary by school and, unfortunately, can be cost prohibitive to some applicants. It isn't that any one college has an exorbitant fee so much as they add up quickly if you plan to apply to many colleges. Each college will list its application fee, so do your research *before* taking the time to fill out the forms. Some colleges will waive the fee for low-income families or for online applications.
- *High school transcripts:* This is your official school record; it lists the classes you completed and your grades for each as well as your overall GPA. You can get these from your high school's registrar or your guidance counselor. Knowing your GPA and having a list of the classes you took is useful for the application process as some schools have minimum GPA and course requirements. For example, your high school may have only required two math classes so you only took two, but a particular college may require three. You will need to include copies of your transcripts with each application.
- *Official test scores:* Do you remember your teachers telling you that your test scores matter when it comes to getting into the college of your choice? Or any college for that matter? They were right. Each college decides how much weight they'll place on your scores as well as which tests they want you to take. Again, *do your research.* Some colleges want the SAT, others the ACT, some will want both. Some colleges now want the SAT II, which is a subject-specific test that shows your mastery on a particular subject (SAT and ACT are general knowledge tests). Each of these tests costs money, but your high school may pay for them so talk to your guidance counselor. If you are serious about a college that requires higher test scores, consider taking the tests your junior *and* senior years of high school to give yourself an extra chance for the best scores. You will need to include official copies of your test scores with your application. Once your tests are scored, you can log into your SAT or ACT account and fill out the request form to have them sent to a particular college. Some colleges offer scholarships based on your scores.
- *Letters of recommendation:* Colleges require different numbers of recommendation letters but the standard is three. You want to think carefully about who you ask to write one for you as colleges read them carefully to find out what kind of a person you are. Most colleges want your recommenders to send the letters directly to them so they are confidential (you aren't supposed to read them though some recommenders will let you). You want to ask people who know you well in different contexts and can

speak to your character, determination, dedication to academics, and willingness to work hard. You also want people who can write good letters. Popular choices are guidance counselors, teachers, and employers. If you are applying for a religious school, you'll want to ask your local pastor/priest/bishop/imam/rabbi. If you are applying to a school so you can join its athletic program, you'll want a letter from your coach, and if you're looking for a music scholarship, you'll want one from your music director. Give your recommenders plenty of time (I'm talking months here) to write your letter. They can write a basic one and then customize it for particular schools but you are still asking quite a time commitment from them, so ask early and politely as it is probable that they have several requests. Remember to send each recommender a handwritten thank-you card.

- *Résumé:* Some colleges request a résumé so they can see "you" at a glance. While there are many templates online and built into your word processing software, it is a good idea to talk to your guidance counselor or the business teacher at your school as he is most likely to be up-to-date on the most recent résumé trends. Create your résumé early and give a copy of it to each of your recommenders so they can speak effectively to those specifics that make you unique. Most importantly, do not creatively alter the facts (lie) on your résumé. You will get caught.

- *Essay:* Twelve years of English classes have provided ample practice for this moment, so I hope you paid attention. The essay is your evidence that you can communicate at an appropriate college level. Yes, the readers are looking to find out more about you beyond the statistics of your transcripts and test scores or the glowing platitudes of recommendation letters; however, they are also looking at your quality of writing, mastery of English language conventions, clarity of thought, and ability to respond effectively and creatively to the prompt. Do not babble, lie, or merely repeat the information you put on your application. Read several samples of good college essays as well as instructional articles on this whole strange subgenre of writing. Your guidance counselor (and, probably, senior English teacher) will have many of these resources and can point you to more.

Did You Know?

While the director of admissions at Princeton from 1922 to 1950, Radcliffe Heermance developed a new admissions policy that included interviews, two letters of personal recommendation, and a social ranking of applicants. Heermance did this in order to limit the admission of Jewish students.[a]

You'll need to keep track of your applications. Most seekers of higher education apply to an average of four colleges. If you apply to more than four, feel free to make several copies of the record page in figure 2.1.

There are, literally (notice, I used *literally* correctly and not in the figurative sense—I beg of you to also learn the difference and use them correctly), hundreds of articles, books, and websites dedicated to helping you apply for college. That isn't the focus of this book so this chapter is exceptionally small.

My College Applications Record

School Information

Name: _____

Web Address: _____

_____
City   *State*

Application Submitted: _____ **Fee Amount:** _____ **Date Paid:** _____
Date

Academic Transcripts: Y N _____ **Resume:** Y N _____
Date Submitted   *Date Submitted*

Application Essay: Y N _____ **Other:** _____
Date Submitted   *Date Submitted*

Test Scores:

SAT Y N _____   ACT Y N _____
Date Submitted   *Date Submitted*

Other Y N _____   _____
Name   *Date Submitted*

Recommendation Letters: _____ Submitted: Y N _____
Name   *Date*

_____ Submitted: Y N _____
Name   *Date*

_____ Submitted: Y N _____
Name   *Date*

How I'm Feeling:

Acceptance: Y N _____   _____
Date

Accept the Acceptance: Y N _____ **Deny the Acceptance:** Y N _____
Date   *Date*

Figure 2.1 A sample applications record

THE COLLEGE VISIT

You wouldn't buy a house without touring the residence or a car without driving it, so don't choose a college without visiting it. With a bit of planning, the college visit can be the best part of the choosing-a-college experience. Plan ahead so that you can best utilize vacation time; start the summer before your senior year, or even your junior year, so you will be able to visit the most places. While it's a good idea to utilize virtual tours through college websites, this is just a way to narrow your choices as virtual tours highlight the best and leave out the rest. Be sure that you personally visit the places you are seriously considering and don't forget to take pictures, especially of the stuff not on the website.

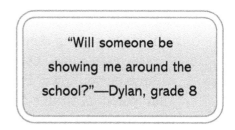

"Will someone be showing me around the school?"—Dylan, grade 8

When planning college visits, the *Princeton Review* suggests keeping the following in mind:[1]

1. *Mind the calendar.* You want to go when school is in session so you get the most accurate idea of the real environment.
2. *Meet the experts.* Talking to current students allows you to get the unvarnished truth of the place. They know the best parts of the school, area, and extracurricular options. Be sure to talk to those in any program(s) you are considering to get the 411 on teachers, classes, internships, and so on. They'll be honest with you about whether they love the place and if you are likely to agree.

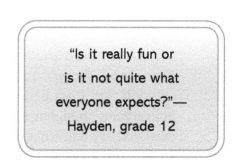

"Is it really fun or is it not quite what everyone expects?"— Hayden, grade 12

3. *Meet the* other *experts.* Stop by the admissions office. Collect information on the school, area, and financial aid options (it's likely they have a ready-

made financial aid packet you can grab). Sign up for their mailing list and grab any free SWAG they offer (T-shirts, water bottles, key chains). Don't forget copies of campus publications such as the newspaper. This will give you an idea of typical events and an uncensored (or at least less-censored) view of current student perspectives.

4. *Take the tour.* No college visit is complete without the official tour. Recruitment will put on a sales pitch and highlight the best and most unique things about the school. This is a great opportunity for you (and your parents/guardians/friends) to ask questions. Be sure to ask *all* the questions and pay close attention to the answers—both what *is* said and what *isn't.* However, answers that are easily discovered online should be avoided. For example, all colleges will list their offered majors, costs for tuition and fees, and sports teams. If you already know what degree you wish to pursue, don't visit a college that doesn't offer that program—even if your significant other is going there.

5. *Explore on your own.* Once the official tour is over, take time to wander the campus on your own. Eat in the cafeteria, explore the buildings that house your potential future degree classes and professors, catch a game/play/concert, check out the library and dormitories. Most especially, investigate the areas of campus that the official tour *didn't* show you. They will cover the highlights—you need to check out any lowlights. Additionally, look lost. Seriously. Stand in the middle of campus with a map and a confused look on your face (this won't be as difficult as it sounds as it is quite possible that you will be lost at some point). Does anyone stop to help you? If you ask for help, how friendly are the students? This is a great way to get a feel for the campus culture.

6. *Be a student for a day.* Plan to take at least two full days at each college. The first half of the first day is the official tour and unofficial wanderings to familiarize yourself with campus. Spend several hours that afternoon sitting in on classes, meeting with professors, and participating in a lab. How do you feel? Are you happy? Do you feel as if this is a place you'd want to spend half of a decade? Listen to your gut and don't settle.

7. *Save the best for last.* You'll want to visit several colleges, and just as with any skill, you'll get better with practice. As you relax and gain confidence in just being in higher education environments, you'll get a better feel for what you like and what you don't want in a college. Saving your top choice for last will allow you to be the best prepared to compare it to the others on your list.

8. *Keep records.* Don't trust your memory. Filling out a personal evaluation form during and immediately after each visit will allow you to make informed decisions as the visits will quickly run together in your mind. No

matter how many questions you ask during your tours, you'll have more afterward. Your records will help you remember the details and remind you who to contact for more answers.

9. *Don't rush to judgment.* Take time to carefully analyze all of your options, and don't let unimportant things (such as bad weather or the way another student decorates her dorm room) cloud your judgment. Be aware of your own moods, energy level, and health at each visit as it is easy to allow non-essentials to affect your decision.

Most colleges will accept walk-ins for campus visits but it is best to schedule them. The admissions page on the school's website will have contact information, and it is increasingly likely that you can sign up for a tour directly on the website. You should also ask for information on local places to stay, eat, and visit while you're there. Some universities have working relationships with local hotels and restaurants and can get you discounts.

Colleges often have different spring break weeks than high schools, so your spring break might be the perfect time for a road trip. Research colleges in the area and book appointments to allow you to visit as many colleges as possible. Once you know which schools and which dates, talk to your high school counselor to see if there is a recent graduate now attending that college—maybe even someone you know. Get in touch and talk to her about her experiences in higher education. You can't beat the personal touch.

Another thing to keep in mind is that some colleges have Instant Decision (ID) Days. An ID Day allows you to reduce the entire application process to one day.

Date

Dear Mr./Ms./Dr. Smith,

Thank you for taking the time to show me around/interview me/let me stay in your room/visit your class on (date of visit). My parents and I particularly appreciated your explaining the program/treating us to lunch/recommending a local restaurant. We enjoyed learning about (name of school).

Sincerely,

(your signature)

(your printed name)

Within a few days of the visit, send a thank-you to your interviewer, host, tour guide, and each professor who welcomed you into her or his classroom. An email is acceptable (though nothing beats the handwritten touch). *Courtesy of the author*

Each university sets different ID Days and has different requirements for what information you'll need to bring, so check the websites ahead of time as you'll need to make an appointment to attend. While you'll find out that day whether you are accepted, you have until National Decision Day (May 1) to accept or decline your acceptance. See chapter 5 for more information on college acceptance.

Appendix A has a list of questions you should ask each school during your tour. Appendix B is a self-check that you'll need to answer. Make copies for each school you visit.

Keep in mind that the tour guide is likely a student who is following a strict script. Your tour guide is there to cheer the campus—point out the best facilities, most interesting history, and prettiest spots. This guide isn't the right person to ask about financial aid or graduation rates, *but* if the guide is a student, ask questions that will give you a feel for how much he or she likes being a student there. Ask about his major or whether she lives on campus. Ask about his favorite on-campus eatery or her favorite local spot. Be judicious if there are others in your tour group and don't bogart (dominate, control, take over, consume, overly utilize, hog, monopolize, or exploit) the time, but it is likely that your guide knows more about the campus than he or she is letting on.

FINANCIAL AID

College is expensive—as are most investments. I remember a high school teacher of mine telling us that a college degree is the only investment guaranteed to pay itself off: cars lose value as soon as you drive them off the lot, real estate is a gamble that depends on many factors that are beyond your control, and the market crash in the late 2000s proved that even retirement accounts you pay into your entire career aren't safe. But—education! A degree means you have a better chance of gaining employment and earning a higher salary and benefits. It used to be that a degree meant that, even after you made your monthly student loan payment, you had more net salary than if you didn't have a degree. Additionally, student loans would be paid off in five to ten years, and the increased salary would be yours for decades.

> "How am I going to pay for it?"
> —Cheznie, grade 12

That is, unfortunately, no longer guaranteed. According to several researchers, the cost of higher education has grown faster than the cost of food and health care and is even more extreme than inflation. This rise is exacerbated with stagnant income so that education costs consume a higher percentage of your net earnings than ever before.[1]

> "Why is college so expensive?"
> —Jersee, grade 10

Between 1971 and 2015, the average cost of one year's college tuition increased 276 percent (from $2,499 to $9,420). In 1971, tuition costs were approximately 7 percent of median income for men (20 percent of median income for women), whereas by 2015, paying for one year's tuition cost the average male 25 percent of his median income and a female 39 percent of her median income (adjusted for inflation).[2]

Vocabulary Moment

Median income is the amount that divides income distribution into two equal halves—with half of earners making more than that and half making less.

You may have family members regale you with stories about how they worked their way through college and can't understand why you can't or won't do the same. The sad, simple fact is that it is improbable, if not impossible, to work your way through school, especially if you are going to school full time, which doesn't leave you enough hours in the day to work full time. Most students work part-time jobs at, or close to, minimum wage. Even if you were able to work twenty hours a week (half-time) at ten dollars an hour for fifty weeks of the year, you'd earn $20,000 before taxes. Thus, the average annual cost of college tuition, which is near $10,000, will cost half of your earnings. A full load of classes is a full-time job (by the time you count up hours spent in class and the time it takes to do the homework for those classes, you are looking at forty hours a week). You are going to need financial aid!

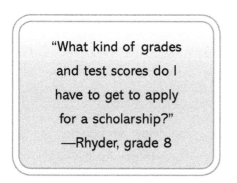

"What kind of grades and test scores do I have to get to apply for a scholarship?"

—Rhyder, grade 8

Federal Student Aid

The Federal Student Aid (FSA) office in the US Department of Education is the largest provider of student financial aid in the country. This office manages programs under Title IV of the Higher Education Act of 1965, which provides grants, loans, and work-study programs for students. At www.studentaid.ed.gov, you can find information on preparing for college, available aid, application process, and repayment of loans. While more than 75 percent of college freshmen were accepted by their first-choice college, less than 57 percent attended, citing lack of financial resources as the reason.[3]

Before any financial aid can be received, you will need to fill out a FAFSA (Free Application for Federal Student Aid). You must complete the FAFSA form *every year* even if your financial circumstances don't change. The FAFSA form becomes available on October 1 but the application deadline depends on your state, and because it's all online now, deadlines are later than when I was an undergrad. (I actually had to move up my wedding date to meet the FAFSA deadline. True story! Stop by sometime and I'll tell you all about it.) But you should

If you need financial aid—loans, grants, scholarships, or work study—you will need to complete a FAFSA every year. Keep secure copies of information and plan ahead. © *iStock / designer491*

still apply early. You will first need to log onto the FSA website and create an FSA ID. You will use this to apply for financial aid every year. When you apply, you will submit quite a bit of personal information so do *not* share your FSA ID with anyone. After creating your FSA ID, you will complete your FAFSA. Information you will need for the FAFSA includes

- your Social Security number
- your parents' Social Security numbers (if they are claiming you as a dependent)
- your driver's license number (if you have a driver's license)
- your Alien Registration number (if you are not a US citizen)
- federal tax information, including IRS W-2 information, for you, your spouse (if married), and your parents (if you are a dependent)
- records of your untaxed income (such as child support or veterans noneducation benefits)
- information on other financial assets (such as investments or real estate)

While your parents shouldn't fill out the FAFSA for you, you can all work on it together at www.fafsa.gov and click on "Start a New FAFSA." There are lots of FAQ areas as well as live chat (in English or Spanish) with experts during business hours.

To submit the FAFSA, you will need to list at least one school to receive your information. For purposes of federal funding, it doesn't matter what order you list the schools in (up to ten of them—but you can add more later), but it *may* matter for state-based aid. There is a link on the FAFSA directions page to help you determine if that is an issue. Every school you list will receive your aid eligibility. Don't worry! Schools will not be able to see what other schools you sent the information to. After you complete the application, be sure to sign and submit!

After the FSA office has calculated your FAFSA numbers (I'm sure it involves a lot of complicated math formulas and, possibly, some sort of ritual sacrifice in a dark room), it will send the information to the schools you included on the form. The school's financial aid office will use the information to determine how much federal student aid you are eligible to receive. If the school has internal scholarships, it may use your FAFSA information for those as well. However, your school might (probably will) have additional paperwork for you to complete. Your FAFSA information also goes to your state's higher education department and may be used for state financial aid.

As soon as you submit your FAFSA online, you can check to see if it was received. If you submit your FAFSA on paper (you Luddite), expect it to take seven to ten days to be processed. Once your FAFSA has been processed, the FSA will send you an SAR (Student Aid Report) (get used to acronyms—higher education is addicted to them), which summarizes the data you included on your FAFSA. *Check it carefully to make certain there are no errors.* The SAR will not tell you how much aid you are getting. That information is calculated by the college that accepts you. Therefore, if you decide to attend a college you did not include on your FAFSA, log back in (remember your FSA ID?) and request the SAR to be sent to that school. The school will send you an award letter outlining the type(s) and amount(s) of financial aid that the school is offering you. Your award letter may arrive as early as winter for the following fall term or as late as right before the term begins. Much of this will depend on when you accepted your acceptance.

Did You Know?

Taking your PSAT (Pre-SAT) your junior year is required to compete for a National Merit Scholarship. Approximately the top 3 percent of test takers will qualify. The easiest states in which to qualify are Arkansas, Mississippi, West Virginia, and Wyoming, while the most difficult locations are the District of Columbia, Maryland, Massachusetts, and New Jersey.[a]

If your SAR says that you have been selected for verification, don't panic. Some applicants are selected at random, and it isn't an indication that you are suspected of falsifying information. Verification just means that you'll need to provide some documents to support what you put on your FAFSA. It is possible that your SAR won't require verification but your school will. This is why it is important to keep all of your documentation together and accessible. Also, give copies! Keep the originals for your records.

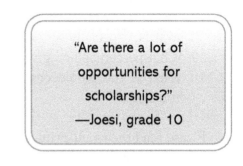

"Are there a lot of opportunities for scholarships?"

—Joesi, grade 10

You do not need to accept all of the aid that the school awards you. Before accepting any financial aid, read the fine print carefully. Be sure you understand if it is a grant or scholarship (you don't need to repay the money) or a loan (you do need to repay the money). Don't accept more than you need as the goal here is to go into as little debt as possible. Also, depending on your career goals, there are certain types of aid that you don't need to repay—even loans. On the flip side, some grants are career based and you will need to repay them if you don't meet the conditions. I know that four years seems like forever in the future, but you really need to pay attention to what you are agreeing to now so you know what you will have to begin repaying six months after graduation (even if you don't have a job).

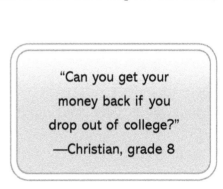

"Can you get your money back if you drop out of college?"

—Christian, grade 8

Federal aid is sent directly to your school and will deal with funds distribution, so talk to your financial aid advisor at your school for details. And remember—you get to do this *every year*!

US News polled financial aid advisors across the country and compiled the top ten questions that they wish parents would ask.[4]

1. Is there alternative financial aid available?
2. How much will my student pay versus how much did he or she initially borrow? (e.g., added interest)
3. How might I decrease my student's loan indebtedness?
4. Is there additional financial aid available?
5. What happens if my financial circumstances change while my student is in school?

6. Do my taxes need to be filed before I complete the FAFSA? (Yes—you can use last year's W-2 and click the button "will file.")
7. How many years is my student's program of study and what will it take to graduate in four versus five or six years?
8. What happens to my student's financial aid after the first year? (Some awards, especially scholarships, may be first-year only.)
9. What percentage of graduates leave without debt?
10. What is the whole cost of attending your school (beyond tuition and housing)?

Please read the small print in your financial aid package that explains that you *must* repay all of the principle (money you borrowed) plus interest even if you drop out, can't find a job after graduation, or are unsatisfied with the quality of your education.

5

THE ACCEPTANCE

All right. You researched. You weighed your options. You visited the campus. You fell in love with the program, place, and people. You filled out the application form. You interviewed. You did everything right and now you wait. Each day you run home to check the mail, visions of thick envelopes with amazing news dancing before your eyes. Then it happens. You see the logo of the university of your dreams in the return address spot. Take a deep breath and open the envelope.

How long did you wait? If you apply for early decision, you can expect a response by December 15. Regular application dates are around the first of the year (early January), and students are notified in March and April. Colleges with rolling admissions typically respond in six to eight weeks.

What did you do while waiting? First, when you applied you should have received a confirmation (probably by email) that your application was received. If you do not receive confirmation of your application within a week of submission, contact the admissions office and politely ask if all of your materials were received. As each university has unique requirements for application, be careful about following the directions. Some schools make their first round of decisions by tossing incomplete or incorrect applications.

As online applications become more common, many schools have you create a login to apply. You can use that login to check the status of your application. You can check back as often as you like but don't expect the information to change until close to the previously mentioned time frames.

If, during your wait time, any of your information changes (such as your address, awards, or additional extracurricular activities), be sure to update your application information. Otherwise, there isn't much you can do but wait.

Don't expect to hear back from all of the schools on the same day even if you applied on the same day. National Decision Day is May 1. Wait until you hear from everyone before making a final decision and notifying the schools of your decision.

College Acceptance

The rule for college acceptance used to be that thick envelopes meant accepted and thin envelopes meant denied. This was because acceptances included forms for you to complete and return as well as more information on housing, finances, and deadlines. It only took one sheet of paper to say "no."

As information has moved online, acceptance letters—even if they are on paper and mailed to you—are increasingly short as schools can save quite a bit of money by having you go online to gather the information and complete and return forms electronically.

In addition to being accepted or denied by a college, it is possible that you will be placed on a wait-list. Some schools have a certain number of spots to fill and will rank application acceptances according to first choice, second choice, and so on. Let's say a school has five thousand spots and ten thousand students apply with six thousand students meeting admission requirements. It may send out four thousand denial letters, five thousand acceptance letters, and one thousand letters to students who are on a waitlist. This means that the school is waiting to hear back from the five thousand students who were accepted to see if each student is actually going to attend (likely not as we all apply to multiple schools). Once an accepted student sends his regrets, the first person on the wait-list is notified that a spot has opened and she has been accepted.

Not all schools have wait-lists and those that do won't tell you *where* on the wait-list you are (you could be number one or number one thousand—you'll never know). A school may wait until May 1 (National Decision Day) and assume that all accepted students who have not responded have decided not to attend and will begin contacting wait listed students on May 2. Likely, if you haven't heard from a school that wait-listed you by May 15, you can assume that you have not been accepted. Rarely, but it does happen, you may hear from that school during the summer. (However, it is likely that you will have made other arrangements and accepted the acceptance of a school that accepted you initially. Yep, that's a complicated sentence to describe a complicated process.)

So, it may help to think of college acceptances as finding a date for prom.

Situation 1: Your parent(s) graduated from a school that honors legacy students. This means that if your parent is an alum (graduated from there), you are automatically accepted. This is much like having a steady significant other—you are guaranteed a date for prom.

Situation 2: You have a 4.0 GPA, excellent standardized test scores, and abundant extracurricular activities that highlight your many talents. You more than meet the minimum qualifications for a school to which you applied. You have no worries about getting accepted and are just waiting for the official notification. This is like being the most popular kid in school and asking out the person who has crushed on you for four years—he or she will say yes; it's just a technicality.

Situation 3: You have spent money applying to a school you are not qualified to attend. You have a 1.0 GPA, you slept through the SAT, and you can't even spell *extracurricular*. This is like asking out someone who has never heard of you and is waaaay out of your league. Not going to happen.

Situation 4: You have a decent GPA, average test scores, and a few extracurriculars. Nothing extraordinary, but certainly enough to qualify for acceptance. However, you have no idea how many others have applied for that school so you really don't know what your chances are. This is like being a decent and cute person, but not particularly popular and not rich at all. You ask out someone in your league but that person tells you he or she is waiting to see if anyone else makes a better offer and will let you know. You've been wait-listed for the prom. While there is a slight chance you'll eventually get a yes, you should ask someone else out and work on a guaranteed yes or you might miss prom altogether.

Financial Aid Offers

As acceptance letters begin to arrive, compare financial aid awards. If your second choice offers you a full-ride scholarship, perhaps it should become your first choice. A "full ride" usually means the cost of your degree program including tuition, fees, and on-campus housing, *but* there could be exceptions. The offer may just cover tuition and fees, or it may be limited to four years (even if you don't finish your degree in that time), or it may be cancelled if you change your major or get injured and can no longer compete athletically. Be sure to read the fine print on all financial aid offers.

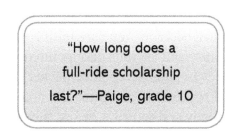

"How long does a full-ride scholarship last?"—Paige, grade 10

As the offers start rolling in, you'll want to compare packages. College Board offers an online tool that allows you to compare up to four financial aid offers.[1]

Not all forms of financial aid are renewable. Clarify with the financial aid office which ones are only applicable for your freshman year, and don't assume that you'll get that much aid every year. © iStock / AndreyPopov

Accepting the Acceptance

Huzzah! You have been found worthy and accepted into an institute of higher education. Perhaps you were accepted into more than one school. Well, aren't you the belle of the ball!

Now you get to decide who the lucky school will be and let everyone know your final decision. You have until National Decision Day on May 1 to accept your acceptance and let your disappointed suitors know you won't be attending their school.

In your acceptance packet (old-fashioned paper or electronic), there will be directions on accepting the acceptance. Fill out the paperwork carefully and correctly and return it before the deadline. Typical information will include financial planning, housing application, advisor contact information, and orientation dates. If you don't officially accept the acceptance (yes, I do like saying that), you risk losing your spot so let the school know you're coming. In addition, schools expect you to submit a deposit (money) to hold your spot. The amount will depend on the school. If you intend to live on campus, expect to pay a second deposit to hold your housing reservation. Additionally, you may need to accept your financial aid package separately from your enrollment and housing.

If you were accepted by a school that you have decided not to attend, it is likely that there are directions for notifying the school that you have rejected it. Let the school know as soon as you have made the decision not to attend so others can have the opportunity.

If you are the typical high school senior, your friends are going through the same processes you are. Be sure to keep in touch about who is being accepted where and don't forget to have genuine sympathy for someone who is rejected from a school. The vast majority of students get a combination of acceptance and rejection letters and may get the rejection letters first. Don't lose hope and don't be *that* person if you get an acceptance first. Again, not everyone gets his first choice for prom date but still enjoys the prom.

While all of this accepting and rejecting is happening, don't forget to finish high school. Seriously. More than one person has failed at the finish line and then all that college planning and stress will have been for nothing.

Another Campus Visit

Well, you've accepted the acceptance (I promise, this is the last time I'll say that) and let all the other colleges know "thanks, but no thanks." As you now know where your next home will be, it's time to make another visit. You can either make a separate trip or go a bit early to orientation days.

Orientation Days

Orientation days are offered in the summer and fall (depending on the school). Parents are welcome but not required to attend with you. Your school may call these days something else (Freshman or New Student Orientation, Welcome Week, Fresh Week, or something creatively unique to the school, such as ThunderU or Fish Camp). It may be a few days or an entire week and is usually the week before classes start, although some schools have shorter orientation days spread out that are not connected to your big move. The purpose of these days is to get you started on your first year of college, and, as such, you

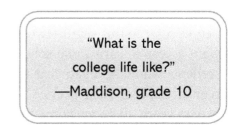

"What is the
college life like?"
—Maddison, grade 10

will receive more vital information in a short time than you can possibly remember. So no matter what your school calls it, consider them note-taking days.

Also use the time to find the various offices you may need, including financial aid, registration, counseling, security, housing, bookstore, and health center.

There may be a specific parent orientation, which may include more information on school finances, housing, Family Education Rights and Privacy Act (FERPA controls what information your parents are and are not able to have based on the fact that you are now an adult), and ways to support the transition for you (and them). It is likely that your parents will take a keen interest in your new roommate(s), resident assistant(s), cuties who live next door, and professors—although we typically draw far less parental attention than roomies, at least until midterms. You may be embarrassed by their level of interest but they will soon leave, and, much to your surprise, you are likely to find yourself wishing for their company. Yes, you may actually miss your parents. Stranger things have happened. Just make sure they have your mailing address so they can send you care packages. If your parents didn't attend, don't worry. There will be plenty of activities to keep you busy and there's a better-than-average chance that you'll be adopted by one of your roommates' parents.

> "Should I wait longer before I go to college, and not go right after high school?"
> —Joesi, grade 10

Once you've accomplished all of this—you're mostly unpacked in your new home, textbooks purchased, and you like your new roomie—you know that you made the right choice in accepting the acceptance (sorry, couldn't resist).

Deferment

Deferment is putting college off for one year after you have been accepted. Some people refer to this year between high school and college as a "gap year." You may want a year to earn some school money, care for a sick relative, or travel. Many students who take a gap year enter college a bit more mature, confident, and career driven than their peers.[2] While college officials have become more accepting of gap years, there are some things you will want to consider:

- *Admission:* Be sure to contact the admissions office of the college that has accepted you to see what they require for holding your spot a year. Contact the office even if you are just considering deferring your enrollment as there may be a deadline.[3]

- *Financial aid:* You will need to reapply through the Federal Student Aid department *and* ask your college what their policy is for deferred admission for any department or college financial aid you have been awarded.[4] Remember that if you are earning money during your gap year, that may affect your financial aid offers.
- *The school "habit":* You have been going to school for most of your life and are in the habit of classes and homework. Taking a year off may make it a little more difficult, but not impossible, to readjust to a school schedule, especially if it is only one year.

STAYING IN COLLEGE

HOGS... 6

HOUSING

You have several housing options available to you. If your family members live close to your chosen school, you may decide to live with them. Be sure to talk with your parents or guardians and clarify if they have decided to *let* you live with them as it is possible that they have already scheduled an interior decorator to transform your bedroom into the game room of their dreams.

If you are living with family, discuss (and consider putting the agreement in writing) to what extent you'll need to contribute to rent, utilities, and household chores. An adult contributes positively to his or her own upkeep. Even if you are not required to, you need to help with cooking, cleaning, maintenance, and finances, and *you absolutely should be doing your own laundry*. If you wish to be treated as an adult, you must act like one. This is especially true, and particularly difficult, if you are living with people who have known you as a child. It is

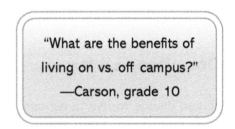

"What are the benefits of living on vs. off campus?"
—Carson, grade 10

up to you to set the new tone of your relationships. If you have a vehicle and are not already paying for your own insurance, maintenance, and fuel, now is the time to budget it into your other expenses.

If you are moving out of your house for school, you can live on campus or off campus. Some colleges *require* all first-year students to live on campus. Others require students to live on campus *unless* they are living with family (be prepared to prove it). Even if you choose a school that doesn't require on-campus living, consider it. Students who live on campus are much more likely to be socially involved and achieve academically. Attendance is higher and satisfaction greater for those who live in the dorms. Dormitories have resident assistants—older students who live in the dorm and who are available to help with the transition to living on your own. If you live in the dorm, your cost is a set rate and includes rent and utilities. A meal plan is also included (at least to some degree) in on-campus housing. You can have the cost added directly to your tuition and fees and have your financial aid cover it. Most experts recommend living on campus—at least for your first year.[1]

If you choose to live off campus, you have several options. In addition to living with family, you could rent a house or apartment. You can live by yourself or have roommates. (This is usually decided by examining your bank account.)

> "Are you required to live on campus for at least one year?"
> —Nathan, grade 10

If you choose to have roommates, you can rent a room from someone else or find a place and look for roommates to help you out. You will need to have clear expectations and understandings (*in writing*) regarding finances, nonpaying guests, noise, chores, and all other aspects of sharing a domicile. Even if you are going to the same school as some friends and are excited to fulfill your lifelong dream of all sharing a place, have honest talks about responsibilities and put everything *in writing*. Most people have different expectations, and the only way to achieve successful cohabitation is through successful communication. (I should put that on a T-shirt.)

Dormitory Living

If you decide to live in on-campus housing (a dorm), your school may have options of coed or single-sex dormitories. Even in a coed dorm, it is customary to have policies against males and females sharing a room and some coed dorms are separated by floors so that males are on odd-numbered floors and females are on even-numbered floors (or vice versa).

The size of the dorm room will determine the number of inhabitants but the typical number is two (you and one roommate). Many schools will have places on the dormitory application form to request a particular roommate if you and a friend want to room together. The two of you may share a bathroom or the rooms may be arranged to have two rooms (four people) share one suite bathroom. Some dormitories merely have a large, general bathroom down the hall (like a locker room), which several people share.

Typically, the school will provide a bed (twin size frame and mattress), desk, dresser, and closet space. You'll need to provide everything else. If you are think-

Did You Know?

Approximately 40 percent of full-time students at public universities and 64 percent of full-time students at private universities live on campus.[a]

"If you live on campus, can you have a friend move in as your roommate
or are you just stuck with someone they assign?"—Sage, grade 10

ing of bringing appliances (e.g., refrigerator, microwave, and coffee maker) be
sure to check with the housing regulations as some dorms (especially older ones)
prohibit these items.

Depending on the school, you may be able to get a single room but it will cost
you more. Living alone also keeps you from experiencing certain social aspects of
college. Newer dormitory buildings are de-
signed more like apartments. For example,
there may be a kitchen(ette), living room,
four bedrooms, and two bathrooms. Up to
eight people will share this space (two to
each bedroom, four to a bathroom). It is still
common for all eight people to be of the
same gender but the gender might vary from
apartment to apartment instead of floor to
floor. If the school has several dormitories, it

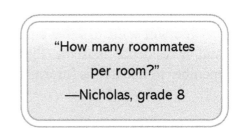

"How many roommates
per room?"
—Nicholas, grade 8

may have a mixture of coed and single-sex dormitories. Be sure to discuss your
options and preferences with university housing.

Dormitories will have resident assistants (RAs)—older students (such as juniors and seniors) who have lived in the dorm for a year or more. Generally, there
will be one RA per hall/floor. An RA is a student who is trained to help others
acclimate to higher education. It is her job to point you in the right direction for
school services such as tutoring or counseling, arbitrate disagreements between
roommates and neighbors, enforce housing policies including noise ordinances
(the technical term for "Shut up, people are trying to study/sleep!"), and help
plan social events.

Pets (with the possible exception of fish and registered service animals) are
not allowed in dormitories. In addition to potential allergic reactions from roommates, it is incredibly unfair to have a pet in your dorm room. You will be far too
busy to take proper care of an animal, so leave Fido at home.

"Are there dorms where I can live by myself or do I
have to have a roommate?"—Alexa, grade 8

> "Are there still events at colleges such as dances or
> occasional college dinners?"—Nicholas, grade 8

If you are under twenty-one, having alcohol in your room is illegal. If you are over twenty-one, having alcohol in your room is probably against school rules. Most schools have a "dry" policy—*no* alcohol on campus. Please abide by this rule. Forget the movies—there is nothing exciting enough about binge drinking to make alcohol poisoning, prison, or sexual assault worthwhile.

If you aren't sure what your shopping list should look like, please make copies of the one in appendix C. If you plan enough in advance, you could list some of these on your high school graduate gift registry.

You will want to leave emergency contact information with your roommate and/or residence assistant. Please make copies of the form in figure 6.1 and remember to update the information each semester.

Moving In

Plan ahead. You'll need moving boxes, packing supplies (newspaper, tape, bubble wrap), and, possibly, a moving van/trailer. Typically, colleges have a move-in weekend for all students, which is part of the orientation days the week(end) before school starts. Yep, that's right. *Everyone* moves in at the same time. All the students and their sumpters (a word that means "pack animal" but in this instance refers to parents and siblings), moving boxes, and furniture, *all at the same time.*

Begin by checking in to get your room assignment. This may be sent to you by housing before move-in day or you may have to wait until you check in that day. Move-in procedures are as follows:

1. Find the building your assigned room is in.
2. Find an available parking space—hopefully within a mile of the building.
3. Carry the first load of your belongings to the building and find your room.
4. Realize it's faster to take several flights of stairs than wait for the overcrowded elevator.
5. Hope you are the first one to arrive at your room so you can pick which bed you want.
6. Meet your roommate(s) and accept whichever bed is left.
7. Continue moving your stuff in.
8. Realize, after a few dozen trips, why so many people were willing to wait for the overcrowded elevator.

Emergency Contact Information

Your Name: _____ Date of Birth: _____

School Address: _____

City: _____ State: _____ Zip Code: _____

Home Address: _____

City: _____ State: _____ Zip Code: _____

Allergies: _____

_____

Medications: _____

_____

Emergency Contact

Name: _____ Relationship: _____

Address: _____

City: _____ State: _____ Zip Code: _____

Home #: _____ Cell #: _____ Work #: _____

Email Address: _____

Alternative Emergency Contact

Name: _____ Relationship: _____

Address: _____

City: _____ State: _____ Zip Code: _____

Home #: _____ Cell #: _____ Work #: _____

Email Address: _____

Figure 6.1 Emergency contact information

9. Become concerned that mom/dad/grandparent/sibling/roommate has begun unpacking your stuff and decorating your room.
10. Accept the help because the person means well and you know you can redecorate.

RAs will scramble around being "helpful," and some schools have faculty and staff who volunteer to help students move in. (Don't get too excited; we mostly hold the door open and talk to your parents.) In addition to hundreds of people and thousands of boxes, the flow of traffic gets interrupted by frequent impromptu hallway reunions, lost siblings, and crying parents. Take calming breaths as it will all be over soon and, much to your surprise, you'll miss them.

Laundry

Often, stress is caused by feeling overwhelmed. You have so much to do that you aren't sure where to begin because you can't conceive of being able to get it all done.

I had a student in my office who was suffering from anxiety. Through her tears, she rattled off a list of things she had to do and ended with, "I don't even know how to wash my clothes!"

I was stunned. My mother had me doing laundry by the time I was eight years old. Out of curiosity, I took a survey of my students to see how many knew how to do their laundry before college. The results? About half. I asked how they managed and several said they went home every two weeks so their moms could do their laundry.

Think this isn't a common problem? I did a quick YouTube search for "How to do laundry in college" and got 947,000 results! Just under 1 million videos to show you how to do laundry in college; from laundromats to dormitory laundry rooms to "8-Year-Old Teaches College Students to Do Laundry," there are step-by-step videos for separating lights and darks, matching temperature to fabric, and the pros and cons of different detergents (soaps) and softeners.

So watch a video (or a thousand), ask your RA, or have your parents teach you before you move out. Having clean clothes lessens your stress level and increases the chances of getting a date (either because you meet the most amazing person in the laundry room or because "doesn't stink" is a priority on everyone's dating list). Win-win.

CLASSES

Full or Part Time

Many factors play into the decision to attend school full or part time, including financial aid, job, and family obligations. Obviously, attending part time means it will take you longer to graduate, and you should keep in mind that while college credits don't "expire," many colleges won't count them after a certain number of years. The college and field of study will determine how many years; it may be five, seven, or ten.

Many colleges have limits on how many credits they will allow you to transfer in from another institution of higher education. For example, if you took 200 credits (seriously though, if you take anywhere near this many you really need to have finished a degree, but we're just using this number for an example) but the college you are transferring to accepts a maximum of 150 credits, those leftover fifty credits are

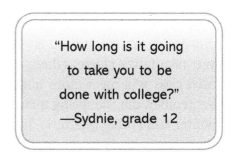

"How long is it going to take you to be done with college?"
—Sydnie, grade 12

lost. Another possibility is that your school determines that a particular class is no longer relevant after a certain number of years. (This is more likely in fields such as medicine or technology where advancements are made often enough that information past a certain number of years is no longer up-to-date.) In this case, you will have to retake those classes.

Typically, a four-year (bachelor's) degree is 120 credit hours. (We'll talk credit hours in more detail in a few pages.) If you attend the full-time minimum (twelve credit hours per semester for two semesters per year), it will take you five years to complete 120 credits. For those of you who are slow at math (or just too tired to count), to complete 120 credits in four years, you'll need to take fifteen credits each semester. Colleges typically count any amount of credit hours between twelve and eighteen as full time, and you'll pay a flat rate for tuition. Anything less than full time will mess with your financial aid, and anything more than full time will mess with your sanity (and will cost more money).

Academic Terms: Dividing the Academic Year

Institutions of higher education divide up the academic year in various ways. By far, the most common is the semester, which divides the year in half—fall and spring—with each semester lasting about fifteen weeks. Fall semester begins mid to late August and ends in early to mid-December for a long winter break (three to four weeks). Spring semester begins early to mid-January and includes a one- to two-week-long spring break before ending, typically, at some time in May. These schools will likely have a summer session with fewer course options, which run more hours each day for fewer weeks. There are dozens of different configurations for summer sessions. They are not required and may be more expensive and utilize less financial aid than fall and spring semesters. Full-time students take between four and seven classes each semester.

Some schools divide the academic year by quarters: fall, winter, spring, and (optional) summer. This is not as common as semesters. In fact, other than some community or trade colleges, unless you are attending college on the West Coast, you are unlikely to encounter the quarter system. However, in case you do (as I did during my undergraduate years), each quarter is about ten weeks long and you take fewer classes (three to four) each quarter. Before you get too excited, each class will meet more hours per week. Fall quarter doesn't start until mid-September, but the spring quarter ends mid-June. Spring break is usually between winter and spring quarters. Summer quarter is available but not usually required though it is likely to run more as a typical quarter than an intensive summer session you'd see in the semester system.

The rarest of academic divisions is the trimester. Dividing the year into thirds (fall, winter, and spring with few or no summer school options), each trimester is twelve to thirteen weeks long and full-time students typically take three to four classes each session. While a trimester system is used in some middle and high schools in America, it is very rare in higher education, as colleges prefer the semester system with modified summer offerings.

Registering for Classes

Your first year, you will be assigned an academic advisor whose job it is to help you understand the requirements for your declared major (even if your declared major is "undeclared") and plan your course schedule to help you graduate on time. *On time* is a catchall term for a variable number of years, the complicated formula for which includes the following:

Declared major ×
Full or part time +/–
Summer courses ÷
Number of times student changes her major –
Which sessions required courses are *not* offered +
Incomplete study sessions abroad ×
Number of failed classes that must be repeated =
Graduation date +/– 2 years

Depending on your institution, your academic advisor may design your schedule, register you for the classes, and simply hand it to you (especially your first year), or he may hand you a list of required courses and leave the majority of the planning and registering up to you. Most advisors fall somewhere in the middle, requiring a sit-down meeting every term to check on your academic progress, decide which courses you need to take in the next term, help you plan which sections of the courses work best with the overall work/school balance, and then register you for them.

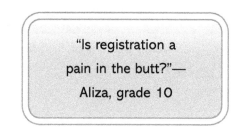

"Is registration a pain in the butt?"— Aliza, grade 10

Your first year, and possibly part of your second year, is likely to be filled with gen eds (general education courses) and pre-reqs (short for prerequisites, which are introductory courses that must be taken prior to upper-division courses in your major), so don't be surprised if you are a sophomore before you get to take classes that you feel have more to do with your chosen degree.

The purpose for gen eds is to help you be successful in college by understanding the breadth of information that all highly educated people are expected to have and, hopefully, find a career path in which you will be happy and prosperous. Pre-reqs provide the foundational knowledge and skills to help you be successful in more complex and time-consuming upper-division courses. My advice: instead of being frustrated with courses you may not find interesting or germane

"Do I have to take math and those other classes before I start my career's schooling?"—Alexa, grade 8

(a college word for "relevant," which is a high school word for "important") to your future career, believe that faculty members in your department and across the school have worked hard to design a degree program that best prepares you for your future career. Each of your teachers has earned an advanced degree, has worked in those areas, and knows more about your college success and future career than you do at this point. So relax and remember that every day you learn something new (even if you didn't want to learn it) is a day you haven't wasted.

It is possible that, due to low grades or test scores, you will be required to take remedial courses. These are high school–level courses and are designed to help you catch up to freshman-level class work. These classes are usually designated by a course number that begins with a zero and do not count toward your degree. If you believe that you do not need to take an assigned remedial course, talk to your advisor about the possibilities of being reassessed. If you do need a remedial course, take it! These courses are designed to help you succeed in college.

Did You Know?

Twenty percent of first-time undergraduates take at least one remedial course.[a]

FERPA and Your Family

FERPA (Federal Education Rights and Privacy Act) is a federal law that protects the privacy of students' academic records. When you are in elementary and high school, your parents have the right to view all of your educational records (e.g., grades and attendance) and discuss your educational progress with your teachers because you are a minor. When you turn eighteen and become a legal adult, the right to access this information transfers to you, the "eligible student." This means that even if your parents are paying for your education, they cannot get copies of your grades or speak with your teachers about your classes *unless* you have signed a form with the school granting them that access. Sometimes, schools include this form as part of your registration or financial aid package. Perhaps it was mentioned during parent orientation and you didn't feel comfortable refusing in front of your parents. Remember, if you have signed the form (often in the registrar or financial aid office), you may revoke that permission at any time by signing another form.

The school retains the right to provide, without your consent, what is called "directory" information about its students. This information includes a student's name, address, telephone number, date and place of birth, honors and awards, and dates of attendance.[1] Each school is required to have a process whereby you can request that the school not provide your directory information. If this is something you wish to pursue, ask the school about its individual process.

Mapping Your Class Schedule

When you meet with your advisor to declare your major, you will receive a list of required courses. You should also request a copy of this list when you do your school visit. Finally, schools have these lists on their websites so there should be no surprises about which courses you need to take.

The year you begin at the school is called your catalog year. This means that, even if changes are made to your program after you begin, the school cannot hold you accountable for these changes. Once you have completed all of the requirements from your catalog year, they have to graduate you. This keeps you from being a student forever, even if, some days, it feels like you will be.

As noted, your first year will likely be fairly set for you, full of gen eds and prereqs. However, you should still have some say in *which* social studies (e.g., history, anthropology, sociology, psychology) or science (e.g., biology, chemistry, geology, astronomy) class you take. Also, schools offer several sections of each course, which allows you to have a bit more say in which days and times (and teachers) you have. It is likely that you will be working at least part time, so having the ability to schedule all morning or all afternoon classes may help you with your work hours. However, most schools register seniors first, then juniors, and down to freshmen last. Also, there may

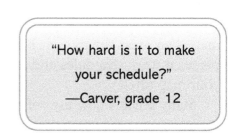

"How hard is it to make your schedule?"
—Carver, grade 12

be more students trying to register than there are available seats. Classes with ideal times and popular teachers fill up fast. There is no guarantee you will get your first (or fourth) choice, so make plans A–D as soon as the schedule for the next session comes out (usually a week or two before registration opens) and register as soon as you are able.

"How do you know what classes to take to be successful in the major you chose?"—Paige, grade 10

When I was in school, I made a weekly calendar (days and hours) and plugged in the classes and work schedule I wanted. Being me, I also color-coordinated it. I highly recommend that you do this *and* add in meals times (it is very easy to schedule classes through lunch) and study times. (In the next section, we'll discuss the number of homework hours per class that you should plan on.) It is easy to fool yourself into thinking, "Wow, I only have four classes, which is only twelve hours each week. I'm going to have tons of time for work and play!" No—no you are not. You may spend fewer hours in a desk than you did in high school, but you will spend *many* more hours doing homework. Also, no matter how popular you were in high school, higher education offers abundant opportunities for socializing. You should take advantage of all of these you can without risking your grades. The parties, sporting events, and other extracurricular activities available in college are not duplicated anywhere else in your life—so enjoy them.

Graduation Map

Essentially, your degree is a journey and your "graduation map" is all of the stops (i.e., courses) you need to take on the way. Just as you should map out your term schedule as a weekly calendar, you should map out your entire degree program. Some schools provide this for you. However, unless the school can guarantee you a spot in every class for every term (they can't), the graduation map is an ideal situation at best, not a guaranteed contract. Also, due to your personal work schedules and interests, don't be surprised if you have to revise your map often.

Many schools now use software programs such as DegreeWorks to help you manage your graduation map. These include options to see what would happen if you changed your major (remember, "undecided" is a perfectly acceptable option your first year) or added a minor. When you register for classes, the program marks them "in progress" and, once grades are posted, marks them "complete." This helps you to keep track of your progress toward completing your degree.

Majors/Minors/Emphases/Endorsements/Certificates

Your major is your primary degree program. When you accept your acceptance for the school and meet with your academic advisor for the first time, you will be asked to declare your major. This is the area that you will study for your degree (chapter 1) and future career.

In addition to declaring your major (this requires more than just telling people what your major is—there is, of course, paperwork involved), you can add minors and certifications. These are best to plan from the beginning as you can often take some of those courses for your gen eds. Most of these additions are to enhance your major and better market yourself for a career.

An emphasis, or concentration, is often used to explain your major. For example, if you earn a bachelor's in fine arts (BFA) with an emphasis/concentration in photography, fine arts is your degree and photography is your major. Another example is a bachelor's in business administration (BBA) with an emphasis/concentration in human resources: BBA (degree), human resources (major). A third example is a bachelor's degree in elementary education with an emphasis/concentration in mathematics. In this example, you may actually have two emphases/concentrations: BA in education (degree), elementary (major), mathematics (major). Got the hang of it?

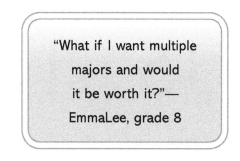

"What if I want multiple majors and would it be worth it?"—EmmaLee, grade 8

A minor is usually chosen to enhance your major. For example, a major in business administration is often enhanced with a minor in accounting, finance, human resources, or another specific field within business. Students working toward becoming doctors may major in biology and minor in chemistry to increase their chances of getting into medical school. A minor is, on average, eighteen to twenty-four credit hours of very specific (and usually upper-division) classes. It may have "hidden" pre-reqs. This means that you can't take a required class without a pre-req, but unless the pre-req is also required for one of your major classes, you may not be aware of it until you try to register. Be sure to talk with your academic advisor about the possibility of hidden pre-reqs.

Credit Hours

To earn a degree, you must earn a certain number of credit hours *and* you must take all of the required classes. A credit hour tells you how much the class is "worth" on your way to the magic graduation number (which varies per degree, major, and school but a bachelor's degree typically hovers around 120 credit hours). The number of credit hours a class is worth also signals how many hours of class time the course will meet with the instructor each week. On average, most classes are three credit hours and you will meet three hours each week. Classes that include extra time for labs—such as chemistry or foreign language—are often four credit hours. Usually, you will meet for three hours per week with the instructor and have one hour per week of lab time that may be run by the instructor but, more likely, will be supervised by a teaching assistant.

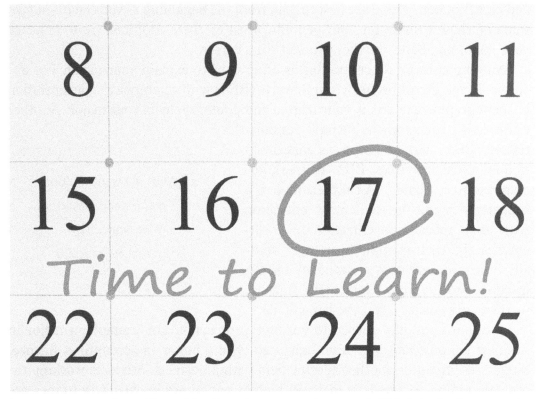

In some cases, a class will meet for three hours, one day a week. This is typically an evening or weekend class and is more common in graduate school. © *iStock / sapfirr*

To make things even more interesting, to give students and teachers time to get from one class to another, most hour-long classes are actually fifty minutes and most hour-and-a-half classes are seventy-five minutes long. For example, if you have a MWF (Monday, Wednesday, Friday) three-credit-hour class, it may meet from 10:00 to 10:50 a.m. with classes starting on the hour, every hour; a TR (Tuesday, Thursday—some colleges abbreviate it as T/TH) three-credit-hour class may meet from 8:30 to 9:45 a.m. with the next class starting at 10:00 a.m. and running until 11:15 a.m. Classes that require a lab are likely to meet MTRF or MTWR for fifty minutes each day or TR for one hundred minutes each day with the lab built in.

Scheduling is determined by the number of students per class, classes per semester, faculty teaching load, available labs and classrooms, and room occupancy. Typically, the department chair (with possible help from a department committee and probable help from ibuprofen) creates and submits a spreadsheet with

"What is the schedule like? Will I be going to school like
I do in high school?"—Maddison, grade 10

all of the classes she needs to offer, when they need to be offered (days/times), expected and maximum class sizes, and the name of the anticipated teacher, to the dean's office. The dean (or, more likely, the last person in the dean's office to call "not it") compiles all of the schedule requests from each department and sends them to the provost's office. There, possibly in a dark and scary room, all of the schedule requests are compiled to create the university schedule. An entire office is dedicated to finding and scheduling classrooms and labs for all of these classes. You can tell how stressed these people are by merely asking for a room change, something faculty are strongly discouraged from doing.

The number of credit hours you take is called your "course load." To qualify for many types of financial aid (and to defer student loan repayment), you must be a full-time student. Usually, full time is a course load of twelve to eighteen credit hours per term (semester, quarter, or trimester). Any fewer credit hours is considered part time and any more is considered insane. In chapter 9, we'll talk more about how much time credit hours actually take up in your life.

General Education Classes

Most degrees require that you complete a certain set of courses collectively called "general education" and typically abbreviated to "gen eds." Especially at a liberal arts college, these classes reflect a range of content areas and may feel like high school part two. Gen eds are lower division (freshman and sophomore) courses that are meant to do a variety of things, including

- test and strengthen your general knowledge
- introduce you to a variety of areas to pique your interest
- help you choose a major
- make you a more well-rounded citizen

In some cases, especially at open enrollment colleges, gen eds are used to weed out students who are unlikely to be successful at that particular institute.

Typically, gen eds include math, English composition, science, and history. Some may include a foreign language class, computer/technology class, and/or physical education class. They may also include a required course that masquerades by many names but is, essentially, How to Do College, specifically at that institution.

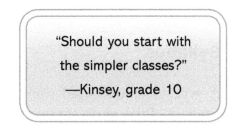

"Should you start with the simpler classes?"
—Kinsey, grade 10

> ## Vocabulary Moment
>
> ● An *open enrollment* or *open admissions* college is a noncompetitive or unselective school that accepts practically anyone with a high school diploma or a GED (General Education Development).

Many gen eds include a service learning component (depending on your school and program, you may have service learning requirements throughout). Service learning is what institutions of higher education call volunteering. (Try not to dwell on the oxymoron of forced volunteerism. Much of education seems contradictory and these inconsistencies are easiest to accept if ignored.)

Service learning requirements are denoted in how many clock hours you need to volunteer. Where you volunteer, as well as how many hours are required, varies by school/program/class and may be set by the school or by individual teachers. Required hours typically land somewhere between ten and twenty for the term. Some schools do not have a designation for service learning classes in their registration schedules so it is possible that you will not know you are taking a service learning course until the first day you attend class. This is just one of the many potential surprises that await you on the syllabus.

> ## Course Numbering
>
> Courses that start with a 1 or 2 are lower division classes, whereas upper division course numbers begin with a 3 or 4 and graduate courses begin with even higher numbers. If you happen to take a class that begins with a 0, it is a developmental or remedial class, meaning it's high school level and you likely won't get college credit for it.

Syllabus

A syllabus (pronounced sill·uh·bus—*not* silly bus) is, essentially, your course contract. Like most contracts, a syllabus (the plural is syllabi, pronounced sill·uh·bye) is full of useful information but not much fun to read. (Personally, I include cartoons in mine because, hey, I have to read them, too.) There are various formats to a syllabus but it should include the following:

- Faculty contact information: teacher's name, email, office location and hours, and phone number
- List of required (and optional) books/materials
- Course description: what the class is about (description should match the one in the university catalog you encountered when you registered for the class)
- Grading scale: what percentages equal what letter grades
- Class policies (such as attendance requirements, late work penalties, and technology usage—some professors have a "no cell phone in class" policy)
- Grading rubrics: how your assignments will be assessed
- Assignment due dates: when your assignments are due
- University policies (such as academic integrity, student notification procedures, tutoring availability)
- Subject-to-change clause: this is a small sentence with big ramifications; essentially, it means that if the instructor deems it necessary to change assignments or due dates, he or she has that right

Keep copies of all of your course syllabi. Many professors are posting their syllabi online instead of handing out paper copies to all students. If this is the case, print off a copy for your own use as you should refer to the syllabus *often*. The vast majority of questions that students ask are already answered in the syllabus. (Several companies offer T-shirts with "It's on the syllabus!" printed on them. Just in case anyone was wondering about a birthday gift for me. No pressure.) In addition to providing you with vital information while you take the class, if you transfer to another school, your syllabus may be necessary for course credit acceptance at your new college.

Attendance—Especially When It Isn't Required

One of the perks of higher education is that you aren't required to go to class. Many teachers include attendance as part of your grade and some institutions have policies that if you miss a certain number of classes, you will be dropped or failed from the class. However, no one is going to call your parents or a truancy officer. You are paying for the course and you are a legal adult, so the choice to succeed or fail is up to you. Welcome to adulthood!

Freedom comes with responsibility, and it is extremely rare (i.e., virtually impossible) to pass a college course if you don't show up. Many college courses are lecture and laboratory based. Professors deliver the information and then give you the opportunity to practice it—if you aren't there, you miss out. Some professors give participation points that can't be made up if you are absent, and many professors don't have a category for "excused" absences—you are there or you are not. Period. Most professors have late work policies that only give you a few days (if any) to make up missed assignments. You will not get to cram it all in at the end and begging for mercy won't matter. A failure to plan on your part will not constitute an emergency on the teacher's part.

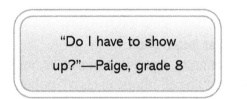

"Do I have to show up?"—Paige, grade 8

Many college classes are lecture format, which means you show up and listen to the professor give you the information while you take notes that you will use to study for the test. You are in charge of your learning. If you need extra help, there are tutors. If you blow off class and fail, you will likely need to take (and pay for) the class again. The professor will help you according to institution policy and what is written in the course syllabus, but there will be no hand-holding, mercy-passing, or caving in to parents.

If you want to pass, show up to class.

Studying

The credit-hour-to-study-hour ratio is one to two, which means professors plan for two times as much homework as class time. If you take a three-credit-hour class, you will spend three hours in class and have six hours of homework each week. This is the average. If you struggle with the course material, expect that you will need to spend more time studying. This doesn't sound like a lot but multiply it by the number of classes you are taking. Remember, a full load is typically twelve credit hours (which is twelve hours in class and an additional twenty-four hours of homework each week). If you are hoping to graduate in four to five years, you will likely take fifteen to eighteen credit hours (which is a total of forty-five to fifty-four hours of class and study time each week). Full-time school is a full-time job.

In addition to scheduling enough time to study, *where* you study is extremely important. Many students do their homework in their rooms, on their beds. This is the worst place you can study as it causes back and neck problems (improper support), limits your ability to focus on the material (too comfy), and messes with your sleep cycle (you are training your brain to stay awake when you are in bed). Your bed is where you (should) sleep and if it is also where you work, then your brain will not let you stop thinking enough to go to sleep. If you like studying in your room, stick to your desk and chair. Many people suggest a standing desk, which helps with posture and blood flow (which brings more oxygen to your brain). Before you invest, consider placing your laptop or desktop on top of your

> "How much time and effort goes into having to get the grades and do the work along with other things?"—Statler, grade 8

dresser or shelf and making your own standing desk. However, getting out of your room to study has many benefits including keeping your room as a relaxation station for sleeping and socializing.

School libraries have private study rooms and open study areas. *Use them!* They are open late and staffed with professionals. Even if you don't need to search the stacks for books and journals, being in an environment dedicated to learning will help you focus. Libraries are quiet, often centrally located on campus, have all the Internet resources, and are home to the books and journals you should be reading, and the library staff is wonderfully helpful. Additionally, it is not uncommon to find other students in your class who are studying for the same test or paper. Finally, college libraries also often have delis or coffee shops that are open during library hours. If you are worried about walking back to your home or dorm late at night, campus security offers escorts from the library. It is the safest, most convenient, and most productive place on campus.

If you are studying for a specific class, many institutions have tutoring centers with students who have taken (and passed) the class you need help with. Often, having an advanced student explain a concept, review a lab, or provide feedback on a paper is more helpful than asking your friends or family to "look it over." These centers may be connected to computer labs, and you are welcome to study there even without an official tutoring appointment. However, if you know you will need help, *make an appointment*, especially if it is during the busy seasons of midterm and finals.

Tutoring

I am often stunned at how many students complain about how difficult a class is and how they are struggling to understand the material but don't go to tutoring. Some students pay quite a bit of money for private tutors, but colleges offer tutoring centers for all subjects. While some colleges may limit the number of hours of free tutoring students can access, the vast majority have unlimited free tutoring (this is one of the things your fees pay for).

The research on the benefits of peer tutoring is near universal in its praise—not just for the tutee (yes, it's a real word!) but the tutor as well. According to the National Tutoring Association, the benefits of tutoring include not only increased academic successes, but improved self-confidence, greater persistence in task and course completion, better studying strategies, enhanced peer relations, improved internal locus of control (the understanding that your actions influence events around you and that you are responsible for your actions instead of blaming everything in your life on others and playing the eternal victim), and skills that transfer to your workplace or parenting.[2]

> "How do you get a tutor or how do you become one?"—Anjelita, grade 8

Many tutoring labs are also open-study computer labs. This means you can spend your study time in there even without an appointment. For example, writing centers are often computer labs where you can write your paper as you would in any computer lab or library computer station. However, with the writing tutors working there, it is easy to ask for help as the need arises. Have a grammar question? Just ask a passing tutor your quick question and keep working on your paper.

Use tutoring centers to work on your homework and tutors for help on specific issues, and use them early and often. Don't wait until you are behind and desperate; make an appointment with a tutor when you are ahead and desperate.

Student Support Services

Student Support Services is an area of higher education that can incorporate several aspects, including disability support. If you have a physical or learning disability, colleges have departments to help you. However, it is a bit different from your K–12 experience. While in elementary and secondary school, the school and your parents initiated assessment, diagnosis, and the creation of a 504 designation and IEP (Individualized Education Program) goals and modifications. Every year (or so), you were reassessed and your IEP was updated. The school passed your information on to the next grade and then to the next school as needed. This is not how it works in higher education.

You are considered an adult (even if you begin college before your eighteenth birthday), and your K–12 disability information is not forwarded to the higher education institution. If you need disability support, *you* are responsible for making an appointment at the disability support services on campus and initiating assessment. You will likely need to be reassessed for accommodations, so prepare yourself by gathering all former records, including doctors' reports. College teachers cannot make modifications for your education until they have the paperwork from the disability support services department. Even if your teachers suspect a learning disability or you tell them honestly that you need a certain modification that you have had in the past, they cannot make accommodations for you without that paperwork. If you know that you will need accommodations such as extra testing time, a note taker, or a sign language interpreter, *you* must take the lead on the process. These services are open (though they may have limited hours) during the summer so as soon as you have accepted your acceptance to the institution, contact the necessary centers and get started on your assessments so they can be in place when classes start.

Online Education

Taking classes online may seem like a dream come true. What? I can sit in my pajamas and binge-watch Netflix *and* get college credit? What a wonderful world we live in!

Um, nope. It really doesn't work that way. Online classes are actually harder to pass for most people. The reason? You have to be super motivated and organized and have excellent self-control. Additionally, there is less help for you if you are struggling with the course content because you don't have personal access to the instructor, teaching assistants, or tutors.

Yes, I hear online teachers and program directors screaming, "Yes, you do have access! We've spent millions on software and trainings to ensure that professors hold online office hours and tutoring centers offer synchronous and asynchronous sessions." This is true. However, no amount of technology can replace face-to-face interaction with the instructor or tutor; especially when so many students take an online class in the area they most struggle with. For example, if writing is not your thing, don't take an online version of Freshman Composition. You need *more* support and *more* structure—not *less*. If you aren't

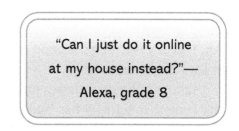

"Can I just do it online at my house instead?"— Alexa, grade 8

good at it and you don't like it, you are less likely to devote the time necessary to succeed. It's easy enough to procrastinate with the things we like, but the things we hate? We can put those off forever.

If intrinsic motivation is lacking, you have to make up for it with extrinsic motivation, such as seeing a classroom full of people working on the same assignment, having a study buddy guilt you into doing the assignment, or having to face the teacher two or three times each week and not wanting to see "that look."

So even when an online section is an option, carefully consider how much more work it is and how much more dedication you will need to be successful. It isn't, necessarily, your best option.

Online classes are not easier nor less time consuming than face-to-face courses. Be honest about your organization skills and ability to avoid procrastination to know if online learning is right for you. © *iStock / fizkes*

Online Class

Ah, I see my warning has gone unheeded. All right, if you insist on an e-education, at least do it correctly.

Taking individual classes online while completing a degree at a ground university (one that actually has buildings and classrooms and cafeterias) is an increasingly popular option. You may decide to take a class online because of a scheduling conflict such as two required face-to-face classes scheduled at the same time; a face-to-face class is during the only time you can work; or a face-to-face class is only offered at night and you don't have sufficient transportation. Sometimes, typically offered face-to-face classes are only offered online during the summer, and you want to take summer sessions so you can take fewer credit hours during the school year. Perhaps the perpetually orange-fingered, Cheeto-eating girl you barely survived sharing a desk with last semester has promised to take the next class with you—and you find yourself less than thrilled with that future. Whatever your reason, you first need to clarify if the class is fully online or hybrid. A fully online class never meets face-to-face, whereas a hybrid class requires that you do meet face-to-face for a portion of class. There are many different types of hybrid schedules. Some only require your personal appearance on the first day for instructions and the last day for the final exam. Others require you to meet once each week in person and do the rest online. Still others may be all online except for a week or two of face-to-face practicum. If the school schedule isn't clear as to how much face-to-face time a hybrid requires, contact the instructor of record.

Some schools charge a different amount for tuition or fees for an online class. Others require specific software that you may need to purchase. Some online classes require a certain number of synchronous hours (you have to be online at a certain time), so it may not be as convenient as you believe. These are all possibilities you'll want to clarify before you begin the class.

Another possible issue with an e-class is getting your books and supplies. If you are no longer in the area of the campus (maybe you went home for the summer and want to take an online class so you can keep up with your planned graduation date while living off of your parents for three months), you'll need to order your books. Most college bookstores offer the option of ordering from them and they'll ship the books to you. You may decide it is preferable to order directly from the publisher or an online dealer such as Amazon. All of these take time and money.

Online Degree

It is possible, depending on your career field, to get most or all of your degree online. As with all types of education, there are pros and cons to the online variety. As the purpose of this book is to help you navigate a ground or brick-and-mortar college, I won't go into detail about online education beyond the warning that, according to the Marketplace at the *Chronicle of Higher Education*, employers rate online schools as "undesirable" in hiring employees.[3] If you choose to do an online degree, do it from a college that has a ground campus.

Dropping a Class

Colleges have strict deadlines. Typically, you won't be able to add a class after the first week of the term. There are a couple of different drop deadlines for different purposes. You may drop individual classes (it isn't an all-or-nothing proposition), but remember that if you drop so many classes that you are now registered for fewer than twelve credits, you are no longer considered a full-time student and this may affect your financial aid.

Keep track of add/drop dates as they will affect your GPA and finances. © iStock / Wavebreakmedia

The first deadline is usually a few weeks into the term—the Drop with a Refund deadline. This means that if you drop by that date, you can receive a full (or partial depending on the school) refund. No record of you ever being in that class will be on your transcripts.

Later in the semester, you will have a deadline to drop with a *W*. This *W* stands for *withdraw*, and while it doesn't allow for a refund and will show up on your transcripts, it will not affect your GPA. Some schools will post a *WP* for *withdrew passing* or a *WF* for *withdrew failing*. It still won't affect your GPA but anyone reading your transcripts will know if you were passing or failing at the point of dropping the class.

If you wish to drop all of your classes, you will need to withdraw from the school. There are deadlines for this type of drop as well, but they often align with the refund and *W* dates for dropping individual classes.

The college will also have a nonpayment deadline, which means they will drop you from all of your registered classes if you haven't paid (or made arrangement to pay) by that date. This deadline is likely to be before classes begin.

Dropping a class means more than just not going. As long as you are registered, you are responsible for paying the tuition. If you are still registered at the end of the term, the teacher is required to give you a grade and it will affect your GPA. The only way to fix that is to retake (and repay for) the class. Even if you change your major and no longer need that class, it will stay on your transcripts and your GPA.

Transcripts

Transcripts are your official academic record and list every class you took (and didn't drop before the refund deadline) and the grade you earned. It will list your term and overall GPA. It may list your major GPA separately. Even if you decide college isn't for you and drop out, whenever you return, your transcripts will be waiting for you. If you transfer to another college and want credit for any of the classes you have already taken, you have to request your transcripts and your old school will send your complete transcript to your new school. Transcripts *are* all-or-nothing. You cannot have the old school just send a record of the classes you passed. If the new school gives you credit for any of the classes you took at your old school, they will also calculate your old GPA into the current one. A student who bombs the first year and decides to try at another college often makes the decision to start with a fresh slate and never admit to attending the old college.

GPA

You probably already know that your GPA is your grade point average. This means that each letter grade is assigned a point value (A = 4, B = 3, C = 2, D = 1, F = 0), and your points are added up and divided by the total number of credits to calculate your average. Many scholarships, programs, honors societies, and graduate schools have minimum GPA requirements (and are often 3.0—B average—or higher).

You may be a 4.0 (straight A) student in high school but don't expect that to be the case in college. Just as high school was harder than elementary school, college is harder than high school. If you go to college with the same study habits and expectations you had in high school, you may be quite surprised at your first set of graded assignments.

Textbooks

Two of the biggest shocks to new college students are (1) you have to buy your textbooks and (2) how incredibly expensive they are. According to the National Association of College Stores, college students spend an average of $655 each year on textbooks. The College Board includes "materials" (e.g., paper and pens) and puts that figure at more than $1,100/year. For-profit college students

"Do I have to buy books? I have heard that you use the books maybe like three times and they cost like $200."—Christian, grade 12

pay even more, as the majority of funding for these schools comes from students' tuition and fees.[4]

Remember, these figures are an average; depending on your major, you could spend far more as it isn't uncommon for some textbooks to be $300 or more. Yep—$300 for one book and you may only use it for three months. Professors are increasingly using OERs (open educational resources) and less-expensive digital materials wherever possible. While we've all heard the stories of professors requiring expensive books they hardly use, most professors are quite aware of the costs of books and try to utilize all relevant resources. Please keep in mind that the publisher—*not the author or teacher*—sets the price. Additionally, there are ways to save money on textbooks.

One way to save money is to buy used books. Some students prefer buying books with someone else's notes and highlights in them thinking an already-annotated book is helpful. Keep in mind that there is no guarantee that the previous owner(s) were good students. Also, while used books are cheaper than new books, they still cost about 80 percent of the new book cost; it isn't as if you

Buying or renting used textbooks could save you quite a bit of money. © iStock / JenniferRae

"What are the cheapest books and materials I can get
that will help my education?"—Kinley, grade 8

are getting them for only a few dollars. Used books can be bought through the campus bookstore or directly from previous students. If you know someone who took the class last term, talk about purchasing or renting their book. Many students post flyers advertising used books for sale and some schools (especially in residence halls) have dedicated bulletin boards for textbook sales.

Another way to save money is to rent textbooks. There are several online textbook rental companies and many schools offer this service through their bookstores. Be sure to read the fine print regarding the required condition of the book upon return. Know if you are allowed to highlight or notate within the book and what the cost will be if your book becomes damaged (coffee spills, broken spine—the book's, not yours—or torn pages are all possibilities that will cost you). You will also want to be sure you have returned the book on time or you'll likely need to pay for a second term of usage.

You will likely have little continued use for a gen ed textbook after the course is completed, but it's quite possible that the textbooks for your major will be something you wish to hang on to. Keep this in mind when purchasing (and lending) books.

Navigating the Bookstore

Yes, I know you've been to a bookstore. An old-fashioned, brick-and-mortar bookstore where you look for genre signs hanging from the ceiling and then authors whose works are alphabetized by their last names is not a "new" thing for you. You've also been to the library, which works on a similar basis.

But, a college bookstore does *not* work this way. When you go to buy your textbooks, they will be organized in a very different manner. First of all, you'll need your course schedule. Each class will have an abbreviated name (usually three or four letters) and a number (again, most schools have either a three- or four-digit numbering scheme).

College bookstores organize textbooks by these course codes that are based on areas of study and alphabetized by these subjects; for example, all of the accounting (which may be abbreviated ACCT) books will be together and will be before all of the anthropology (ANTH) books. Within these subjects, the books will be arranged by the course number; that is, books for 1000 level will come before 2000 level books, and within that, books for a course numbered 1020 will come before 1030.

Let's look at a concrete example. Imagine it is your first semester and you are taking the following fairly typical courses:

- Freshman English (ENGL 1010), three credit hours
- College Algebra (MATH 1020), three credit hours
- Introduction to Computer Programming (CSIS 1010), three credit hours
- Human Biology with lab (BIOL 1020), four credit hours (remember that extra lab requirement)
- Cultural Anthropology (ANTH 1010), three credit hours
- Introduction to Yoga (PE 1057), one credit hour (typical of physical education classes)

With this schedule, you'll have seventeen credit hours of first-year (1000-level) classes.

Some university bookstores have workers who collect your books for you. You give your schedule to one of the "runners," who disappears for a few minutes and returns with all the books for your classes. While this might seem preferable to finding your own books, there are drawbacks. You may have less choice over new versus used books, and you certainly wouldn't get to pick which used book to purchase.

However, the odds are that you will get to find your own books so let's take our hypothetical schedule and continue our imaginary trip. College bookstores do not have shopping carts; they have little baskets. Textbooks are heavy. Consider this your first academic workout. Also, all students are trying to buy their books within the same few days. Prepare for long lines, shortened tempers, and very busy bookstore employees (most of whom will be students themselves). Add in several hundred parents trying to "help" their kids navigate the bookstore and realize that your trip will not be a quick one. This is *not* something you can take care of in the few minutes between classes.

Okay—you've got a copy of your schedule and have found the campus bookstore. You've managed to make your way past clothes racks and shelves of school merchandise to the back or the basement where textbooks are kept. Hopefully, you haven't forgotten to grab a basket. Alphabetically, which class do you head for first? Right! Anthropology. There are four ceiling-to-floor bookshelves in this section. On the front of each shelf, there are tags with ANTH and a variety of numbers. You scan the shelves for ANTH 1010 (probably on the top shelves) and realize there are fifteen sections of ANTH 1010. And they all have different required textbooks. *What?* Breathe!

Look back at your schedule and find the section number after the course code (ANTH 1010). You learn you are in section seven. Back to the shelves and you find "ANTH 1010 Sec 07." Before putting the book(s) in your basket, double check the professor's last name on your schedule and make sure it matches the professor listed on the tag. *But* is there only one required text? Check the shelf tags to see if there are multiple books, extra workbooks, and/or any optional or recommended materials. These last ones are materials that the professor is not requiring, but suggests you consider getting as they may be useful for best understanding course information. Most people decide whether to purchase these materials based on personal budgets. OK, you've checked the tags and realize there is only one required textbook. The used ones look to be in fairly good shape and are twenty dollars less than a new one so you grab one and put it in your basket. Next stop? Yes, B for Biology.

Here you find eight shelves of BIOL 1020 materials, so you narrow it down to section and double-check the professor's name and discover that there is a required textbook and an optional study guide. Get the study guide. Remember there's a lab component for this class so you'll need to see which lab section you are in and repeat before moving on to CSIS (Computer Science and Information Services).

By the time you get finished, you have a thirty-seven-pound basket and a yoga mat tucked beneath your arm. As you politely make your way toward the cash registers, you pass shelves of three-ring binders, pens, T-shirts with the college logo, and two hundred people. By the time you get to the checkout line, your basket is over forty pounds and your fingers are starting to cramp. Feel free to place your basket on the floor and nudge it slowly forward as the line moves incrementally. But don't lose hope! Keep your temper and your smile and look around you. Many college students have secured their first date while waiting in line at the bookstore. Use the time wisely.

Note Taking

It amazes me how few students know how to take notes effectively. So many of them sit in class and try to transcribe every word the teacher says. The new thing is to take pictures of the board or screen with your cell phone and pretend you will actually use them to study from. You won't. Do you know how much text we can fit on a white board or a PowerPoint slide and how small it all looks on your phone? Even if you transfer the picture to your computer screen and the resolution is good enough to read, who wants to do that? Also, professors *hate* it when you ask them to wait to continue with their lecture so you can take a picture. Seriously. Stop it. Most of us put the PowerPoints on our course LMS anyway (learning management system such as Canvas, Blackboard, or Moodle).

Taking clear and organized notes is vital to doing well in college. If you don't know how to take notes effectively, ask your college about a note-taking workshop. © *iStock / Jacob Ammentorp Lund*

Some students prefer to take notes electronically but the research[5] has shown that comprehension and recall are lessened by typing notes instead of handwriting them. And those touch screen keyboards? Even worse for learning than actual keyboards. So take paper and a writing utensil and *take notes*.

There are several ways to improve your note-taking skills. Many colleges have classes or workshops you can take (some are free) on improving your learning and studying habits. These include speed reading, organization, and note taking. If your school offers these, take them.

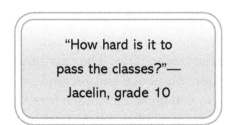

"How hard is it to pass the classes?"— Jacelin, grade 10

Just in case your school doesn't offer these workshops, I'll include a couple of note-taking methods my students have had success with.

The Cornell Note-Taking System[6] is so popular that several universities offer tutorials as part of learning strategies. If that isn't available, you can watch YouTube videos describing the system. This method is so effective that there have even been tutorials created so you can use Microsoft Word to create Cornell notes templates.[7] Some high school teachers utilize this system so it is possible you are already famil-

> **Did You Know?**
>
> There are several shorthand systems, including Pitman, Gregg, and Teeline. The Groote system was invented by a Dutch general and is specifically for taking shorthand on horseback. And, yes, there are YouTube videos as well as free online lessons for all types of shorthand.

iar with using Cornell notes to organize your summaries. If not, take the time to learn—even if you already believe you have a system that works for you.

If you learn better with visual aids, mind maps may work best for you. Mind maps utilize pictures, graphs, and color coding to help you see the progression of an idea. These visual aids help you see sequential information without writing long paragraphs of text. GoConqr has an app as well as an explanatory article to walk you through mind mapping.[8]

If you like copying down as much of the lecture as possible but can't write as fast as the professor can talk, consider learning shorthand or creating your own version of shorthand using abbreviations, symbols, or skipping vowels. Remember to transcribe your notes into longhand or type them out as soon after class as possible so you are most likely to transcribe correctly.

Underlining or highlighting text as you read can be useful unless you underline everything, in which case you get a useless, although colorful, page. I suggest creating a color-coding system such as names in yellow, dates in blue, terms in green, and so on. You don't need to underline or highlight everything—just key words or phrases. Your eye will be drawn to the color when you reread and study. Additionally, color-coded text is easily transferred to your note-taking system. If you do use highlighters, be sure to splurge on the ones specifically for textbooks so you don't get bleed through on the pages.

Binder Organization

Remember those three-ring binders you grabbed in the bookstore? It's time to put them to use.

One of the biggest mistakes students make is to underestimate the power of organization. There are many ways of organizing your school materials, and if you have already found a method that works for you, stick with it. However, if you aren't getting at least a B average and/or have a history of turning in assignments late or having to explain to your parents about "missing" assignments, you might want to read through this section.

To try to make some of this information more useful to you, I'm going to reuse that course schedule I created for you (see table 7.1). These sample classes are a fairly typical beginning schedule with course title (course code: prefix and number) and number of credit hours:

- Freshman English (ENGL 1010), three credit hours
- College Algebra (MATH 1020), three credit hours
- Introduction to Computer Programming (CSIS 1010), three credit hours
- Human Biology with lab (BIOL 1020), four credit hours (remember that extra lab requirement)
- Cultural Anthropology (ANTH 1010), three credit hours
- Introduction to Yoga (PE 1057), one credit hour (typical of physical education classes)

Once you have your schedule figured out for *when* each class meets, look at your registration to see *where* each class meets. Pull out a map of your campus and

Table 7.1 Sample First-Term Course Schedule

Monday	Tuesday	Wednesday	Thursday	Friday
8–8:50 BIOL 1020		8–8:50 BIOL 1020	8–9:40 BIOL 1020 lab	8–8:50 BIOL 1020
	10–11:40 ANTH 1010		10–11:40 ANTH 1010	
10–10:50 ENGL 1010		10–10:50 ENGL 1010		10–10:50 ENGL 1010
11–11:50 MATH 1010		11–11:50 MATH 1010		11–11:50 MATH 1010
	2–3:40 CSIS 1010		2–3:40 CSIS 1010	
				4–4:50 PE 1057

find each classroom. Walking your schedule each semester (going from biology to English to math) will help you not feel stressed or lost when there are hundreds or thousands of people trying to accomplish this at the same time.

Organization Method 1: The Per-Class Method

Get a ½-inch binder for each class. Either create sticky labels for the spines or get the binders with clear covers and make card stock labels to slide into the spine covers. Label them with the course code (ENGL 1010) or course name (Freshman English)—or both. Put loose-leaf paper and a pocket folder in each. This way, all of your notes and handouts for the class will remain together. Once you get a copy of the course syllabus with assignment due dates, put it in the binder.

Designate a shelf in your domicile (dorm, apartment, parents' basement) that is just for your class materials. I find it preferable to have each binder in a different color and to put the binder and books on the shelf in the order of the classes: all MWF materials together and all TR materials together (remember, in academia we often abbreviate Thursday as R). Keeping your course materials together as well as a supply of pens, pencils, calculator, candies, and tissues in your backpack will increase the likelihood of you getting to class with the necessary materials, even at 8 a.m. after a particularly "fun" night.

Organization Method 2: The Per-Day Method

Get two 1½–2-inch binders and divide the loose-leaf paper and pocket binders into a MWF binder and a TR binder; this cuts down on the amount of materials you have to carry to class. Also, you may look at your MWF schedule and think, "I'll just take stuff for Biology right now. I can come back and get my stuff for English and Math between 9 and 10." The thing is—you won't. You do not want to spend that time running back and forth from campus to home or your car. Use the time wisely to study or get the breakfast you missed out on when you woke up at 7:45 for your 8:00 a.m. class (yes, you will). Or use the time to ask out the cute boy in your biology class who doesn't care that you have worn the same sweat pants all week and that you have completely forgotten how to put on makeup. (Keeping emergency deodorant and breath mints in your backpack is a necessary part of college.)

It is easy for backpacks to get very heavy, very fast. If you have even three classes on Monday, each with only one textbook, and one 2-inch binder, along with materials, a laptop, cell phone, headphones, and power bars (you know, the essentials), you've already got several pounds to carry with you. It is likely that you'll have even more items stuffed in your bag and colleges don't have lockers (except for physical education lockers but that won't help you between classes). Interestingly enough, many colleges are built on hills (my theory is that all the flat land was claimed for farming and livestock) and the larger the school, the more acreage you'll have to cover in fifteen minutes or less.

Summer School

Most colleges offer summer sessions. The traditional view of summer school is to retake courses you failed, and while this is an option, the priority for summer school is to get ahead on your degree or so that you don't have to take as many credit hours during the regular terms.

Summer classes are not like those during regular terms. They are usually more hours during the day and more days during the week, but for fewer weeks. For example, you may have class two hours each day, five days each week, but for only four weeks. Summer classes are intense! Expect to have the same requirements you would have if you took the class during a regular term because if you want full credit, you need to do full work.

Possible summer course issues include the following:

- Some schools have limitations on tutoring services during the summer (usually fewer tutors and fewer open hours).
- Some schools don't offer as many courses, so the class you need might not be available.
- Sometimes, summer classes are more likely to be cancelled because they didn't "make" (what we call a course that gets enough students so that the budget department decides it isn't costing the school money).
- Sometimes, financial aid doesn't cover summer classes—tuition and/or living expenses.
- Students often take their hardest/least favorite course during the summer. This is under the (false) assumption that summer classes are easier. It is natural to want to avoid that which we hate or that with which we struggle; however, it is likely that you need *more* help with that class—not less. If you have time in the summer to take only that one class (and you don't have work or life interference), and you can dedicate abundant time to that class, summer session may be a great opportunity. Just be aware of the realities of summer school.

Academic Integrity

Some colleges will have honor codes that require you to not only avoid dishonest activity yourself but also to turn in any student you know who is violating the honor code. All colleges have an academic honesty policy that forbids cheating of any kind. This includes plagiarism.

Plagiarism is taking another author's expressions, ideas, language, or thoughts and misrepresenting them as your own. This could be a straight copy and paste from a website, journal, book, or newspaper, or restating their writing in your own words but not giving them credit (citing) for the information/ideas. Plagiarism can be intentional or unintentional (often because you aren't diligent about citations). Hopefully, your high school teachers were adamant about citing your sources because college teachers are brutal about it. You can be expelled from school for plagiarism or, at least, failed from the course in which you plagiarized. Minimum penalties are a zero for the plagiarized assignment. Often, professors start with a failed assignment and a warning that further instances of plagiarism will result in a failing grade for the course and a referral to the dean for potential expulsion.

You will likely submit your written work digitally (through the course's LMS such as Canvas or Blackboard, or through a broader platform such as Google Classroom), and these all have integrated plagiarism checker software. This software compares your paper against millions of sources including previous student papers that have been checked for plagiarism. Once you submit your paper, a digital copy is added to the repository of student work so that future papers are checked against it. When your professor opens your assignment, she will get a plagiarism report stating the percentage of your paper that may be plagiarized. It also marks which section(s) were found duplicated elsewhere and provides a link to those sources. Your professor can do a side-by-side comparison of your work and the possible source(s) it came from to determine if plagiarism happened.

Of course, you are allowed to reference another author's work—that's what research is! But you must absolutely, positively, unequivocally, cite *all* the material you used (whether through direct or indirect quotes), according to the citation and format style required by your teacher. Humanities fields tend to use MLA (Modern Language Association) while the sciences use APA (American Psychological Association). There are several others and your professor will tell you which she wants. Your library will have reference manuals for each and you can also find the latest editions online. Purdue University has an excellent online resource called the OWL (Online Writing Lab) at owl.english.purdue.edu that includes research and writing tips in addition to style help.

> ### Helpful Tip
>
> Do *not* use citation engines to create your in-text citations and works cited/bibliography page. They are not reliably accurate. *Do* use the research librarian at your university and the latest printed version of the style guide.

Remember that having another person do your homework for you (even if you pay them or are related to them), using someone else's unpublished work (such as your roommate's paper because she took this course last semester), or giving your work to someone else to use are all cheating. Paying someone else to write your paper for you doesn't mean you "own" it in a non-plagiarism sense. Claiming another's work as your own, even with their permission, is plagiarism.

One last thing. If you happen to have a professor who has you hand in your work on actual paper, don't think you can get away with plagiarism. He has likely read so many papers, and all the research on the topic, that he can spot a copied text a mile away. He can always confirm his suspicions by typing that part of your paper into our user-end plagiarism checker.

General Safety

Campuses provide security escorts for students who feel unsafe, particularly after dark. You should also get in the habit of not walking around alone; there is more than one reason to have a study buddy.

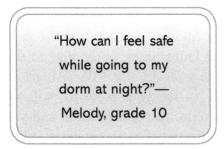

"How can I feel safe while going to my dorm at night?"— Melody, grade 10

When I was an undergraduate, I liked to study at the library in the evenings (it was quieter than my dorm room). I was often there until well after dark but all I had to do was pick up the phone and call my dorm's main line and within a few minutes, two of my friends would arrive at the library to walk me back to the dorm. They would do this for anyone who called and asked for company, and I'm willing to bet that you'll have friends who will do the same.

Your campus may have emergency call boxes with a phone or a speaker with an emergency button that connects directly to campus security (which will know your location). Push the button or pick up the phone handle and the light will illuminate and a siren will sound. Know the locations of these boxes so that, if you are being chased, you can (literally) sound the alarm.

Campuses have alert systems you can subscribe to so that, in the event of an emergency, you will receive a text and/or email notifying you (and everyone else) of the situation. Stay calm and follow the given emergency protocols. Campus security are well trained and, in some cases, fully trained police officers. Many colleges have a city police substation on or very near campus.

Student IDs

One of the steps for registering at your college will be to get your student identification (ID) card. Your ID card may be used for many things, depending on your college. Some schools require you to present your ID to get into school events. Others allow you to put money on it (you will likely need to do this in the cashier's office) but then you can use it like a debit card at on-campus eateries (and vending machines). If you live in a dormitory, you may need to use it as your passkey to get in after curfew (most schools don't expect you to be in your rooms after a certain time, but they may lock the outside doors for safety). Many schools require a current sticker on it proving you're registered for that term (you don't get a new ID every term). There's probably a fee if you need to replace a lost ID.

Many businesses offer discounts to students and your ID is your proof. Even if the business doesn't post student discounts, ask.

WHO'S WHO

As we've discussed, academia is its own world with its own rules and idiosyncrasies. Part of knowing how to navigate this world is knowing the players and their roles. As such, this chapter is dedicated to helping you understand the structure of higher education.

Faculty

Everyone who teaches is considered a member of the faculty (or faculty member). There are many different types of faculty, however, and they are designated by rank (like the military but without the cool uniforms).

However, before we discuss faculty rank, we need to take a moment to explain tenure. Many people believe that tenure means a teacher can't be fired. This is not true. Teaching, as a paid profession, existed for centuries before labor laws, which include due process protection and the employee's right to know why he or she is being terminated (fired, not killed). Before earning tenure, a teacher is a contract employee who can be fired at any time without cause. A nontenured teacher doesn't have any protection against retaliation from administration. There are many things that teachers have to do to earn tenure, including a minimum of six years of positive teacher evaluations from students and administrators, several peer-reviewed publications that contribute to the discipline (some places require a book), and years of service contribution to the department, college, university, and community. Then the faculty member has to go through a rigorous application process that includes having her teaching, scholarship, and service scrutinized by her department, dean, provost, president, and the board of trustees. At any point in this yearlong process (which is usually the seventh year of employment), tenure can be denied. Once a faculty member earns tenure, it simply means that if the university terminates her employment, it must be for a legal and legitimate reason and the university must tell the teacher *why* she was fired. Tenured faculty may still be fired for poor teaching, illegal activity, or failure to continue to contribute to the scholarship of the discipline and service to the institution. Tenure does *not* guarantee lifelong jobs for poor teachers. That is a myth.

When an open teaching position is posted, it is either a tenure-track or non–tenure-track position. Teaching positions such as adjunct, instructor, and lecturer are, typically, nontenure track. This means that even if the person hired for the position fulfilled all the requirements of a tenure-track position, he wouldn't be granted tenure. A tenure-track position just means that earning tenure is an option. If the tenure-track teacher does not meet every requirement for tenure within the allotted time, his employment is terminated. This is where the term *publish or perish* comes from—a phrase all tenure-track and tenured teachers know all too well.

OK—back to faculty rankings.

Graduate Teaching Assistant

If you attend a university with graduate programs, your introductory courses may be taught by a graduate teaching assistant (GA or GTA). This is a student who has completed his bachelor's degree in the field and is working on a master's or doctorate. Graduate students often teach freshman-level courses as part of their scholarship package for graduate school. GTAs are supervised and supported by full-time faculty members. One of the perks to attending a community or teaching-focused college is that fewer courses are taught by GTAs as fully qualified faculty who have earned their terminal degree teach courses at all levels.

A "terminal" degree is the highest degree possible. The fact that it also refers to death is coincidental. At least, I think it is a coincidence. © *iStock / LemonTreeImages*

Adjunct Faculty

An adjunct teacher is a part-time member of the faculty. This teacher is hired to teach a few classes (sometimes only one or two) during the term. His employment is on a term-by-term basis and is often utilized for filling in for full-time faculty who get a course release for a special project, committee work, research and publication, or for a temporary increase in student enrollment. An adjunct teacher must meet all the academic requirements of full-time faculty. He must have a graduate degree appropriate to the discipline/content he is teaching. Often, adjunct faculty have master's degrees but not doctorates and may be working on their doctorate while adjuncting. They are not required to publish and have few service obligations beyond faculty meetings.

Instructor/Lecturer

An instructor/lecturer is, usually (depending on the institution), hired full time but on a year-to-year basis. An instructor often teaches lower-division (freshmen and sophomore) courses, especially in research institutions. Like adjunct faculty, an instructor has a master's degree but not necessarily a doctorate. Because an instructor is not eligible to earn tenure, she does not have scholarship requirements (although most will keep up with scholarship to remain relevant in their field, especially if they are working on doctorates) and have minimal service requirements that are typically focused on the department.

Assistant Professor

An assistant professor is a tenure-track teacher with a terminal degree in his field (usually a doctorate but there are some areas, such as business and fine arts, where a master's is considered the highest degree). Because an assistant professor is working toward earning tenure, he has teaching, scholarship, and service commitments. He will teach a full load (usually three or four classes per term), publish an article every one to two years while also working on a book, and serve on committees at the department, college, university, and community levels. This lasts for about six years before the application for tenure is due, and the seventh year (or year-of-stressful-waiting) begins.

Associate Professor

An associate professor has earned tenure. She is still required to earn positive teaching evaluations from her students, publish on a regular basis, and provide ample service to all levels of the university. Often, an associate professor is also required to take advanced leadership roles such as department chair or associate dean. If she wants to earn a promotion to full professor, she continues to work on her book.

Full Professor

A full professor is a tenured professor who has earned the final level of rank advancement. Some universities do not require an associate professor to earn full professor rank—it's a choice. Typically, the rank advancement requirements are similar to moving from assistant to associate professor (teaching, scholarship, and service) and require a minimum of five years of positive employment at the associate professor level and a published book.

Professor Emeritus

A professor emeritus is a retired professor who may teach on a limited basis, such as a specialized topics class once a year. A professor emeritus is considered an expert in her field, and the university is fortunate to have its best teachers still willing to teach after retirement. The word *emeritus* is from the Latin *e–* "out of" and *meritus* "merit." As such, some schools do not bestow the title on all retired professors, whereas other institutions do so as a sign of respect for the years of service. The female equivalent word is *emerita*, though because English isn't a gendered language (notice that a female professor is not called a *professoress*), *emeritus* is typically used in America for retired professors of either gender. (Note: if you happen to win a jeopardy tournament with this information, I expect a percentage of your winnings.)

! Vocabulary Moment

Course release means a professor teaches fewer courses so that he can do other scholarship or service obligations. Typically, a teacher may have a one or two course release during a term depending on the time commitment of the scholarship or service. Course releases are usually temporary, and the teacher returns to a full load (three or four classes per term) when the scholarship or service commitment is completed.

Department Chair

A department chair is typically a faculty member of the department who is on a course release to take on the administrative duties of the department. While she may occasionally be hired specifically to fulfill this position long term, most departments rotate full-time, tenured faculty members through this position. Depending on the size of the department, there may be another faculty member serving as associate chair. The dean appoints some department chairs, while department colleagues elect others. She may work with scheduling and course substitution and oversee new faculty hires and student workers. However, her primary purpose is to manage the daily department operations and advocate for her department with the college and university.

If you are close to graduation (I'm talking last semester close), and a required course isn't offered that semester, the chair may be able to work out a course substitute (you take another, approved, class and it counts for the required one) so you can graduate on time. However, there is no guarantee, so don't put off a class you don't want to take in the hopes of a course substitution; the gamble isn't worth the risk of a delayed graduation.

Are you still wondering what to major in? Are you curious as to whether that department would be a good place for you? In larger universities, department chairs don't always have the time to counsel students on decisions about their majors, but often in smaller departments, the chair will happily sit and discuss specifics about her department, major, and future career possibilities. Some departments have another faculty member designated for this, and the chair can point you in the right direction. Many departments house multiple majors (for example, the communication department may have majors in journalism, media studies, advertising, public relations, or several other subspecialties) and the chair may have appointed a specific faculty member as liaison for each specialty.

If the class you need is full, don't expect the chair to sign you in. He is also a teacher and works with his department members as colleagues. Some of these professional relationships go back decades, and, especially in a department that rotates faculty members through the chair position, we are all acutely aware of the "do unto others" principle of not screwing over your colleagues. Likewise, if you don't like your grade from a class, don't expect the chair to override the teacher and change it just because you complain.

If there is a legitimate issue with grading, such as the professor not following the grading scale outlined in the course syllabus (you kept a copy, right?), and you have already had a reasonable (you were calm and listened to the professor's explanation) conversation with the professor, there is a process for each department to handle grade complaints. The first question the chair will ask is about your communication with the professor. Teachers are human and we make mistakes. (Personally, I have dyscalculia and am prone to adding or inputting numbers backward—such as 18 points instead of 81. I ask my students to double-check my math on every grade and let me know if they find an error. Like most teachers, I'm happy to correct a legitimate—and kindly worded—request.) If you have not talked to the professor, don't bother starting with the chair—you'll end up in a loop. And if you have talked to the professor and you believe there is a legitimate issue with your grade? When you talk to the chair, take all of your documentation: syllabus, graded assignments, copies of communication with the professor—such as emails or notes on conversations. As always, be mature and calm. Oh, and leave your parents out of it. You are an adult; bringing mommy or daddy to arbitrate (fight your battles) for you will not help your case.

Staff

Staff is a catchall term for everyone employed by the college who are not faculty or administration. A staff member could be an administrative assistant, janitor, grounds crew member, academic advisor, financial aid clerk, food services worker, nurse, or a librarian. Staff members may be full or part time and may be current students as well. Many colleges offer tuition discounts for staff and certain family members (spouses and children) of staff.

If you need something signed, sealed, or delivered, they're yours. (If you aren't familiar with Motown music, you are missing out!) If you get a student job on campus, you will work closely with various staff members and many staff members are college alumni. It isn't uncommon to find a staff member who has made the college his work home for decades. Be nice to him—he knows all of the secrets and is invaluable in navigating your way through the piles of paperwork and hoop jumping that college requires.

Administration

Administration makes up the upper echelon (a college word for level or rank) of the institution. Deans, vice presidents, provosts, and the president are considered administration. Some administrators are former faculty members and others continue to teach, although on a reduced load. Unless you work in an administrator's office, get into trouble, or are involved in campus politics (such as a student association officer), it is unlikely you will meet, much less know, a campus administrator.

Dean

Especially in large universities, there may be several kinds of deans. An academic dean is in charge of a college (such as humanities or business, education or science). Each of the department chairs reports to their academic dean and the dean reports to the provost (hold on, I'm getting there). An academic dean is someone who has a terminal degree in her area and taught courses before moving to a full-time administrative position. She may still teach a course or two in her discipline, particularly if the school has a graduate program in that field. The dean is involved in budgeting, employee hiring and firing, and serious complaints against faculty (such as ineffective teaching) or students (such as cheating). Often, academic deans are highly involved in student recruitment and retention, as well as fundraising for scholarships, new or refurbished facilities, or special projects to enhance student programs.

A nonacademic dean may also be called a vice president and may be in charge of financial aid, recruitment, admissions, student life, or another nonteaching department. This person may have some experience in teaching but it isn't necessary to his position. He will often have a graduate degree in a related discipline (such as business, human resources, and finance).

If you are challenging a course grade or are accused of breaking school rules (such as cheating or possession of illegal substances), you will likely meet the dean. Some department or school clubs, honors societies, or committees with student representation may bring you into the sphere of the dean. Otherwise, just know the deans are working to keep the school running at peak performance for your tuition dollar.

Provost

The provost is the chief academic officer. Typically, academic deans report directly to the provost, who oversees the quality of educational programs, the recruitment and retention of outstanding—and increasingly diverse—faculty, and earning and retaining accreditation for the university. Other names for this position are chief academic officer or vice president of academic affairs.

Did You Know?

The word *provost* meant "chief" and was someone who was placed in charge. While the word usually refers to academia, it also describes the "keeper of a prison."

> ### ⚠ Vocabulary Moment
>
> *Accreditation* is quality assurance from outside agencies who evaluate educational institution on a regular basis. There are several different types of accrediting bodies but when you are shopping for a school, be certain to attend one that is accredited through an agency recognized by the US Department of Education. *Note:* Some financial aid sources will only work with accredited schools.

Vice President

Typically, the title of vice president may take the place, in a particular university, for a provost or dean. Occasionally, a college will decide to title academics as deans and nonacademics as vice presidents.

Chancellor

In some schools (usually those with only one campus), a chancellor is another name for president. In large university systems (such as the University of California system, which has nine schools, and even more campuses, across the state), each campus may have a chancellor who serves many of the same functions as a president. The entire university system has a president that the campus chancellors report to while working closely with one another to ensure programmatic continuity.

President

Like the CEO of a company, the president leads the overall strategic plan for the school. The president recruits donors; oversees fundraising for campus expansion and facility renovations; acts as liaison between the school, state, and federal political concerns; and builds relationships with other schools across the state, nation, and (in some cases) the world.

Board of Trustees

The board of trustees is a group of people who have the ultimate responsibility for the welfare and governing of the school. These advisors rarely hold any position within the school itself (though it isn't uncommon to have school alumni on the board), with the exception of the college president (who, sometimes, is a nonvoting member). The size and makeup of the board depends on the school (small or large, public or private, and teaching or research) and their job includes big picture items such as determining the overall goals of the school, approving policies, finalizing tenure, hiring the president, and reviewing the budget.

YOUR HEALTH

School-Life Balance

In chapter 7, we talked about the ways that the academic year is divided into terms and the number of credit hours per class. The number of credit hours for a course is also a signal for how many hours of homework you will likely have for the course. The general rule for higher education is two hours of homework for every one hour spent in class. So, if you take a three-credit-hour class, expect to spend three hours in class and an additional six hours of homework every week. Remember, this is an average. If you are a quick reader or exceptional at math, it may not take you six hours each week to get through the assignments. However, if you are taking advanced courses or have difficulty in a particular subject, expect

"How can I balance everything?"—Samantha, grade 10. © iStock / 3D_generator

to spend more than six hours/week doing homework for that class. And before you get too excited about having "only" six hours/week of homework remember—that is per class. The minimum number of credit hours to be considered a full-time student in most schools is twelve. This means that you will spend twelve hours per week in class and an *additional* twenty-four hours per week doing homework. This is thirty-six hours per week, which equals a full-time job. And that's what school is in many ways—a job. It is certainly preparing you for your future job.

Likely, you will also need to work a paying job. Most college students work part time (ten to twenty hours per week) depending on needs and opportunities. If you are the typical eighteen-year-old freshman, it is likely that you will be working a minimum wage job. That amount will vary depending on where you live, but it is likely that the higher the minimum wage, the higher the cost of living. This means that you may make more money in some places, but things will cost more so you don't actually have more net (take home) pay.

Your financial situation will most likely determine the number of hours you will need to work. However, keep in mind that if you work so many hours that you do not complete your homework or you miss class, you will likely fail. Yes,

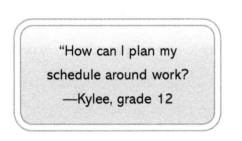

"How can I plan my schedule around work?
—Kylee, grade 12

you can retake a class *but* you'll have to pay for it again. This, obviously, costs more money. As you are paying for school (either as you go or taking out loans you will have to pay back), remember that passing your classes is your top priority. You may have scholarships or grants (money for school you don't have to repay) that are contingent on your GPA. You may lose this money if you fail a class or if you get poor grades (some scholarships require nothing lower than a B). It is easy to feel an urgency to work extra hours and earn more money. But keep the big picture in mind. Finishing your degree is the goal, and the faster you can do that, the less expensive it will be and the sooner you can start earning a much higher salary and benefits.

In addition to school and work, you'll have family obligations. These will vary greatly depending on your family situation. You may have a small family who are far enough away that weekly phone calls are enough to keep up with what's happening at home. You may have a huge family that expect you to be home every weekend for church or *quinceañeras*. You may think that you'll be able to do homework at your parents, but don't bet on it. You'll have travel time there and back, and your family will want to spend time with you while you are there. It is common for freshmen to begin the year going home often but then have to explain to family why that just isn't the best thing for their education.

"How can I plan my time so that I can enjoy quality time with friends/family without wasting or slacking?"—Emily, grade 10

It is likely that you have friends back in your hometown and promised faithfully to come back often for visits. Expect that this, too, will taper off. A fact of college is that you'll make many new friends. It is natural that you will find much in common with others in your classes, clubs, and dormitory. College exposes you to new people and new ideas and new experiences that your friends who are still in high school or going to a different college may not understand. We'll talk more about this in chapter 11.

Finally, you'll want time to spend with all these new friends and significant others. College offers many opportunities for extracurricular activities. Chapter 10 explains these in detail. You can participate in as many or as few as you want but it's all about balance. So let's do a little math.

We figured you'd spend about forty hours per week on academics (attending class and completing homework). Let's assume you got some good scholarships (yay, you, for taking high school seriously!) and only need to work ten hours per week. OK, we're up to fifty claimed hours (plus travel time for work but that will depend on you so we'll just pretend that you have figured out how to instantly teleport yourself there and back). You should eat three meals a day, and you should take time to eat healthy. Ideally, you'd have one hour per meal so let's say twenty-one hours per week to eat. Please do *not* cut into your eating time or consumption of healthy foods—you're going to need the energy and relaxation/digestion time. If you experience food insecurity (not having money or access to enough nutritional food), read chapter 10 for campus and community resources.

Another thing that college students short themselves on is sleep time.[1] Sleep is essential for clear thinking, lowering stress, and building your immune system. College students do best with eight hours of sleep each night. Any less creates a sleep debt[2] that, like all forms of debt, can grow exponentially and cost you a lot. If you are wise and get your recommended eight hours each night, you'll get fifty-six hours of sleep every week. Keep in mind that trying to survive on four to five hours each night and then sleeping for twelve hours on the weekend *might* get your fifty-six hours of sleep each week *but* it will still create a sleep debt during the week and your ability to focus in class, understand your homework, and function properly will be negatively affected.[3] You are also more likely to get sick, which will also have a negative effect on your schooling.

OK, let's see where we are after scheduling the essentials. There are 168 hours in each week. You'll spend 40 with academics, 10 at work, 21 eating, and 56 sleeping. Keeping up with your requirements and giving yourself the healthiest eating and sleeping habits, uses 127 hours per week. This leaves you with 41 hours each week for nonessentials.

Nonessentials you need to pack into these hours include family, friends, dating, cleaning, and entertainment. Can you see how spending every weekend at home (or traveling anywhere) will quickly become unsustainable?

The key to balancing the areas of your life is to learn to separate essential from nonessential activities. I've gotten you started but please don't think I'm labeling friends and family as "nonessential," meaning that they don't matter. Family and friends are your biggest support group and you'll need them. Rather, I've listed them this way to help you remember that your number one priority in school is—school. And staying healthy is as important as studying to your ability to be successful in school. People generally mean well, but it is easy for them to not realize how many things you are trying to juggle. They may each only want a few hours of your time every week and are very reasonable about it. But it's up to you to keep up with the math and realize that, as much as you may want to, you can't give everyone else everything he or she wants and still meet your obligations and care for yourself.

Learn to say no (or no, thank you), and not feel guilty about it. Learn to explain, "I'd love to, but I just can't this weekend as I have a paper due and I can't study when I'm at home because it is too much fun to be with all of you." Learn to make deals, "I can only come home one weekend this month and next weekend is Sally's bat mitzvah. I'll be home for that."

You'll have to explain things to your friends as well. "I'd love to go the movies tonight, but I have three chapters of chemistry to read because Dr. Osgood loves pop quizzes." Or study together: "I can't go out for dinner but if you want to split a pizza, we can have one delivered while we work on the group presentation for communication."

Be honest with yourself about where you study best. Does the game being on actually distract you even though you claim that you study better with background noise? Do you prefer to study alone but keep letting people study with you because you don't want to be rude and it's affecting your grade? Is your significant other just

> "What's amazing is, if young people understood how doing well in school makes the rest of their life so much more interesting, they would be more motivated. It's so far away in time that they can't appreciate what it means for their whole life."—Bill Gates, cofounder of Microsoft

too much of a distraction but you are afraid to say anything? Do you prefer studying in the library but aren't sure about the walk back?

Turn off the TV. Tell your friends or significant other that they are too much fun and you need to study alone. Head for the library and remember that most colleges have late-night escorts so you don't have to walk back on your own.

Put school first—you are spending a lot of money to be successful so give yourself the best chance to succeed.

Physical Health

Freshman Fifteen

Dramatic weight gain or loss causes long-term health issues. However, this change in weight is so well known that it's called "the freshman fifteen." The main causes for this are eating high-calorie foods (a.k.a. fast food), alcohol consumption, stress, not eating on a schedule (especially late-night binges), and not getting enough exercise.

A few extra pounds is not a huge health disadvantage, so don't panic. In no way do I want to worry you into developing an eating disorder such as anorexia or bulimia. If you notice your waistband getting a bit tight, cutting back on late-night snacking and parking on the far side of the lot to increase your number of daily steps will help you back onto the healthy path.

For a number of short-term and long-term health benefits, you want to stay in your ideal weight range. *Medical News Today* reports four ways to determine your ideal weight.[4] The experts caution you to take several factors into consideration, including your age, height, gender, muscle-to-fat ratio, and bone density. Additionally, comparing yourself to those around you is not an accurate way to determine your healthiest weight.

1. *Body mass index (BMI).* According to the National Institute of Health,[5] your height determines your ideal weight range. There are many online BMI calculators and health experts *mostly* agree that an index under 18.5 is underweight, 18.5–25 is ideal, 25–30 is overweight, and over 30 is obese. However, BMI does not take body measurements or bone density into account. At best, your BMI is a general estimate and "experts say that BMI underestimates the amount of body fat in overweight/obese people and overestimates it in lean or muscular people."[6]
2. *Waist-to-hip ratio (WHR).* To determine your WHR, measure the smallest circumference of your waist (usually just above your bellybutton) and

Table 9.1 Waist-to-Hip Ratio Chart

Risk of Cardiovascular Health Problems	Female	Male
Low risk (increased fertility)	Less than 0.8	Less than 0.9
Moderate risk	0.8–0.89	0.9–0.99
High risk	0.9 or over	1 or over

your hips at their widest part. Divide the first number by the second to calculate the ratio. For example, if your waist is twenty-seven inches and your hips are thirty-four inches, your WHR formula is 27/33 = 0.79. The WHR takes gender into consideration. However, WHR does not accurately measure total body fat percentage for muscle-to-fat ratio. Table 9.1 shows the relationship between WHR and cardiovascular health.

3. *Waist-to-height ratio (WHtR)*. Dr. Margaret Ashwell reports that keeping your waist circumference less than half of your height will help increase longevity and decrease health risks.[7] For example, if you are six feet three inches tall (seventy-five inches), your waist circumference should be less than thirty-nine inches. If you are five feet two (sixty-two inches), you should keep your waist circumference under thirty-one inches.

4. *Body fat percentage*. This may well be the most accurate calculation, and it is certainly the most complicated. This percentage is calculated by dividing the weight of your fat by your total body weight. You'll need to use a method such as "near-infrared interactance, dual energy X-ray absorptiometry, and bioelectrical impedance analysis."[8] Medical offices and gyms often have the ability to calculate your body fat percentage.

The most important thing is to pay attention to how you feel. Do you have ample energy? Are you pain free? Do you sleep well? Is your digestive system healthy? Then don't overly focus on the number on your scale. It should never be the most important number in your life.

Cooking

Depending on your home life while you were growing up, you may have little experience with planning a well-balanced meal, grocery shopping, and cooking.

Never fear—it isn't as hard as it seems. If you are new to meal planning, check out the clickbait BuzzFeed[9] for thirty-three tips and tricks for easy and healthy eating.

Your kitchen(ette) availability may limit your inner chef but you can accomplish much with little. When I was in college, my friends and I made a recipe book *101 Things You Can Cook with a Coffeepot*. As a coffeepot was our only allowed appliance, we got *very* creative. The easy ones are pasta such as ramen noodles, mac and cheese, and spaghetti. Just put the pasta in the pot and run water (nothing in the grounds basket) through the maker into the pot. It will be boiling hot and will cook your noodles. Drain the water (if needed for the recipe) and add seasonings or sauces. Bonus: if you eat directly out of the coffeepot, you only have it and a fork to clean! Professional tip: If your pasta tastes like coffee (and you consider that a *bad* thing), run a cycle of water through before cooking.

Do you have a microwave? Anisha Jhaveri provides twenty-two recipes you only need to microwave.[10] Her breakfast recipes for overnight oatmeal and yogurt parfaits in mason jars are easy to grab on the way to class and most professors don't ban eating in the classroom as long as you aren't loud or messy.

Are you a seasoned chef or just want a (little) challenge? Check out www.fromvalerieskitchen.com for a plethora of recipes. In particular, Chef Valerie has reached out to food bloggers and compiled more than forty easy and healthy recipes specifically for college students.[11]

Grocery Shopping

Rule Number One: Do Not Shop Hungry

Seriously. If you go the grocery store when you are hungry, you will become the proud owner of aisle 6, your pantry will be stocked with easy-to-consume junk food, and you will still claim you have nothing to eat.

Rule Number Two: Make a List

Even if you think you are only going to pick up two or three things, you may forget them and purchase ten others. An amazing amount of money is wasted on impulse buys so make a list and stick to it.

Rule Number Three: Make Your List Based on Planned, Healthy Meals

Plan out your meals for a week and list all the ingredients you will need. By limiting the number of trips you take to the store, you save time and money. If your storage capacity doesn't accommodate a week's worth, plan as many days as you can consume before the food goes bad.

Rule Number Four: Don't Waste Money on Organic

I'm not going to argue; I'll let the experts do it for me.[12]

Rule Number Five: Storage Matters

If you plan on doing any kind of cooking or baking that requires staples (flour, sugar, baking powder, baking soda, and vanilla extract), you'll be required to purchase an amount that is much more than you need for one meal. Flour and sugar come in bags and you will want to invest in a plastic or glass container that you can seal. In addition to preserving freshness and preventing spills, sealed containers also help keep out vermin and bugs.

If you are going to school in an area with high humidity, you'll want sealable containers for cereal, crackers, cookies, chips, and all crunchy food to preserve freshness and ward off staleness. Stackable containers save space, and plastic containers will allow you to write your name on them with permanent ink.

In addition to containers, you'll want a set of measuring cups and measuring spoons, and one or two mixing bowls. The ones with handles are easier to use but take up more room and are harder to stack. You'll need one or two basic cooking knives for slicing and dicing. Grab a spatula (the kind you stir with) and a spatula (the kind you flip pancakes with), to finish off your basic set. I prefer the silicone ones as they are harder to destroy, easier to clean, and less damaging to cookware. Unless you have a stovetop and/or oven, don't worry about pots, pans, and baking sheets. You may, however, want to grab an extra-large mug (or even an extra, large mug—get it? It's a grammar joke!) as there are many dessert recipes for microwavable mug cakes and cookies.

Did You Know?

Do not use the same box of baking soda to control refrigerator odors *and* to cook with.

Rule Number Six: Snack Healthy

Instead of filling your cupboards with chips and cookies, shop for fruits and veggies. Grapes are yummy, convenient, and help keep you hydrated. In addition, the physical snacking motion mimics eating popcorn, chips, or other less-healthy snacks and can help fight off boredom or stress snacking. Carrots and celery provide the crunch you may crave and tropical fruits (e.g., mangos, papaya, and pineapple) will sooth your sweet tooth. If fresh fruit isn't available or economical, grab a package of the dehydrated variety.

Exercise

Running from your dormitory to class to another class to work to the cafeteria and back to class sure seems like you're getting enough exercise. However, if you take a look at your phone's step counter (if you don't have that app, get it), you'll see that you aren't exercising as much as you think. Between those quick sprints, you'll spend hours sitting in lecture halls, cafeterias, and libraries. While walking provides amazing benefits, short jaunts don't necessarily give you the workout your body needs.

Fortunately, there are several ways you can work a workout into your schedule. The most convenient is by taking physical education classes. Not only will you get a scheduled workout multiple times each week, you'll earn college credit for it. Additionally, most colleges have gymnasiums that students can access for free (or at least much less than an off-campus gym membership). If you are worried that a workout might cut into your study time, double up by reading or listening to lecture notes while on a stationary bike or treadmill. Or lower your stress level by leaving your books behind to take a swim or grab a friend for a game of racquetball. If you prefer a group workout, join an intramural team (chapter 10 gives you more information on intramural sports).

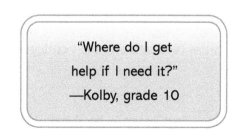

"Where do I get help if I need it?"
—Kolby, grade 10

Ideally, you'll get a solid thirty-minute workout at least three times each week. If you can't fit in thirty minutes at a time, break it into two fifteen-minute workouts. Additionally, there are several ways to increase your daily steps:

- Park on the far end of the parking lot
- Walk, bike, or skateboard to classes (check the school policy for bikes and boards)

- Take the stairs
- Choose an eatery on the far side of campus
- Take regular study breaks to run up and down the stairs, walk around the block, and/or stretch

Mental and Emotional Health

Psychology Today reports that mental health issues have reached crisis levels on college campuses.[13] In addition to the eating disorders and various addictions we'll discuss in chapter 10, depression, anxiety (stress), and suicidal thoughts and actions are all increasing. According to the National Alliance on Mental Illness (NAMI),[14]

- one in five youth and young adults lives with a mental health condition
- half of all lifetime cases of mental illness begin by age fourteen and 75 percent begin by age twenty-four
- the average delay between onset of symptoms and intervention is eight to ten years
- 80 percent of college students feel overwhelmed (stressed) by their responsibilities
- 50 percent of college students have become so anxious that they struggled in school

If untreated, mental health issues lead to suicidal thoughts and actions. The Centers for Disease Control and Prevention report suicide as the second leading cause of death amongst college-age students,[15] and researchers from the University of Texas at Austin report that more than half of college students have had suicidal thoughts with one in ten seriously considering a suicide attempt.[16]

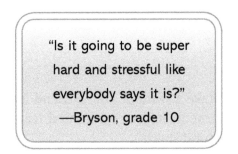

"Is it going to be super hard and stressful like everybody says it is?"
—Bryson, grade 10

This guide is in no way to be taken as treatment. I am merely providing information to help you identify commons signs and symptoms of various mental health issues. Even the suggestions I provide are just for in-the-moment help and are not long-term solutions. If you or anyone you know is exhibiting signs of depression, anxiety, stress, suicide, eating disorders, risky behaviors, or addiction, *please* tell someone: a family member, close friend, teacher, counselor, coach, faith leader, campus security, resident assistant, or doctor.

If you aren't sure how to begin the conversation, please know that you cannot "suggest" suicide to a person so don't fear that your bringing up the topic will encourage the act. QPR (question, persuade, refer) suicide prevention training encourages you to ask the following:[17]

- Have you been feeling overwhelmed lately? Has it caused you to have suicidal thoughts?
- Have you thought that ending your life would be easier for you or those around you?
- Do you ever want to go to sleep and never wake up?
- Have you had any thoughts about harming yourself or others?

Also, if you are struggling with suicidal thoughts, don't let fear of freaking someone out keep you from seeking help. You can begin with[18]

- I haven't felt right lately and I don't know what to do. Can I talk to you about it?
- I'm worried about stuff that's going on right now. Do you have time to talk?
- I'm having a really hard time lately. Will you go with me to see someone?

If you need help, call the National Suicide Prevention Lifeline at 1-800-273-TALK (8255).

Millions of American teenagers and college students deliberately injure themselves as a way of handling stress. Judy Dodge Cummings tackles this serious subject in *Self-Injury: The Ultimate Teen Guide*, which is aimed at teens who need to find healthier ways to handle the pressures of everyday life. This book will also assist friends and families who want to help their loved ones.[19]

Stress

No one is immune to stress, but college students are particularly vulnerable due to the number of life-changing events that happen during your freshman year. It is likely that you will be moving, making a new social group, finding and keeping a job, and balancing increased personal and academic responsibilities. College students report[20] top stressors as

- change in sleeping habits
- change in eating habits

- new responsibilities
- increased class workload
- financial difficulties
- change in social activities

Dr. J. David Forbes describes stress as having your tension level exceed your energy level. This overloaded feeling "can result in a state of anxiety, depression, and feeling overwhelmed."[21] If you don't effectively manage your stress, it can lead to panic attacks and long-term mental, emotional, interpersonal, and physical damage.

The American Psychological Association explains that there are four types of symptoms that may be present in stress sufferers:[22]

1. Physical symptoms:

    - Irregular bowel movements
    - Irregular periods
    - Involuntary twitching or shaking
    - Decreased immune system (getting sick more often than usual)
    - Chest pain
    - Nausea
    - Headaches
    - Trouble sleeping
    - Fatigue (even with sleep)
    - Clenched teeth
    - Unusual changes in weight

2. Emotional symptoms:

    - Less than normal patience/irritability
    - Feeling overwhelmed
    - Reduced desires for once-favorable activities
    - Increased pessimism
    - Sense of isolation

3. Cognitive symptoms:

    - Impaired concentration
    - Trouble remembering things
    - Chronic worrying
    - Impaired speech (mumbling or stuttering)
    - Unwanted thoughts

4. Behavioral symptoms:

- Change in eating habits
- Change in sleeping habits
- New or increased use of drugs, alcohol, tobacco
- Nail biting
- Increased procrastination/delay in completing everyday assignments
- Frequent lying
- Trouble getting along with people

If you go to college, you will experience stress. If you do not go to college, you will experience stress. It is a part of life. So let's look at ways to manage your stress.[23]

- Get plenty of sleep
- Eat well
- Exercise
- Avoid unnatural energy boosters (e.g., caffeine and prescription meds to stay awake)
- Get emotional support
- Don't give up your passions
- Try not to overload yourself
- Avoid relaxing with alcohol
- Breathe
- Get a massage

How important is it to manage your stress? Extremely. The American Psychological Association reports a 30 percent increase in the number of students seeking counseling at college centers.[24] Forty-five percent of college students who seek counseling, do so for stress. Add in the 61 percent who seek counseling for

Did You Know?

Carlton College in Northfield, Minnesota, has several coordinated stress-relief traditions. In addition to the pre-finals Primal Scream event, during reading days (designated study days before final exams begin) students download the same hour-long play list and meet at the library at 11:00 p.m. They dance through the library and across campus to the same music they only hear through headphones.

anxiety and the 49 percent who are looking for help with depression (many people who struggle with one of these issues, struggle with two or all three), and it is easy to see that there has been a meteoric rise in stress-related counseling.

This rise has created a crisis on many campuses due to the lack of professional counselors employed by colleges and universities. The Association for University and College Counseling Center Directors reported in 2016 that the average student to professional staff (trained counselors) ratio is 1,737 to 1.[25] Smaller schools have a better ratio but average-sized schools (ten to fifteen thousand students) have an average ratio of more than two thousand students for every trained counselor. At the same size college, 25 percent of students wait for six to ten weeks for an appointment.

College counselors are incredibly overwhelmed with the rise in numbers of students seeking services. Some colleges offer group counseling or other stress-relieving workshops. Some universities have created Care and Support Teams, which give faculty and staff greater training to help counsel students.

While colleges offer counseling services, you may find long wait times before you can see a counselor. This is especially true during high-stress times such as midterms and finals. This is why it is important to care for your mental health as much as possible and that means planning ahead and keeping up.

A leading cause of stress is falling behind in your classwork. You may have gone to a high school that had a very open policy for submitting work; perhaps you could even turn in several weeks of work on the last day of the quarter and still pass. You cannot do this in college. Missing an assignment is like a snowball that quickly turns into an avalanche. If you are struggling in coursework, seek tutoring and talk to your professor *before* you get too far behind. If you are having trouble managing your time, your academic counselor or professor can provide organizational and work-life balancing tips.

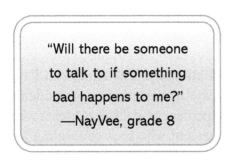

"Will there be someone to talk to if something bad happens to me?"
—NayVee, grade 8

If you are stressing over money issues, talk to your financial aid advisor. In addition to having the 411 on grants and scholarships, this office keeps track of emergency funding you may be eligible for.

Your resident assistants can help with housing problems. Perhaps a roommate shift or intervention is needed. If you are living off campus and having difficulties with landlords or neighbors, you can still talk to residence services for advice.

If your school has medical services available on campus, you can get help with any health issues you may be having, including eating/weight management or sexual concerns. Often, campus health services (and women's centers, which are sometimes additional and separate offices) have free condoms because there is *no* excuse to not protect yourself and your partner (if you can't afford a condom, you can't afford a baby). Women's centers also stock free menstrual cycle items such as pads and tampons.

If your school doesn't have a medical or health center, ask about which community services work closely with the school. Before you need them, find out where the closest urgent care, hospital, and pharmacy are. Get a recommendation for a local doctor if you are attending school away from home. You may be able to wait on an annual checkup, but you will get sick before the year is over. Guaranteed. You can't have that much stress and be around so many new people (and germs) and not get sick.

Panic Attack

If you don't manage your anxiety, you are headed for a panic attack. Symptoms include

- increased heart rate
- weakness, faintness, or dizziness
- tingling or numbness in hands and fingers
- cold sweat or chills
- breathing difficulties
- chest pains
- feeling a loss of control or impending doom

If you feel as if you are having a panic attack, take deep breaths. Anxiety can cause you to breathe quickly and shallowly (like a panting dog), so counter that with long, slow, deep breaths. If you are standing, find a safe place to sit down. If you don't get your breathing under control, you could pass out.

Once you are sitting and breathing, get your thinking under control. Panic attacks are often caused by feeling overwhelmed, so organize your thoughts and remind yourself that you only need to do one thing at a time. Breathe. Decide what is the one most important thing to do first, and concentrate on accomplishing that one thing. Once it's done, you can concentrate on the next thing to do.

Think positive thoughts. I recommend having a calming mantra and repeating it to yourself in time with your breaths. If you've seen *The Unbreakable Kimmy Schmidt*, she does this by bouncing in place and repeating "I'm not really here, I'm not really here." My personal mantra to lessen stress is "Not my circus, not my monkeys." I use it to remind myself not to get stressed over things I can't control.

Relax your muscles. Start with your toes and tighten and relax as you move to feet, legs, hips, and all the way up your body and down your arms. Imagine pushing all your stress to your fingertips and them releasing it like a magic spell.

If your current situation is causing you to panic, such as someone is fighting with you, give yourself permission to leave or tell the other person he or she needs to go. You are allowed to stand up for yourself.[26]

You don't need to wait until an attack to practice regaining control and calming yourself. The relaxation technique helps you get to sleep at night. Controlled breathing can be done anywhere. Yoga and meditation are also useful in learning to manage anxiety, and many colleges offer yoga for physical education credit.

Depression

Everyone feels moody, crabby, less patient, and sad at various times. Not enough sleep, too much caffeine or sugar, even the weather can alter your mood. A failed test, a bad date, or PMS can cause you to feel the blues. Depression is more of a consistent and prolonged (two weeks or more) sadness or irritability. Not everyone experiences depression the same way. For some, it is more a sense of touchiness and sorrow. Depression could feel more like a sense of worthlessness or hopelessness. It may show in a lack of energy, change in sleeping (either not being able to sleep or oversleeping), or difficulty in remembering things or concentrating. However, if you are having thoughts of hurting yourself, don't wait two weeks to seek help—*get help immediately.*

Things you can do to combat depression are similar to fighting anxiety: get sleep, eat well, exercise, take a break and have some fun with friends, break large tasks into smaller bits to make them more easily managed, avoid depressants such as drugs and alcohol.

Depression is a risk factor for suicide. If you or a friend is experiencing any of the following, please get help immediately.[27]

- Talking about wanting to die or to kill oneself
- Looking for a way to kill oneself, such as searching online or buying a weapon
- Talking about hurting others
- Talking about feeling hopeless or having no reason to live
- Talking about feeling trapped or in unbearable pain
- Talking about being a burden to others and that others would be better off if you were gone
- Increasing the use of alcohol or drugs
- Acting anxious or agitated; behaving recklessly

- Giving away prized possessions
- Sleeping too little or too much
- Withdrawing or feeling isolated
- Showing rage or talking about seeking revenge
- Displaying extreme mood swings

Your campus counselor, resident assistant, or professor can help you find the help you need. If you are in crisis, you can call the National Suicide Prevention Lifeline for free, any time of day or night, at 1-800-273-TALK (8255). You can also visit the website for more information at www.suicidepreventionlifeline.org.

If someone you know is considering suicide, don't leave him or her alone. Encourage your friend to seek professional counseling and *take* him or her to the professional. You can seek immediate help through campus resources such as counseling, security, or your resident assistant, or contact the nearest hospital or call 911. Don't be afraid that your friend might be angry with you for seeking help—better to have someone angry with you than to grieve his or her death.

Notice that many of the symptoms are the same for anxiety and depression. Anxiety doesn't always make you feel jittery or anxious. Depression isn't just about being "sad." If you feel depressed but can't look at anything particular in your life that you are sad about, it is likely you are experiencing anxiety. A professional can help you identify which (or a combination as you *could* be experiencing both) and discuss treatment options.

Going to therapy or taking medication for anxiety or depression does *not* mean you are weak or abnormal. There may be an underlying physical condition. There may be a more significant mental issue. You are dealing with a *lot* of new things at this point in your life. Give yourself the best support and never be afraid to seek help.

Serious depression afflicts more than two million teenagers each year in the United States alone. Despite being a widespread illness, it can often be difficult for teens to recognize it and get help. Tina P. Schwartz helps teens and young adults learn how to deal with this often-debilitating affliction in *Depression: The Ultimate Teen Guide*.[28]

Choosing the "Wrong" Major

Remember in chapter 7 when we talked about choosing a major? Remember how I said the majority of college students change their major at least once? That is not just because they started as undecided. *Many* students who have their whole life planned out before they get to college realize that they really don't want to stick to that plan. What too many of them don't admit is that it is *perfectly normal and common* to begin a degree program and realize that you aren't enjoying that field of study. If you can no longer see yourself being a doctor, engineer, registered dietician, professional musician, software developer, whatever—don't keep taking classes in that area. If you don't know what you want to change your major to, you can change it to undecided and take a variety of classes (see, there is a purpose for gen eds) until you find your passion.

Are you worried about telling your parents that you want to change your major? While it can be scary, it is much better to tell them now than the term before graduation. If you have spent years dreaming about a particular career and are no longer interested in that field, of course your friends and family will question your new decision. They are worried that you might be abandoning your dream. Just clearly and rationally explain that you have a new dream. If you aren't certain what your new dream is, explain your reasoning for focusing on gen eds or taking a year off. Your academic and career advisors can help you find the right words for those conversations.

And changing your major does *not* mean that you made a mistake or wasted your time. It doesn't mean that you are a flake who will never finish college or get a job. It doesn't need to cause an existential crisis. It is perfectly fine if you change your mind. Just as you shouldn't stay in a relationship that makes you miserable just because of the time you've already devoted to it, don't stay in a major that makes you miserable just because of the time you've already devoted to it. Changing your mind and moving forward in a different direction is a healthy response to unhappiness. It is OK not to have your life already mapped out. It is OK to admit that you don't like something as much as you thought you would. It is not OK to keep pouring time, energy, and money into a toxic relationship, even if that relationship is between you and your major.

Loneliness/Homesickness

You may not expect to miss home, but don't be surprised if you do. Homesickness doesn't mean that you made the wrong decision or aren't ready for college—it just means you are going through a very natural transition that most (if not all) college students experience to some degree. Essentially, you have stepped outside of your comfort zone and homesickness is more about missing the "usual."

Now that you've accepted that what you're feeling is normal, realize that frequent trips home or regular visits from parents/siblings actually make the transition to school more difficult. Instead of rushing home or begging home to come to you, explore your campus and community. Making the new surroundings more familiar will help the unusual become the new usual. Join school activities by going to a game or discover your new favorite place to eat.[29]

RISKY BEHAVIORS

College will provide many life-changing opportunities but not all of them will be worthwhile. You can do a lot to stay safe by making good choices. Don't get me wrong; bad things happen to good and careful people and I am not blaming the victims. I just want you to realize that avoiding risky behaviors, places, and people will lessen the possibilities of you getting hurt or participating in life-destroying behaviors. Avoiding risky behavior will greatly increase your chances of staying in college and having a happier, healthier, and more successful life.

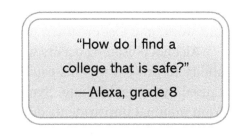

"How do I find a college that is safe?"
—Alexa, grade 8

Alcohol

According to BestValueSchool.com, college students attend an average of sixty-two parties per year.[1] If you are the typical age college freshman, you are not yet old enough to legally drink. However, there will likely be several opportunities to consume alcohol before you turn twenty-one. While many schools are actively against the kinds of frat parties portrayed in many Hollywood movies (e.g., *American Pie 2*, *Van Wilder*, *House Bunny*, or *Animal House*), there will be plenty of off-campus or underground opportunities for you to get drunk enough to do things you won't remember but will still regret.

Binge drinking is defined as consuming multiple drinks in one occasion (four for women and five for men). According to a *Morbidity and Mortality Weekly Report* by the Center for Disease Control and Prevention, "Excessive drinking accounted for approximately 4,300 deaths each year among persons aged <21 years during 2006–2010, and underage drinking cost the United States $24.3 billion in 2010." Additionally, "Most high school students who drank were binge drinkers (57.8%), and 43.8% of binge drinkers consumed eight or more drinks in a row."[2]

Binge drinkers are at risk for several major health problems, including alcohol poisoning, liver disease, heart disease, and cancer. Alcohol also contributes to sexually transmitted diseases and unplanned pregnancies by lowering your ability to make safe choices. Binge drinkers are more likely to be involved in car accidents and violent behaviors.[3] Studies found that, annually, alcohol contributes to 1,800 deaths, approximately 600,000 injuries, and nearly 700,000 assaults relating to college students.[4] Furthermore, students at the University of Washington reported experiencing blackouts, hangovers, missed classes and work, and lost or stolen possessions due to drinking.[5]

> "Are there parties in real life like there are in movies?"— Jacelin, grade 10

Alcohol poisoning occurs when the consumption of alcohol exceeds the body's ability to process it. This causes your blood alcohol level to rise and is typically caused by binge drinking. Symptoms of intoxication "are progressive, and range from minimal impairment, decreased judgment and control, slurred speech, reduced muscle coordination, vomiting, and stupor (reduced level of consciousness and cognitive function) to coma and death." An individual's response to alcohol

Excessive alcohol consumption and violence are closely linked. © *iStock / deeepblue*

depends on more than just how much, and how quickly, alcohol is consumed. Your overall health, the consumption of any other drug, metabolism, gender, weight, and basic tolerance play roles in how quickly you will progress through the levels of intoxication and how much, or how little alcohol it will take to poison you.[6]

Should you manage to survive the immediate potential disasters of binge drinking, long-term effects abound. Researchers have also found that "young adults who drink heavily have abnormalities in the gray and white matter of their brains,"[7] and "college students who reported that they participated in binge drinking scored lower on a verbal learning test than college students who don't binge drink."[8]

Another survey of almost two thousand former college students reported that, ten years after binge drinking in college, there was an increased likelihood of alcohol dependence and abuse. Furthermore, there had been a higher drop-out rate of this group compared to their non-binge-drinking peers. They had experienced poorer job opportunities due to their drinking and incomplete college degrees.[9]

Underage drinking will also put you at risk of expulsion and arrest, which will affect you negatively for the rest of your life. If you are of legal drinking age and provide alcohol (directly or indirectly) to a minor, you face misdemeanor or felony charges (depending on the state), which may result in jail, fines, court costs, and probation.[10]

Binge drinking can lead to alcohol use disorder and alcoholism. Warning signs include[11]

- experiencing temporary blackouts or short-term memory loss
- exhibiting signs of irritability and extreme mood swings
- making excuses for drinking such as to relax, deal with stress, or feel normal
- choosing drinking over other responsibilities and obligations
- becoming isolated and distant from friends and family members
- drinking alone or in secrecy
- feeling hungover when not drinking
- changing your appearance and friends

If you or someone you know is struggling with alcohol use, get professional help immediately.

- Recovery Worldwide: 1-866-280-2474
- Alcohol Rehab Guide: www.alcoholrehabguide.org
- Rethinking Drinking: www.rethinkingdrinking.niaaa.nih.gov
- College Drinking: www.collegedrinkingprevention.gov
- Alcoholics Anonymous: www.aa.org

Don't struggle alone. Visit the professionals at your college counseling center for confidential treatment options. © *iStock / andriano_cz*

Smoking

Smoking, in any form, is bad for you. I know that you already know that—just like you know that binge drinking or doing drugs is bad for you. But, according to statistics, more and more of you are smoking, vaping, or juuling.[12] Therefore, I'll dedicate a few pages to reminding you of just how dangerous this habit (or "hobby" as some crazies are calling it) is for you and everyone around you.

The Centers for Disease Control and Prevention's 2016 figures show the following:[13]

- Cigarette smoking is the leading cause of preventable disease and death in the United States. More than 480,000 (or one in five) deaths every year are caused by smoking.
- More than fifteen of every one hundred US adults aged eighteen years or older currently smoke cigarettes. This means almost forty million adults in the United States currently smoke cigarettes.
- More than sixteen million Americans live with a smoking-related disease: cancer, heart disease, stroke, or lung disease.
- Thirteen percent of college-age adults (eighteen to twenty-four years old) smoke.

While e-cigarettes may be used to help smokers wean off the traditional form of the habit, vaping isn't safer than smoking. Additionally, early research shows that, instead of helping smokers quit, it is more likely that vapers will become cigarette smokers.[14] In addition to nicotine, vape solutions include poisonous chemicals that cause cancer in many areas of the body, including lung, esophagus, larynx, mouth, throat, kidney, bladder, pancreas, stomach, and cervix.

Four thousand chemicals are found in cigarette smoke, more than 250 of which are harmful. Some of the most toxic chemicals include hydrogen cyanide (used in chemical weapons), carbon monoxide (found in car exhaust), formaldehyde (used in embalming fluid), ammonia (found in household cleaners), and toluene (found in paint thinners). These chemicals are also found in vape solutions. When you smoke, you are not just killing yourself. Everyone sharing your oxygen is at risk.

Secondhand smoke from cigarettes, e-cigarettes, cigars, or juuls isn't the only way your habit negatively affects those around you. I had a student in freshman composition who chewed tobacco. I didn't realize this at first. I noticed that he brought a water bottle to class each day with brown liquid in it (I thought he was adding some kind of flavor packet). By the second week, no one would sit by him. Once everyone had cleared out, I realized that he was chewing tobacco and spitting his disgusting brown saliva into the water bottle. Actually, he wasn't "spitting." Because of the smallness of the water bottle's neck, he would just put it under his chin and drool into it. The sound, sight, and smell of this habit literally drove everyone away. And when he participated in class discussions, little brown drops went flying. Three desks in any direction were like sitting in Shamu's splash zone without a raincoat. Gross. And he wasn't the only chewer I've had in class.

If you haven't begun using nicotine in any form, don't start. If you have started, *stop*! There are many programs to help you kick the habit. Call 1-800-QUIT-NOW (1-800-784-8669) or visit www.teen.smokefree.gov to begin reaping the benefits of quitting which include the following:[15]

- You will feel better. Your heart rate and blood pressure will drop, you will produce less phlegm, your circulation will improve, and you will breathe more easily.
- Your energy will improve. As more oxygen reaches your heart, lungs, and muscles, you feel stronger and more energetic.
- You will reduce the risk of illness. Your body will be able to fight illnesses such as colds much better because your immune system won't be focused on fighting the toxins you are putting in your body.
- Food will taste better. Your sense of smell and taste will return and your appetite will improve.
- You will save money. Figure out how much you spend each week on tobacco products, and then multiply that by fifty-two weeks to find out

how much you spend per year. Many people find they are spending about $1,000 per year on tobacco products! Think of something nice to buy with the extra cash you will save. Put a picture of your dream where it can remind you to stay focused on your health.

- You'll look better. Your teeth will be whiter and your clothes and breath will smell better.
- Your self-esteem will improve. Quitting will help you feel more control over your life. Depression that is caused or exacerbated by nicotine will lessen. Also, you will feel good because you are doing something to help yourself!
- You will protect those around you. Quitting will help protect your friends and family from the dangers of secondhand smoke.

Benefits will begin within minutes but can take years to be complete.[16] The sooner you quit, the sooner your body can heal.

Drugs

We've talked about two drugs already—alcohol and nicotine—and, by far, alcohol is the most abused drug by college students. Of course, not all college students begin binge drinking and getting high the moment they step on campus. Most users begin with routine social drinking that escalates into an addiction. In addition to wanting to be accepted in social situations, stress, curiosity, and peer pressure contribute to drug use. Beyond alcohol, the three most commonly used drugs in college are Adderall, marijuana, and Ecstasy.

Adderall (Ritalin, Concerta, or other brand name), nicknamed the "study drug," is used by students to stay awake and focused on their studies, athletes to overcome fatigue, and those with eating disorders to suppress their appetites. As an addictive combination of two stimulant drugs—amphetamine and dextroamphetamine—Adderall affects people similarly to cocaine. Adderall is legal only by prescription but is frequently obtained and used illegally. It is possible to build up a tolerance, which requires higher doses and speeds up the addiction. Common signs of an amphetamine addiction include[17]

- needing larger doses to feel the drug's effects
- taking the drug despite knowledge of the harm it's causing
- not being able to finish work without the drug
- spending a lot of money getting the drug
- being unable to feel alert without the drug

You *can* overdose on a study drug. If you or someone you know is using it and develops chest pain, nausea or vomiting, uncontrollable shaking, a fever, or faints, contact 911 immediately.

Adderall is often paired with alcohol, cocaine, or marijuana. Sixty-seven percent of patients admitted to the ER (emergency room) for Adderall complications had additional drugs in their system.

Adderall (a.k.a. speed, uppers, Addys, pep pills, or black beauties) can be ingested in pill form or crushed and snorted. Adderall should never be taken without being under a physician's care as it is a schedule 2 controlled substance, due to its strong addictive potential.

As legal restraints on marijuana loosen across the country, access to this addictive substance has increased. More than four million Americans are reportedly dependent on pot, making it the most abused illicit substance.

Signs of marijuana abuse include[18]

- bloodshot eyes
- increased appetite/weight gain
- lack of motivation
- nervous or paranoid behavior
- impaired coordination/slow reaction time
- panic attacks
- impaired cognition (ability to learn)
- mood swings
- heavy breathing
- impaired memory

Marijuana isn't harmless. Use may increase the chances of developing or worsening mental disorders such as depression, anxiety, motivational disorder, and schizophrenia.[19]

Ecstasy, otherwise known as "the party drug," is an illegal drug with hallucinogenic properties. Ecstasy is the name of MDMA in pill form but is called "molly" in its powder or crystal-like form. Adding to its harmful properties, MDMA is often cut with other drugs such as[20]

- cocaine
- LSD
- heroin
- amphetamine
- caffeine
- rat poison

For help, call or visit your college counseling office, or other organizations that provide confidential services, such as Integrated Treatment of Substance Abuse and Mental Illness, Addiction Center, or Substance Abuse and Mental Health Services Administration. © iStock / stanciuc

As a schedule 1 substance (highly addictive), a high from this drug can last several hours, but the effects from the crash can last for days. Users can experience heightened senses and lowered inhibitions. Overdosing can cause seizures, foaming at the mouth, and a spike in body temperature that can cause heatstroke or aggravate an underlying heart condition. As with all drugs, an overdose can kill you.

While these four drugs (alcohol, marijuana, Adderall, and Ecstasy) are, statistically, the most commonly used and abused by college students, all drugs are harmful. If you personally experience, or notice someone else experiencing, any of the following symptoms,[21] seek help immediately.

- Poor academic performance
- Drastic changes in weight
- Isolation
- Withdrawal from friends and activities
- Unidentified pill bottles
- Trouble with the law
- Traffic accidents
- Violent outbursts

- High-risk sexual behavior
- Skipping classes
- Agitation
- Excessive sleepiness
- Decreased focus
- Forgetfulness
- Lack of motivation
- Depression

For more information on the process of substance use to substance abuse, from curiosity and experimentation to full-blown addiction and recovery, read Sheri Mabry Bestor's *Substance Abuse*.[22]

Sexual Decisions

According to Kate E. Lechner and her co-researchers, college students see it as the school's responsibility "to provide resources and the responsibility of students to access resources."[23] Depending on your college, the availability of information and services will vary. However, the most important thing for you to know is that *you* are responsible for your sexuality. If your school, parents, partner, friends, or church doesn't provide you with the information, support, or protection you need, *go find it out for yourself*.

The authors also report on a variety of studies from the Centers for Disease Control and Prevention showing that emerging adults (late teens through early twenties) "experience a disproportionate risk of negative sexual health outcomes compared to all other age groups."[24] These negative sexual health outcomes include not using condoms (29 percent) or any form of birth control (11 percent). Without the constant use of a reliable barrier contraception, "it is not surprising that over one-third of new cases of gonorrhea and chlamydia occur in young adults between the ages of 20–24."[25]

A sexually transmitted infection (STI) is often the first step of a sexually transmitted disease (STD). In the infection stage, there may be no symptoms while the bacteria, microbes, or viruses multiply. Once symptoms appear, the infection will have progressed to a disease such as chlamydia, gonorrhea, genital warts, syphilis, hepatitis, pubic lice, scabies, or HIV/AIDS. While some bacterial STIs can be treated, most STDs are permanent and can cause infertility, destroy relationships, or even cost you your life.

To prevent STIs and STDs, *always* know the sexual history of your partner and use condoms *every time*. (Don't be a fool; wrap your/his tool!) If you are sexually active, get tested regularly just to be sure you haven't contracted a disease.

Did You Know?

While a sophomore at the College of New Jersey, Kyle McCabe created CondAm (Condom Ambulance). This on-campus condom delivery service lets students order condoms by phone, text, or Internet to be delivered to their dorm room within minutes of placing the order.[a]

Before you choose to become sexually active (and if you already are, it's never too late to make healthier choices), be certain that you are ready emotionally, physically, mentally, and medically.

The Center for Young Women's Health has a series of questions you should ask yourself (male or female) before becoming sexually active.[26]

1. Is your decision to have sex completely your own (you feel no pressure from others, including your partner)?
2. Is your decision to have sex based on the right reasons? (It shouldn't be based on peer pressure, a need to fit in or make your partner happy, or a belief that sex is the only way to make your relationship with your partner better or closer. If you decide to have sex, it should be because you feel emotionally and physically ready. Your partner should be someone you trust.)
3. Do you feel your partner would respect any decision you made about whether to have sex or not?
4. Are you able to comfortably talk to your partner about sex and your partner's sexual history?
5. Have you and your partner talked about what both of you would do if one of you became pregnant or got an STI?
6. Do you know how to prevent pregnancy and STIs?
7. Are you and your partner willing to use contraception to prevent pregnancy and STIs?
8. Do you really feel ready and completely comfortable with yourself and your partner to have sex?

Before having sex with someone, talk to him or her. You should both be free from the influences of drugs, alcohol, or heightened hormones when you have this discussion. Speak honestly and pay attention to your instincts. If anything feels "off," you should back off. During these discussions you need to clarify the following:

- Sexual history. Have either of you been exposed to any STIs? When was the last time you each were tested? What were the results? You should get a medical report showing the test results. Keep it and ask to see your partner's report.

- Are you and your partner planning to be monogamous or will either of you be having sex with other people?
- What form(s) of birth control will you be using? Who will be responsible for each type?
- What types of sex are you comfortable with? In addition to oral, anal, and vaginal sex, you need to discuss your sexual desires and boundaries. Consider having each of you make a yes/no/maybe list on your own and then compare them.

Having trouble figuring out how to start the conversation? The American Sexual Health Association provides accurate and straightforward information including suggestions on communicating with your partner about your sexual expectations and needs.[27]

In *Sexual Decisions: The Ultimate Teen Guide*, L. Kris Gowen discusses the choices teens can make regarding sexual activity—from practicing safe sex to abstaining—and how to decide *what* is right for each individual. This book helps readers make decisions based on both logic and practicality.[28]

Potential negative effects go beyond sexually transmitted disease and unwanted pregnancy. Sexual safety has become as much of a concern on college campuses as all other forms of safety.

The US Department of Justice reports one in four undergraduate females will experience sexual assault by the time she finishes college.[29] *Sexual assault* is a term applied to a broad range of unwanted or forced sexual contact. This includes rape (the penetration of someone's body against that person's will) and attempted rape (unwanted sexual touching). Forcing someone to participate in sexual acts against his or her will through physical, mental, or emotional manipulation, force, or intimidation, is an assault. Most victims know their attacker at least to some degree (you may attend class together or belong to the same club).

While sexual assault is never the victim's fault, there are some things you can do to help protect yourself. Alcohol is a key factor in many assaults. If you are going to a party, make a plan to go with a trusted friend or two and look out for each other. Additionally, make sure that someone who is not going with you knows where you are going and with whom. This person should have access to your emergency numbers in case the cavalry needs to be called when you miss your check-in time.

Know your alcohol limit and understand that other factors (such as lack of sleep, lack of food, and mood) may lower your limit. Be sure you have a designated driver (someone who consumes absolutely zero alcohol) or use a taxi, Uber, Lyft, or other Safe Ride option. Keep track of your drinking, and that of your friends, and leave immediately if one of you feels particularly tired or drunker than usual. You may have been drugged.

I know your parents told you that lying was bad (and it is), but in certain circumstances it is completely acceptable. If you are feeling uncomfortable in a particular situation, much less threatened or pressured, get out, even if you have to lie. Perhaps you have a sick family member you need to check on or you are suddenly not feeling well. It doesn't matter what the lie is if it gets you to safety. The same works for getting a friend out of a bad situation.

Before my first date, my older sister gave me two valuable pieces of advice that I now pass on to you:

1. Always have enough money to pay for your part of the date (even if the other person says he or she will pay) and a cab home.
2. It is always better to call a friend or family member to pick you up than stay in a bad situation, even if you think that person may be less than thrilled at where you are or what you have been doing. Don't let embarrassment cause you to make bad decisions.

If you are the victim of sexual assault, you need to get to a hospital as soon as possible. In addition to getting medical attention, the hospital staff will help you contact the police. Your campus will have a Title IX office that can also help you with getting medical attention, talking with the police, and accessing counselling.

In *Sexual Assault: The Ultimate Teen Guide*, Olivia Ghafoerkhan describes the various ways sexual violence can be perpetrated, discusses myths many teens believe about the subject, and outlines how young adults can get the help they need to begin the healing process.[30]

Eating Disorders

According to the National Eating Disorders Association (NEDA), "Eating disorders are serious but treatable mental illnesses that can affect people of every age, sex, gender, race, ethnicity, and socioeconomic group. National surveys estimate that twenty million women and ten million men in America will have an eating disorder at some point in their lives. While no one knows for sure what causes eating disorders, a growing consensus suggests that it is a range of biological, psychological, and sociocultural factors."[31] NEDA provides information on eleven eating disorders. The information I'm including here is just an overview. If you suspect that you or anyone you know may have an eating disorder, contact a medical or mental health provider immediately.

NEDA has a hotline at 1-800-931-2237 and an instant chat feature at www.nationaleating disorders.org. For emergencies, text "NEDA" to 741741 to be connected to a crisis counselor. © iStock / gearstd

1. *Anorexia nervosa:* characterized by weight loss through the restriction of calories and/or compulsive exercising.
2. *Bulimia nervosa:* characterized by a cycle of binge eating and purging through vomiting and/or laxatives.
3. *Binge eating disorder (BED):* the most common of eating disorders, characterized by recurrent episodes of consuming large quantities of food in a short period of time, accompanied by guilt, shame, or distress. BED is different from bulimia in that binging is not followed by purging.
4. *Orthorexia:* characterized by a fixation on "healthy eating." Sufferers are obsessed with checking nutrition labels, become stressed if "healthy" or "safe" foods aren't available, and take an unusual interest in the eating habits of others. Many individuals with orthorexia are also obsessive-compulsive.
5. *Other specified feeding and eating disorder (OSFED):* an important catch-all diagnosis that allows those with eating disorders that don't fall exactly in line with diagnoses for anorexia or bulimia to qualify for insurance coverage for treatment. OSFED is just as dangerous and potentially deadly as any other eating disorder.

6. *Avoidant restrictive food intake disorder (ARFID):* a newer diagnosis characterized by limitations in the types and amounts of food a person willingly consumes. Similar to anorexia, ARFID does not have accompanying body image distress. While it is common for people, especially in childhood, to go through picky eating stages, a person with ARFID doesn't consume enough calories to develop or function healthfully.

7. *Pica:* characterized by eating items not considered food such as dirt or hair.

8. *Rumination disorder:* characterized by repeated regurgitation (vomiting). Regurgitated food may be re-swallowed or spit out. Although similar to bulimia, people with rumination disorder do not appear to be trying to vomit, emotionally distressed, or disgusted.

9. *Unspecified feeding or eating disorder:* characterized by an eating disorder that causes social or occupational impairment or distress but does not meet the full criteria for a more specific diagnosis.

10. *Laxative abuse:* characterized by the repeated and frequent use of laxatives to "feel" empty or thin. Often, the individual mistakenly believes that laxatives will flush the food from his or her system before the calories are absorbed. This is incorrect and the corresponding loss of water can cause extensive organ damage.

11. *Compulsive exercise:* characterized by excessive exercising that interferes with other aspects of life and may be used as an excuse to eat (binging) or purge (burn off calories beyond consumption). Although compulsive exercise is not currently recognized as a disorder, this can be as dangerous as any compulsion. If the exercise is hidden or used to manage emotions, or if the exerciser becomes irrational, anxious, or depressed if someone or something interferes with her exercise schedule, she may be developing a compulsion and should seek professional help.

Eating disorders are considered serious but *treatable* mental illnesses and are not a choice, are not caused by parents, are not a "girl thing," and can be developed at any age. Biological, psychological, and sociocultural risk factors include the following:

Biological:

- Having a close relative with an eating disorder
- Having a close relative with a mental health condition
- Negative energy balance
- Having type 1 diabetes

Psychological:

- Perfectionism
- Body image dissatisfaction
- Personal history of an anxiety disorder
- Behavioral inflexibility

Social:

- Weight stigma
- Teasing or bullying
- Appearance ideal internalization (using a sociocultural definition of "beauty" as a guide for what you "should" look like)
- Acculturation (changing your appearance to fit in with a particular culture)
- Limited social networks
- Historical trauma

According to the research on eating disorders in college students, the percentage of female students with an eating disorder increased from 23 percent in 1995 to 32 percent in 2008, while the increase of eating disorders in males over the same thirteen years increased from 8 percent to 25 percent.[32] If you suspect someone you know has an eating disorder, be supportive.

- Get the facts about eating disorders.
- Be honest with the person about your concerns.
- Be caring, but firm and avoid making promises you cannot keep.
- Compliment your friend's strengths and remind him or her that the most important things aren't about a person's looks.
- Be a good role model in your own food and exercise choices.
- Tell someone in a position to help such as your residence assistant or a school counselor.

In her book *Eating Disorders*, Jessica R. Greene provides a thorough examination of causes, effects, and interventions. This book will help young adults who are struggling with this illness, as well as their parents and peers.[33]

Food Insecurity

As colleges increasingly recruit students from poor families, more and more students experience food insecurity. Attending school with limited or unreliable access to a sufficient amount of nutritious and affordable food affects 56 percent of college students.[34] Thirty-three percent of students have a high level of food insecurity. Students report purposefully cutting meal proportions or skipping meals several times each week due to not having enough money to afford to eat. The meals they did eat were often earned by dumpster diving (eating food that someone has thrown away). Some students subject themselves to various experiments or sell their plasma for a few dollars for a meal.

The food they can access is rarely nutritious, which leads to both malnutrition and obesity. Marilyn S. Townsend and her team reported that obesity and obesity-caused chronic illnesses increase as food security decreases.[35]

These statistics are similar across location, race, ethnicity, citizenship, and gender, at both urban and rural schools. However, the rate is higher for first-generation students (56 percent) compared to those who had at least one parent who had attended college (45 percent).[36]

To add to the problem, 64 percent of students reporting as food insecure also reported experiencing housing insecurities (e.g., unable to afford full rent or utilities, moved two or more times in a year, or had to share living conditions to avoid homelessness), and 15 percent experienced some form of homelessness (e.g., living in car, crashing at a friend's place, staying at a shelter). In 2013, fifty-eight thousand students listed "homeless" on their Free Application for Federal Student Aid.[37]

These insecurities are exacerbated during school vacations such as winter and spring breaks. Many colleges shut down their dormitories and cafeterias during these breaks. Other campuses charge students ten to fifteen dollars each day to stay there. It doesn't sound like much, but to many lower-income students, that amount is substantial enough to require some to sacrifice food for shelter.[38]

If you or someone you know is experiencing food or housing insecurities, contact your college's student services office as many schools partner with local community organizations to help provide food and shelter. Additionally, you can research government benefits (some of these are especially for expecting parents or parents of young children) at www.benefits.gov for a variety of assistance programs, including

- Supplemental Nutrition Assistance Program
- Medicaid
- Special Supplemental Nutrition Program for Women, Infants, and Children
- Temporary Assistance for Needy Families

Organizations that also help those experiencing food and/or housing insecurities include[39]

- Campus Kitchens Project: www.campuskitchens.org
- College and University Food Bank Alliance (CUFBA): www.cufba.org
- Food Recovery Network: www.foodrecoverynetwork.org
- Swipe Out Hunger: www.swipehunger.org
- uAspire: www.uaspire.org

Take advantage of free food opportunities on campus. Many departments sponsor events that include free or cheap food (e.g., Pizza and Politics or One Dollar Bread and Soup Night). Colleges often partner with local restaurants and grocery stores to donate food that is past its sell-by date. Local churches may have "student feeds" or even a weekly potluck after services.

Being poor is not a risky behavior you can avoid, but not seeking help because you are concerned about the social stigma is risky. Talk to your academic advisor, counselor, student services office, or a professor. We'll help you get to the agencies that can help you.

RELATIONSHIPS

Friends

Even if you choose to attend a small university, you will make many friends. In fact, many students who begin at a large university and transfer to a smaller one report it is easier. Most people begin lifelong friendships between the ages of fifteen and twenty-five.[1] Even the smallest college is likely to have more students than your high school, and the variety of living conditions, classes, and socializing opportunities will bring you into contact with a cast of characters beyond your wildest dreams.

I understand concern about making friends. It's difficult to leave the familiar and start over. Before I left for school, my aunt told me not to worry so much, that there were thousands of people just waiting to find out what an incredible person I was. I don't know about thousands, but I met hundreds and, more importantly, I found dozens who appreciated me just the way I was. Throughout high school, I worked to act like the person I thought I was supposed to be. I imagined what others wanted me to be and twisted my personality to try to become a person others wanted to be around. It caused me a great deal of stress, and I didn't feel like me because I was trying so hard to be the perfect friend, perfect girlfriend, perfect student.

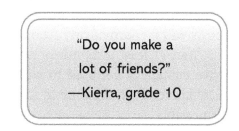

"Do you make a lot of friends?"
—Kierra, grade 10

In college, I found people who liked me just the way I was. They appreciated my warped sense of humor. They accepted that I was intelligent and didn't expect me to pretend to not know or be able to do something just to make them feel better. I discovered who I really was and surrounded myself with people who valued me just as I valued them. If someone didn't like me, that was OK. No one is universally adored. It is better to be disliked for who you really are than to be liked for who you pretend to be; that way, you know that the people who like you, really like *you*.

Did You Know?

In 1980, Robert Shafran enrolled at Sullivan County Community College in New York, where he found his identical twin brother, Eddy, who he knew nothing about. When their story was published, their triplet, David, contacted them. The three had been separated at birth and adopted by three separate families.[a]

In *Shyness: The Ultimate Teen Guide*, Bernardo J. Carducci and Lisa Kaiser provide strategies to help shy teens control their shyness by changing the thoughts, feelings, and behaviors that hold them back from reaching their true potential.[2]

Dating

While dating trends change with each generation, the basics remain the same. Someone has to ask and someone has to accept. Dating is a chance to get to know a variety of people. You don't have to spend money to have fun. Be honest and kind. Know your value and don't compromise your standards. You are better off alone than with someone who is abusive. However, there are a few additional tips for dating in college in the twenty-first century.

First, get off social media. Whether you're looking or have found someone, conduct relationships in person and not in front of the world. Your pictures and posts will be permanent, even if your relationship isn't.

Wait at least a month or two after beginning school to begin dating. You'll have enough to get used to with classes, work, making friends, and setting up a new home. Take the time to make many friends and get to know as many people as possible.

If you and your significant other from high school go to college together, expect that relationship to change. The odds are that both of you will experience so many changes that you will grow apart. This is why I advocate not choosing a college based on a high school relationship. When the relationship goes south, you want to be in the right place to focus on your school and career goals. Even if you stay together, you'll both become very different people, and those people might not want to be together forever.

If you and your significant other chose different schools because you just know you can handle the long-distance thing—you can't. Freshmen are notoriously optimistic (and we love you for it), but the longer two people are apart, the more they have trust issues and communication errors. You are more likely to feel isolated and depressed because you avoid all social activities that either make you uncomfortable, because everyone else there is in a couple, or make your boo uncomfortable, because everyone else there is single.

When you start dating, date out of your comfort zone. No, this is not in contradiction to my advice to not lower your standards. Lowering your standards means dating someone who doesn't realize your value. Dating out of your comfort zone means, if you normally go for the athlete, say yes to the nerd from art appreciation class. If you prefer outdoor adventures, accept the invitation to a play. In addition to having memorable dates and being exposed to a variety of experiences, you'll also have the opportunity to meet people with different interests. Who knows? Maybe they'll become your interests, too.

Don't get serious too quickly. Dating is an opportunity to spend time with many different people. Just because you have dinner with someone, don't expect, or accept, a relationship. Think of it as March Madness. You've got to work your way through a lot of brackets to get to the championships.

Whether casually dating or more formally relationshipping, do *not* get involved with someone who is already attached. Especially as a freshman, you don't know who all of the students are yet. That gorgeous senior may already have a significant other who can destroy your reputation when word gets out that you "made" her cheat. In addition to your reputation, you may end up having your person or property damaged in a fit of jealousy. You'll also lose friends and better dating opportunities as you are seen as untrustworthy. And *always* remember: if a person cheats on someone else with you, he or she will likely cheat on you with someone else.

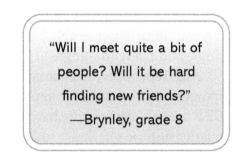

"Will I meet quite a bit of people? Will it be hard finding new friends?"
—Brynley, grade 8

If at all possible, don't date anyone in your own dormitory/apartment complex. First, you want to know that person is willing to make an effort to see you (more than just walking next door) and that you are more than a relationship of convenience. Second, when the relationship sours, you don't want to bump into her coming or going from the bathroom or hear every other date he brings home.

When you do find someone, do *not* disconnect from the rest of your world. Spend as much time with your friends, your activities, and your studies as you did before dating. It is easy and understandable to want to be consumed by your new romance (that chemical rush of testosterone/estrogen, norepinephrine, and dopamine is amazing), but this is just physical attraction—lust, not love. Testosterone (males) and estrogen (females) is activated by your genetic drive to procreate. Norepinephrine boosts your body's energy and keeps you awake and ready with a sense of action. Dopamine spurs your fantasy life and attraction to the newness of the other person. Additionally, your serotonin decreases, causing you to become a bit obsessive.[3] This may sound like love, but it's lust. These hormones will wear off, and when they do, you don't want to add lack of friends and failing your classes to your heartbreak.

Don't text each other constantly. If you text your bae a minute-by-minute replay of your day, what will you talk about when you get together? Concentrate on what you are doing in the real world and not on your phone. A couple of updates is fine, but more than that is annoying and likely to have the opposite effect you're looking for. A mature and self-assured person will see the constant intrusion as a red flag. Why do you need to be so clingy and suspicious? Is the constant checking a sign of a controlling person? A jealous one? An insecure one? Probably. Run.

Statistically, most relationships end, so taking your time to get to know each other is a smart choice. It is easier to part on friendly (or, at least, nondestructive) terms the less serious the two of you were, emotionally and physically. An ended relationship does not signal the end of your love life forever. Give yourself a set amount of time (no more than one hour for every week you were together) to wallow and then get back to life. Grab some friends for pizza and bowling (or whatever you like but be aware that consuming alcohol when you are emotionally vulnerable leads to very regrettable decisions) and enjoy being single and ready to mingle.

And remember, it is completely acceptable for you to remain single, date sporadically, or look off-campus for potential partners. What may work for your BFF doesn't, necessarily, have to work for you. Just because he is in a long-term relationship or she has a different dinner companion every weekend doesn't mean you have to make the same choices. The best relationships (friends and romances) happen when you are least looking for them. It's a strange truth that relies on those around you observing your happy and confident freedom and finding it attractive.

During college, many young adults prefer the hookup to a relationship. There's nothing wrong with it if you are honest with your partner, absolutely certain it is what you want, and safe. A hookup means different things to different people so talk about your desires, needs, and expectations, *before* getting naked.

Likewise, staying a virgin until your wedding night is an awesome and respectable choice. (Rushing into marriage just so you can have sex is a less-than-awesome choice. Marry in haste—repent in leisure.) You can avoid a lot of drama, embarrassment, and health issues by staying abstinent.

Never feel as if you have to justify your decisions. Your sex life is no one else's business.

In chapter 10, we further discussed sexual decisions and avoiding risky sexual behaviors. Reread that section before you begin dating and again if you are considering becoming sexually involved with someone.

Roommates

Even more than finances, the high school students I interviewed were worried about having a roommate. I get it. Living with family is hard enough, but with strangers? People are weird. Much like when dating, being honest, respectful, and responsible are key to a healthy roommate relationship.

Start the discussions early, even if you know the person (e.g., you and a friend have decided to room together). Talk about preferences for cleanliness; how the chores will be divided; what the signal will be if you have "special" company over and time limits for how long you can be "sexiled" from your own room; bathroom habits (do you shower at night or in the morning?); when you each prefer to go to bed and get up in the morning (or afternoon); whether the alarm rings once or there will be fifteen hits of the snooze button; media preferences; study preferences; sounds (e.g., snoring, humming, pen tapping); smells (e.g., body odor, clothes, smoking); illness (do you expect to be pampered or left alone when sick?). Have discussions *before* there are problems. Consider writing up a roommate contract listing agreements and responsibilities. If you are sharing expenses, absolutely put those details in writing.

Don't expect your roommate to be your new best friend. Sometimes, successful roommates are friendly but not friends. It can be much tougher to discuss problems you are having with your friend. When issues do arise, communicate early; don't let resentment build up. Focus on the behavior not the person (e.g., "It's difficult to study when you are talking" rather than "Why are you always so noisy?"). Stay focused on the positive so that when a pet peeve crops up, you can ask yourself honestly if it is really a deal breaker or if you are overreacting (possibly because you let the resentment build or you are stressing midterms). If you can't live with it, can you compromise? Discuss issues when you are both calm and have the time to discuss it completely and not in bits between classes. Talk

"Are roommates hard to live with?"—Carver, grade 12

"Is it better to have roommates or just live solo?"—Catalina, grade 10

"Are you able to turn down an assigned roommate?"
—Jaycee, grade 10

"Would I be able to switch roommates if they
don't fit in with me?"—Dylan, grade 8

in person. Body language and tone of voice are essential to communication and that can't happen except face-to-face. If necessary, bring in an arbitrator such as a resident assistant. Don't be passive aggressive (putting the dirty dishes he was supposed to wash in his bed to "remind" him). Don't complain on social media. Don't try to get even by not holding to your promises.

There are a few things you don't need to compromise on. Any violation of housing rules (e.g., smoking indoors) or illegal activity (e.g., underage drinking, drugs, theft, abuse) needs to be dealt with immediately. If you live on campus, speak to your resident assistant or housing administrator as soon as possible. If you live off campus, contact your manager/landlord or local police.

Professors

Professors are there because they want to be (trust me: we aren't in it for the income; we are in it for the outcome). We are invested in your future and are happy to answer your questions in and out of class. We hold office hours (location, days, and times will be listed in the syllabus and posted on our doors) and encourage you to stop in. If you have work and classes during all posted office hours, email us and we'll find a time to meet with you.

If you have questions or concerns about a class, talk to your professor sooner rather than later. © iStock / KatarzynaBialasiewicz

Most professors have an open-door policy, which means that, if her door is open (even if it isn't a scheduled office hour), you are welcome to drop in. If there is already a student meeting with a professor, pop your head in so he knows you are waiting.

Don't be upset if, especially at the beginning of the term, we haven't memorized your name (there are many students), so begin by introducing yourself with your name and what class you are in. Expect us to pull up your information in the system to help remind us of where you are academically. Speak clearly and honestly. Speaking with your professors is excellent practice for talking to future bosses.

A few things to look out for when speaking with professors:

- If you have multiple absences, don't expect sympathy if you don't understand the material—that's why you are supposed to show up to class.
- If you have missing assignments, don't ask why your grade is so low.
- Don't expect sympathy because you have several other classes that take up all of your time. Telling us you are putting our class at the bottom of your priority list is not a great way to begin a conversation.
- If you forgot an assignment was due, that's your fault and not worthy of extra time. You are literate and know how to operate a calendar. In addition to having all due dates listed on the course syllabus, most professors utilize an online class calendar in the learning management system (an LMS such as Canvas or Blackboard) that states all due dates and (if you set up the option) sends a message to your email when due dates are approaching.
- If we said it in class or assigned it in reading, it may show up on the test.
- We are sympathetic to students balancing school and work but we expect your priority to be on school. If you chose to pick up an extra shift, you are still responsible for course material and assignments without an extension.
- If you stopped by the office when it wasn't a posted office hour, don't complain that you couldn't find us. In addition to the several classes we teach, we have service and scholarship commitments that consume an incredible amount of time. Again, if you can't make it during a posted office hour, email or talk to us about setting an appointment.
- If you have technology issues (e.g., computer crashes or the Internet goes down), don't expect an extension unless it was a campus outage. Save often and back up everything. Plan ahead and expect difficulties. A lack of planning on your part does not constitute an emergency on our part. Oh—and *never* tell us that the LMS was down if it wasn't. Our LMS engineers are amazing and send reports when the system is down, so we'll know if you are lying.

Honesty goes a long way, as does getting ahead of a situation. If you know that your uncle is getting married and you'll have to miss class, talk to us about turning the assignment in early. If you completely spaced an assignment, review the syllabus for the policy on late work and expect a penalty. If you decide to earn extra money by working over the weekend, complete your assignments early or expect there will be academic consequences. Adults take responsibility for their choices.

If you have a legitimate emergency (e.g., you are hospitalized or there's a death in your immediate family) we will work with you to keep up or catch up. If necessary, and your situation qualifies, you can request an Incomplete. You would create a course completion plan with your professor (this gives you a few extra weeks or months depending on the school's policy) after the term ends to get your work in. You will have an Incomplete on your transcripts until you submit your makeup work and your professor submits a grade. Make certain you speak with your academic advisor and professor so you can fully understand your school's policies. If you do not submit required work by the deadline, your Incomplete will become an F.

Professional Communication

Part of being an adult is learning to communicate professionally. It should be obvious that emailing your professor is not the same as texting your friends; yet I am horrified each time I get an email from a student who begins with "Hey" or gets my name wrong.

Teachers are friendly but they are not your friends. These are the people who you take classes from and from whom you will want letters of recommendation. These are the people who may be your future bosses (on-campus jobs are quite convenient) or may know people you would like to be your future bosses. From your first communication, you want to be professional, which includes using proper grammar, correct spelling (*no* text speak), and punctuation.

When speaking to a higher education employee, do a little homework. Your first step is to find out what this person's title is. Your second step is to use it! Most employees have web pages or at least a directory listing so you can find out his or her name, job title, and office location. Administrative employees usually have name plates and staff members often wear name tags. This is useful if you go into an office for help (such as financial aid or the bookstore) and you aren't looking for a specific person you have previously researched. If there is no name plate or name tag, ask the person his or her name. If the person just gives you a first name, you may use it. If the person gives you a first and last name, use their title and last name.

If the person doesn't have a doctorate, use Mr. or Ms., unless you know for certain the woman is a Miss or Mrs. If you haven't done your research and you aren't certain if the person has a doctorate (most professors and higher administrators do), you want to err on the side of calling them Dr. or Professor. If you make an honest error, most will correct you so pay attention to how they introduce themselves.

Also, while it may seem old-fashioned, using Sir and Ma'am when speaking with others is a sign of respect. Warning: some women believe that being called Ma'am is an "age thing" and get offended. This is silly but if a person tells you not to refer to them as Sir or Ma'am, honor their (silly) wish. You should not use a person's first name until they give you permission to do so.

When you email a teacher, use her title and last name (either Dr. or Professor). Begin your first paragraph with a reminder as to your name and which class and section you are in. You may only have one biology teacher but that teacher may have several hundred biology students. Keep your messages brief and to the point. If you are making a request, be very clear as to what you are asking. Do not include threats, whining, or rambling narratives about your personal issues. End with a proper closing (Sincerely, Gratefully, etc.) and your first and last name.

Do not expect a quick response, especially if you are emailing at night or on the weekends; just because you are up at 2 a.m., don't expect your professor to be. It is likely that they use part of their scheduled office hours to respond to emails, and your request may take a bit of investigation so be patient.

You should use your official school email for all school communication. Some schools let you forward your school emails to a personal account, but if you do this, make sure you set it up to respond with your school address. Many people have personal email addresses that are not professional and you should not use these for school or work. If you do not wish to use your school email for job applications, make sure you get an appropriately named personal email account (stick as close as possible to just your name).

Dear Professor (Last Name),

My name is _____ and I am in your (class name), (section). I am writing to request

_____ . My reason for this request is _____ .

Please let me know if you need further information or clarification.

Sincerely,

(Your first and last name)

Sample email to your professor. *Courtesy of the author*

Addressing Envelopes

Not everything is digital and there will be times when you want or need to send something by snail mail. Some colleges will have an on-campus postal service (often combined with a copy and print shop). Additionally, it is likely that your dormitory will have an outgoing mailbox where you can leave properly addressed and stamped envelopes and packages. Whether it is a campus station or the city's post office, you need to learn to correctly format an envelope.

On the back side (the side you seal), you'll want to be sure the sealing flap is on the top. On the front side, in the top left corner, write your name and address (this is the return address and enables the letter to get back to you if it cannot be delivered). Starting in the middle of the envelope (top to bottom and left to right), write the recipient's name and address. The stamp(s) are placed in the top right corner.

If you are mailing a package and affixing a label, you can address the label with the same format *or* place the return address on the top left and the recipient's address on the middle of the package. Either way, the stamps still go in the top right corner.

Postage amount is calculated by size, weight, delivery location, and how quickly you wish the letter or package to arrive. You can calculate United States Postal Service postage at postcalc.usps.com/.

Thank-You Notes

Decent human beings send thank-you notes for a variety of reasons. Depending on the circumstance, a thank-you can be sent as an email but, whenever possible, a physical card should be sent. You can purchase thank-you cards for specific reasons or blank cards in small packs to have on hand for various occasions.

Thank-you cards should be neatly handwritten and sent within a few days of receiving the gift, interview, or help. The inside message should be short and specific and the envelope should be addressed as with any letter.

The greeting card professionals at Hallmark instruct that you begin with your greeting and then the two most important words: Thank you. Follow your statement of gratitude with specifics about the gift or help. If you received cash or gift cards, mention how you intend to use the money. Next, mention the next time you'll see them or let them know you're thinking of them. Restate your gratitude and end with your regards.

There are several ways to say thank you such as "I'm grateful," or "I appreciate," but a simple "Thank you" never goes amiss. Sincere appreciation is more important than flowery phrases, but if you are having trouble finding the right words, check out the suggestions at ideas.hallmark.com or on Pinterest.

According to Miss Manners,[4] there are a few occasions when a verbal thank-you or even a grateful email is acceptable.

In the case of verbal thank-yous, the following occasions are acceptable:

- When you receive a gift as a thanks (e.g., a bridal attendant or hostess gift)
- Holiday gifts you open in front of the giver
- Gifts you receive from close friends or family members that you open in front of them
- A simple favor from a close friend or relative (e.g., a ride or picking you up something while they ran an errand)

Email thanks are not the best but are acceptable in the following situations:

- Email contact is standard in your relationship. This is most likely a work scenario where you thank someone for sending you particular documents or for joining you on a working lunch.
- If you only have the person's email and not physical address. If this is the case, clearly note that you do not have the person's physical address but wanted to thank them in writing.
- A small act of kindness such as a neighbor picking up your mail for a few days while you were on vacation.

Even if you have several thank-you cards to send (e.g., birthday parties, wedding, graduation), resist the temptation to go digital either through emails or printing your gratitude. The person took the time to pick out a gift, wrap it, and either send it or bring it by; the least you can do is take a few minutes to write a thank-you. Schedule enough time to take breaks in case your penmanship tends to lose quality with quantity writing.

Social Media

For the record, I'm glad I was out of college before social media became such an overwhelming part of our culture. The fact that the minutia of my youth was not documented for all eternity is a blessing. However, there are worse things than awkward pictures lasting for all eternity on the World Wide Web.

While social media provides us with amazing opportunities to explore the world and stay connected in ways that aren't physically possible, it also costs us

Protect your current and future self by maintaining a healthy social media profile. © iStock / XiXinXing

social skills and can be incredibly dangerous if we aren't careful and kind. Situations where you have a right to expect privacy, such as a locker room, are no longer safe and even an innocent Facebook page can be used to bully children into killing themselves.

Everything on the Internet is forever. The Instagram pictures of your fun-filled Vegas weekend with friends may cost you a future job or admission to graduate school. According to Snelling.com,[5] a leader in the employment industry, 86 percent of employers are checking social networks even before they grant an interview. Along with that, 94 percent of grad schools also care about a potential student's online reputation while an undergrad. So even if you're still in high school, it's never too early to start making these adjustments. Your Twitter rant could get you expelled.[6] Your hours of Facebook stalking may keep you from building a relationship with a real person.[7] The Internet will not allow you to mature into a better human as you will be judged forever based on what was posted during your youth.

CollegeXpress[8] advises ten steps to fixing and maintaining a healthy online profile:

1. Get rid of any negative posts and pictures.
2. Highlight the good stuff.
3. Remember that *nothing* is permanently gone once it has been posted. So post wisely.
4. Allow someone whose opinion you value (parent, grandparent, mentor, aunt/uncle) to connect to all of your social media sites and ask them to let you know if something you post is inappropriate.
5. Keep your accounts private.
6. Set up a Google alert for your name.
7. Check on what your friends post about you and talk with them *before* an event about not making every aspect of a private life, public.
8. Utilize resources such as SecureMe.me and Reputation.com.
9. Give your phone a break.
10. Think through all of the possibilities and responses before posting anything.

You may think you're an awesome multitasker but Professor Jeff Platt states,

Social media can interfere with learning if students believe multitasking is possible. Research suggests that people actually are just switching between tasks rather than doing several things at the time. Thus, learning is more effective when we just focus on the task of learning and avoid the temptation of distractions.[9]

Social media is an incredible distraction that encourages procrastination on an epic scale. Even a brief study break to check your friend's latest Snapchat message can easily cost you an hour's worth of study time as you get pulled into a web-surfing tidal wave. Additionally, take breaks from social media to "detox." Vow to spend at least one day every week and a full week every few months, completely unplugged from the online world. The more difficult it is, the more you need it, as technology addiction is very real.

Social media isn't all evil. There are many ways it can improve academics such as creating study groups through Google Hangouts or working on group projects with Google Docs or Google Drive. YouTube has millions of videos that you can utilize to review or extend your learning on every subject. You can follow the blogs or Twitter accounts of favorite authors or subject matter experts. Instructables offers a variety of how-to tutorials for science, home repair, cooking, and other activities. Quizlet has almost a quarter of a million study sets with diagrams, flashcards, and games to help you study.

Like most things in life, social media can be used positively or negatively. You have the ability to decide if it will enhance or destroy your life. Like Uncle Ben told Peter Parker, "With great power comes great responsibility," so choose wisely.

FINANCES

···

In chapter 4, we discussed financing college. In this chapter, we'll specifically talk about budgeting the other areas of your life.

Personal Budget

Math has a great many purposes, the most practical application of which is keeping track of money. It is nearly impossible to earn a degree and not find yourself accruing some amount of debt. Unfortunately, *many* students accrue far more debt than necessary as student loans are incredibly easy to get. Additionally, credit card companies flock around college students like vultures over a fresh kill. They want to establish a relationship with you that will last a lifetime—mostly through your paying them a fortune in interest.

It is vital to have—and stick to—a personal budget. Knowing your income versus outgo is part of being an adult. It's a crappy part, but a necessary one. Not understanding how to live within your means and budget your finances is one of the biggest problems a person can have (that they can control) and the leading cause of relationship distress.

To develop a personal budget, you can go simple with paper and pencil, low-tech with an Excel spreadsheet, or online through banks or credit unions such as Wells Fargo, which has a tool specifically designed for college students to track their spending.[1]

Begin with the happy—your income. List your sources of income (most people budget monthly but considering how little you'll likely make during college, I suggest you break it down to weekly income and expenses). Include fixed income from all sources such as work (job or work study), allowance, utilized savings, and financial aid (loans, scholarships, grants). Note: only include financial aid that you'll have for expenses. If you have taken out just enough to pay for tuition and fees (bravo on a wise decision, BTW!) don't count it as income. Next to each source, list the amount received weekly (remember, if you receive it every other week—like most paychecks—divide by two). When listing income, be conservative with your figures. Plan on having less money than desired.

Next, list your expenses. This is likely to be a longer list. It is helpful to categorize your expenses like housing, utilities, entertainment, food, and clothes. Because this is so helpful, I'll get you started.

School expenses (anything and everything your loans aren't covering):

- Tuition (the base cost for classes)
- Fees (additional costs for attending class, library, athletics, student association, activities, labs, and a dozen other possibilities so ask for a complete list from the registrar or financial aid)
- Books
- Materials
- Other

Lodging and utilities (a perk of apartment or dormitory living is that most or all of these are included in one price, and you don't have to set up and balance multiple accounts):

- Rent
- Water
- Gas
- Electricity
- Renter's insurance
- Trash
- Sewer (often paid for as part of the water bill, but double check)
- Other

Debts:

- Student loan payments (you may defer repayment of student loans until six months after you graduate or quit school)
- Credit cards
- Other

Transportation:

- Vehicle payment
- Automobile insurance
- AAA or other motor club membership
- Gas (budget high as gas prices can change at any time and often go up during summer months and around holidays)
- Maintenance (budget extra, especially with an older vehicle)

- Parking (campus parking can cost you annually anywhere from $40 to $2,500)[2]
- Public transportation (bus, taxi, Uber)
- Other

Communication:

- Cell phone plan
- Internet
- Streaming services (Hulu, Netflix, Amazon Prime, etc.)
- Cable/satellite
- Other

Entertainment:

- Movies (calculate how many you can afford each month and stick to it—if you know several movies are coming out in May, skip going in April)
- Music (MP3/CD)
- Video games
- Concerts
- Eating out (*no*, this is not part of the food budget. Eating out is part of entertainment as it is more expensive than eating in and generally involves other people.)
- Going out with friends/dates
- Entertaining friends/dates
- Other

Personal expenses:

- Personal products (e.g., health care, grooming, hygiene, birth control)
- Clothing
- Salon services (e.g., haircuts, professional shaves, waxing, coloring, massage, facial, manicures and pedicures)
- Other

Household expenses:

- Food (remember: no grocery shopping when you are hungry)
- Household goods (e.g., cleaning supplies, toilet paper, furniture, decorations)
- Other

Gifts (if you have at least twelve people in your inner circle, you'll average a birthday each month, plus Christmas, graduations, and other important events):

- For family
- For friends

Medical:

- Health insurance
- Copays
- Prescriptions (recurring such as birth control or insulin, and incidentals like antibiotics because you will get sick)
- Nonprescription medicine (e.g., cough drops, nasal spray, analgesics [pain killers such as ibuprofen or aspirin], allergy medicine, bandages, antibiotic and burn ointment)
- Other

Pet expenses:

- Food
- Medical care
- Boarding
- Grooming
- Treats
- Other

Savings:

- Long-term goals (e.g., car, home, and living expenses from graduation until you get a well-paying job)
- Short-term goals (e.g., vacations, cell phone replacement, study abroad)

When listing expenses, be liberal with your figures. Plan to spend more than you expect.

Another important part of budgeting is learning to separate *wants* from *needs*. It is easy to label a want as a need. For example, you don't *need* cable or satellite or even *Internet*. Calm down—it's true. Take deep, reassuring breaths while I explain.

If you recall from our discussion on budgeting your time (full load of classes, triple time for homework, part-time job, and some semblance of a social life) you really won't have much TV time. In fact, many college students tend to binge-watch over vacation and watch very little during the school year and much of that is just having on a favorite movie as background noise. If you have a collection of movies/shows on MP4 or DVD, you'll be fine. Additionally, you can trade with friends and roommates. Many college and local libraries have DVD collections of movies and TV shows that you can check out for free. Utilize these options instead of cable or satellite (which may not even be an option if you are living in a dorm).

Streaming services are increasingly popular options. Having a monthly Netflix and/or Hulu account is much cheaper than traditional services. The drawback is that you'll need Internet service. If you do decide to have Internet—or it's included in your rent or dormitory costs—remember that you do not *need* a streaming service. You can live without TV. Much of the world does. If you do decide to pay for streaming, consider these cost-saving options:

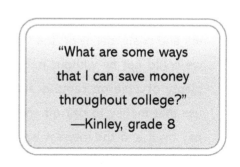

"What are some ways that I can save money throughout college?"
—Kinley, grade 8

- *Netflix:* Get the cheapest level where you watch on one screen and no DVD service.
- *Hulu:* Get the cheapest level and use commercial breaks to exercise, use the restroom, or talk to another human being.
- *Amazon Prime:* Did you know that Amazon has a special college student deal? Yep. After the first *free* six months, the cost is less than six dollars a month (or fifty dollars a year) and that includes free two-day shipping; unlimited streaming of movies, TV, and music (of Prime options); unlimited reading on any device; and unlimited photo storage.
- *Roku, Apple TV, Amazon Fire, or other:* Get a streaming device that you only need to pay for once. You can add streaming channels (stick to the free ones) and plug the device into any screen without having to search for owned programs/channels or download software.

Sharing streaming services with roommates would allow you to spend less than ten dollars a month each and have access to multiple sources on your room/apartment TV. If you go this route, be sure to create a service password that has *nothing* in common with any other password any of you use for other sites. When you decide who is paying for which, write it down and have each person sign the contract. Roommate relationships can be tricky so it is best to have honest discussions and put all decisions in writing.

If you are living in on-campus housing, it is likely that Internet service will be included in your housing cost. Some apartment complexes offer it in their rental package. If it isn't, consider not getting it. You will/should be spending

---

True Story

When my wife and I got our first apartment while attending school, we learned the apartment did not provide Internet. I immediately began researching providers and costs, believing the Internet was a necessity. My wife, however, believed we could get by without it. She made the argument that we (1) already spent plenty of time on campus and could use the Internet there and (2) we could use that money to pay off the debt on my car. I still had a few thousand left to pay on it and the interest was going to make it even worse over time. Eventually, I agreed. We didn't get Internet and spent more time on campus to do our homework. I can definitely say it was the right choice. We ended up being able to pay off my car much sooner than planned, saving hundreds on accruing interest. Because the car was paid off, we also paid less on our auto insurance. Choosing to not buy Internet and pay off my auto loan was the right choice.

—Josh, college senior

---

most of your time on campus, and I don't know of a single campus that doesn't have extensive wireless services. Typically, you can access the Internet from *anywhere* on campus from any device as you will be assigned a student access account upon registration. Additionally, many fast food restaurants have free Wi-Fi that you can access, even from the parking lot. I know of more than one student who drove to the McDonald's parking lot at 11:30 p.m. to log into his student account and submit an assignment. I had a student who would type her papers (without Internet access) and then take her little kids to the public library for story time. While the kids were entertained by the children's librarian, mom would log into the library Wi-Fi and submit her assignments. There are so many options for Internet access on and around a college that you really can do just fine without having it at home.

Many local businesses give student discounts, even ones that don't advertise this policy. Keep your student ID (identification card) on you at all times and get in the habit of asking each business you patronize if they give student discounts. It never hurts to ask, and you'll be surprised at how many will give a 10 to 15 percent discount on meals, coffee, books, clothes, craft supplies, sporting equipment, and more.

Jobs

If you have to work your way through college, don't be surprised at how little sympathy you get. Almost *everyone* has to have a job while going to school. Having a job will not get you extra time to do your assignments, or easier grading, or excused absences. Balancing your responsibilities is part of being an adult and, even if you enter college at sixteen or seventeen, you are considered an adult. I'm sure you want to be treated as an adult, so get ready to be treated as an adult. Quite likely, your professors had to work their way through college (bachelor's, master's, and doctorate), balancing family obligations with work and school commitments. As such, it is unlikely that we'll be overly impressed by your workload.

Additionally, we may be sympathetic but we've heard all the excuses and have good BS detectors. Teachers are more willing to work with honest mix-ups than dramatic whining. Your having to work while you go to school does not make your situation unique, does not earn you special consideration, and is not the end of the world. If you miss class for work, it's a choice. You may have to make that choice based on your bank account, but be prepared to deal with the consequences of missing that class. Don't ask your professor to excuse the absence or late penalty—your professor

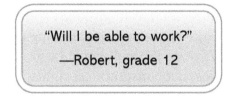

"Will I be able to work?"
—Robert, grade 12

(shockingly enough) is going to see class as the priority. Don't ask for special treatment for something that more than seven out of ten students in your class are balancing.[3] Some professors (individually or as a school policy) have attendance policies that require you to attend a minimum number of classes or you automatically fail. Others count attendance as part of your course grade. Be sure to read the syllabus.

Colleges offer many on-campus positions for student workers. Working on campus provides a number of benefits, including short commute (especially if you live on campus), more available hours as you don't need more than a few minutes to transition from work to class, on-campus jobs aren't allowed to schedule you during class hours so you won't have that potential conflict, ability to build relationships with faculty/staff/administration, and you get to know more students.

"Television is not real life. In real life, people actually have
to leave the coffee shop and go to jobs."—Bill Gates

> "A complainer is like a Death Eater because there's a suction of negative energy. You can catch a great attitude from great people."—Barbara Corcoran from *Shark Tank*

Also, on-campus jobs are more sensitive to your needing to change your work schedule each semester as well as needing more time off during finals week. On-campus jobs typically begin paying minimum wage and have a set raise schedule (usually each year). Because of work study, colleges can offer more hours without worrying about pay reduction.

Off-campus jobs may pay more, especially if you have already been working there, but if it is your first job anywhere, you'll likely begin at minimum wage without benefits. Businesses that are willing to hire students usually do pay minimum wage with little or no benefits. That is because these are entry-level jobs. You are an unskilled worker. As a teenager, you are also (statistically) a hire risk—more prone to slacking off, turning up late, and calling in sick. You do not *deserve* a job and should be grateful that anyone will hire you. Jobs are opportunities, not constitutional rights. Keeping your job is up to you. Getting promoted and earning a raise is up to you. In the real world, people get fired. Even in an on-campus job, you can be fired for poor work performance, attendance, or inappropriate behavior. The college isn't required to provide you with a job any more than any other place.

Want a better job? More money? Benefits? Do your job and do it well. Be there, on time, every shift. Be ethical. Be responsible. Be kind. Be clean. Go out of your way to help people. Don't complain. Work for the job you *want* because people won't promote you if you haven't proven yourself dependable.

> "The world won't care about your self-esteem. The world will expect you to accomplish something *before* you feel good about yourself."—Bill Gates

Paychecks

Let's take a moment to look at your paycheck.[4] *Gross* pay is the total amount you earn (hourly rate of pay times the number of hours worked). *Net* pay is what you get to take home after deductions. Deductions include several areas including taxes, employee benefits, and retirement contributions.

Your personal situation will determine your tax bracket (how much you need to pay).
© iStock / TheaDesign

When you are hired, you will need to complete and submit a W-4 to your employer. The purpose of this form is to determine how much tax should be withheld from your paycheck. Obviously, you'd prefer that amount to be zero but then you'd have to pay all that tax on your own. It is easier to have your employer take it out of your paycheck and send it to the IRS for you.

Taxes are levied (imposed) at several levels. Federal tax withholding will be determined by your W-4. Everyone who works (legally) pays federal taxes. If you earn below a certain amount, you are likely to get most/all of it returned when you file your taxes (the deadline is April 15).

Most states also take a portion of your paycheck as income tax. Only Alaska, Florida, Nevada, New Hampshire, South Dakota, Tennessee, Texas, Washington, and Wyoming do not have state income tax.

Local taxes depend on your state and city and not all localities tax incomes. You can check your locality at www.payroll-taxes.com or wait for your first paycheck to see if there are any surprises.

FICA stands for Federal Insurance Contribution Act and covers Medicare and Social Security. These will be calculated based on your income, so it is likely that you will only have a small amount taken for FICA at this point in your life. Even if you don't believe that there will be Social Security when you retire, you cannot opt out of paying into the system.

Voluntary contributions include health insurance (dental and/or vision may be separate) and retirement. If you are working part time at a minimum wage job, you may not have the option of (or desire for) voluntary contributions. If you are under twenty-six years of age, you can stay on your parents' insurance, and it should be much cheaper than buying your own.

Involuntary contributions are types of wage garnishment (money taken from your paycheck and given to someone else through a legal matter) such as child support, defaulted student loans, unpaid previous taxes, or unpaid court fines. It is unlikely that you will have to worry about any of these but keep in mind that if you try to avoid repaying your student loans or filing taxes, your wages will be garnished. The government *will* get its money.

After all of these deductions, the amount you get to take home is your net pay. You likely planned your income based on your gross pay and so your first paycheck will be a shock. I suggest that you sit down when you look at the figures. Many of us, even after decades of working, are still traumatized by our gross versus net pay.

There are different categories of jobs available to you. In addition to various on-campus and off-campus office, fast food, and retail jobs, you may qualify for an internship or work study program.

Internships

It is unlikely that, as an undergraduate student with little or no training or job experience, you would be able to get a job in your future career area. An internship is a job opportunity in a company that does what you want to do for a career. For example, you may be an accounting major and an internship would give you an opportunity to work with an accounting firm learning real-life job skills. If you are a fashion design major, an internship with a clothing company may allow you to participate in a professional fashion show.

An internship looks much better on a résumé than generic work experience, and studies report that "internships came back as the most important thing that employers look for when evaluating a recent college graduate," says Dan Berrett, senior reporter at the *Chronicle of Higher Education*. Some companies believe that

Did You Know?

Villanova University, a Catholic institution in Villanova, Pennsylvania, has a Vatican internship program where students manage the pope's social media accounts.

an internship is "more important than where they (the student) went to college, the major they pursued, and even their grade point average."[5]

Internships vary in length (they may be a few weeks or an entire year), and they may be paid or unpaid. You may get college credit for an unpaid internship, but occasionally, the experience is all you get. Additionally, the National Association of Colleges and Employers says interns who get paid are almost twice as likely as their unpaid counterparts to get a job offer when they graduate.[6]

Companies expect employees to be able to do the job on day one and a solid internship can help prepare future employees to get, and keep, the job. Many colleges are listening to the research and feedback from employers and increasing internship opportunities during college.

Keep in mind that not all internships are created equally when it comes to quality. Some colleges work closely with businesses to ensure that interns are participating actively in the company and are gaining experiences that will translate directly to necessary career skills. Some colleges are not as involved in building those relationships and supporting students beyond allowing for course credits. Unpaid internships are more likely to suffer in quality and those businesses might utilize unpaid interns for menial tasks (e.g., making copies and custodial work) that don't provide skills-building opportunities. If a business is paying you to work, they are more likely to give you substantial and relevant work to accomplish.

Even in an unpaid internship, you can be fired. In addition to learning the hard skills relevant to the career, you are learning soft skills such as interpersonal communication, customer service, collegiality, work ethic, flexibility, time management, and problem solving. Take advantage of the opportunity by showing up on time, working hard, getting along with others, and not complaining.

In addition to listing your internship on your résumé, you will want a letter of recommendation from your supervisor. If you are fired or didn't get along with colleagues or had an attendance problem, you will not get a good letter of recommendation. Thinking of putting the internship on your résumé but not getting a letter of recommendation? Employers see that as a red flag and wonder what you are trying to hide. When you receive a letter of recommendation, save it (or scan and save it if it is a hard copy) for future use.

The types and levels of support that the college has for internships is one of the questions you'll want answers to while you are deciding on which institute of higher education to grace with your presence.

Work Study Program

The Federal Work-Study (FWS) Program provides money to participating colleges to support part-time employment for needy students. A participating school (there are more than 3,400 in America) applies each year for FWS funding. The amount awarded is based on a complicated formula you really don't care about but does include the word *aggregate*. If you are eligible for FWS (this is part of the Free Application for Federal Student Aid process), the school can hire you to work (for no less than minimum wage) and use FWS monies to subsidize your pay. This means absolutely no difference in your paycheck as you don't get one from your employer and another from FWS. What it does mean is that because your school is using school money to pay for only part of your salary, it can offer more positions and/or more hours to workers. Therefore, certain on-campus jobs (such as teacher's assistant or tutor) are more likely to be filled with a student who qualifies for FWS due to budgeting concerns and the ability to use a higher percentage of FWS monies.

You don't have to work on campus to receive FWS. Federal, state, local public agencies, as well as private for-profit and nonprofit organizations, can apply for and utilize FWS funding. Education institutions are required to use at least 7 percent of FWS monies to support community service jobs such as elementary school reading and math tutors or emergency preparedness and response.

It costs you nothing to qualify for FWS so be sure to complete your FAFSA and select "Yes" on the question "Are you interested in being considered for work-study?" under the Student Eligibility section. This does not guarantee you FWS nor are you bound to accepting FWS if offered.

When you receive your financial aid award from the school, it will list FWS, if you are eligible, and the amount you are eligible for (such as $5,000). You do *not* automatically get that money. You still have to find a work-study eligible job and work enough hours to earn that amount. Additionally, you are expected to use that money to pay your school bill. You can use that money for tuition, but many students use it for daily cost of living such as food and supplies because the amount is paid to you (through your paycheck) and not directly to the school. This is similar to working a non-FWS-supported job and using your income to pay for school. The difference is that it is more likely, especially on campus, that you will get a job if you qualify for FWS. Working to pay for school as you go (any amount possible) is better than loans as you won't accrue interest and have to pay back more than you originally borrowed.

Because it is income, FWS is taxable and you need to be sure to report it when you file taxes *and* when you reapply for FAFSA the next year.

Schools have jobs portals where you can search for on-campus (and sometimes, off-campus) jobs. Some will be marked FWS optional or FWS only. Be sure to state in your application packet (at least in your cover letter), that you are FWS eligible. When offered the job, clarify if you can keep working after FWS funds have run out. For example, you may earn your FWS limit before the term/year is over. Some places will let you keep working and pay your salary entirely from their budget. Others may not allow you to work there once FWS funds are exhausted. Don't assume anything!

Résumé

Your résumé is, essentially, a list of your skills and previous work experience. You may have little or no work experience upon entering college. Fortunately, there are many jobs that do not require previous experience (entry-level jobs such as fast food or retail), and on-campus jobs cater to students who have little or no experience. Don't panic if your résumé has a lot of blank space; it is expected at this point in your life. Do *not* try to overcompensate with creative inclusions (i.e., lies) as you will get caught and you'll probably be fired.

There are *many* online sites to help you create your résumé. Word processing programs contain multiple templates but resist the urge to go that way as you want your résumé to stand out instead of looking like everyone else's who chose the same template. However, beginning with a template so that you can see what kinds of information you should include and various ways of organizing said information, is a good start.

Some of the things you can put on your résumé now are not things you want to include on your career résumé (such as GPA). However, depending on the job you are applying for in college— such as tutor or teacher's assistant—your GPA might be relevant. List your major (and any minors), as well as any academic awards you have received. Other information to include on your résumé:

- *Work experience.* Even babysitting or yard work is acceptable. Additionally, you can list volunteer or community service experience.
- *Leadership experience.* Again, this could be from work or through involvement in clubs or sports.
- *Extracurricular experience.* You won't have much work experience so highlight your extracurricular involvement.

Use action verbs and highlight your skills in leadership, communication, problem solving, and team work. For example, if you worked the cash register at a convenience store, highlight that you provided excellent customer service to over two hundred people every day.

You could describe your babysitting experience as "cared for three children under the age of six, including feeding, diaper changes, transportation, and homework help, for a family for three years." This shows commitment, responsibility, and a range of skills. If someone entrusts their children (you don't have to admit they are your younger siblings) to you, it says something about your character. Be sure to list any certifications (such as CPR or Red Cross) that you've earned.

Did you mow lawns around your neighborhood? Highlight that you created a customer base and provided excellent customer service by telling how long some of these customers kept you employed. If you had any friends or younger siblings working with/for you, highlight your leadership skills. You also had to advertise and manage budgets to set your prices, collect payments, keep your equipment running, and make a profit.

Employers are looking for skills in leadership, communication (verbal and written), problem solving, work ethic, initiative, flexibility, and collegiality (getting along with others). Find ways of highlighting these skills in your résumé. Still stuck? Visit your college's career center and have a professional help you out.

Cover Letter

In addition to an application and a résumé, most jobs require a cover letter. Your cover letter should match the format (font and layout) of your résumé as potential employers will look at them side-by-side.

A cover letter allows you to highlight your skills in greater detail. While you should have an open and friendly tone, this is a formal letter and there are specific rules that govern how you communicate. Look closely at several templates to familiarize yourself with the rules.

- Do your homework on the advertised job and the company and make sure you can address the letter to a person and not "To Whom It May Concern."
- The first paragraph should address the job you are applying for and how you learned about the position.
- The second and third paragraphs should describe what you have to offer the employer. Do not talk about what the job can do for you. Make direct connections between their needs and your skills so you can convince them that you are the best choice for them.
- The final paragraph should be short and thank the employer for considering you and reiterate your availability for an interview.
- Finish with a complimentary close (such as Respectfully or Sincerely), your signature, and your printed name.
- Somewhere on your cover letter, you need to include your name and contact information. This can be at the beginning or after your signature and should match your résumé format.
- Do not use slang or text speak. Keep it to one page. Be sure that you have changed all the names (e.g., contact and company) to the correct job. Many people create a basic cover letter and then adjust it for various jobs. Make sure you don't send a cover letter to a company with a different company's name on it.

Finally, proofread, proofread, proofread. As with your résumé, a typo or the wrong homophone (e.g., their, they're, there) will relegate your employment chances to File Thirteen. Proofreading speaks to your attention to detail and commitment to quality—two important soft skills.

Remember to print off a copy of the job description and keep it on hand in case you get called for an interview. Don't assume that you'll be able to find the description again as many companies remove the listing when they begin interviewing candidates.

Interview

You matched your formatting, used action verbs, and had your English major friend proofread your résumé and cover letter. It all paid off and you now have an interview. Congratulations!

Interviewing for a job is a lot like meeting your significant other's parents for the first time—a *lot* is riding on your first impression. Everything matters: what you say, what you do, what you wear—*everything*.

First, head back to the campus career center. It will help you with potential questions and role playing the job interview. Some centers even have professional clothing you can rent/buy/borrow for the interview. It doesn't matter if you are interviewing for an office position or as a fast food worker—dress professionally. It may be that you'll wear jeans and a company T-shirt at work, but you'll want to wear something more formal for the interview. The Career Services Network at Michigan State University[7] recommends clean, pressed, and comfortably fitting conservative dress suits in blue or black, avoiding flashy "loud" colors, keeping jewelry to a minimum, and doubling the deodorant while avoiding cologne or perfume. Your interviewer might be sensitive (or even allergic) to certain odors so go easy on lotions and hair care products, but be sure to brush your teeth and avoid eating or smoking before the interview.

Whether it is with a professional or your roommate, practice your interviewing skills. If your campus doesn't have a career services department where you can get a list of common interview questions, there are many online sites with interview questions *and* suggestions for answers that you can practice. You aren't meant to memorize and recite answers, just get a better idea of what the interviewers are looking for so that you can feel more confident during your interview.

Using a webcam or other video recording device (with sound), record yourself responding to the questions and watch the video paying particular attention to whether you're making eye contact and how many times you say "uh" or "um" or "like." After each question, take a breath and a few seconds to collect your thoughts. Make eye contact and smile and answer the question directly and honestly without babbling.

The questions you'll be asked will likely fall into two categories. The first consists of straightforward questions about your education, experience, and character. Many of the answers will be in your résumé or cover letter but do *not* be snarky and point this out. Just answer the questions simply and honestly. You should be able to do this without looking at or referring to your résumé.

Character questions will focus on your strengths and weaknesses. Personally, these are my least favorite questions as I don't like bragging about my accomplishments and I really don't like admitting my shortcomings, especially to strangers. However, you can turn the usual, "What is your greatest strength?" and "What is your biggest weakness?" questions to your benefit by not getting personal. Don't talk about how you've dated more people than anyone else in school or that you have trust issues because of your parents' divorce.

The interviewer is trying to determine if you can do the job and if you understand what the job is. For example, if the job requires using computers, don't say your biggest weakness is technology. If the job is service oriented and you are a people person, you can say that you are friendly and work well with diverse groups of people.

Sometimes, interviewers will get tricky and ask you things such as "Why are you the best person for the job?" or "How do you handle failure?" These are variations on the strength/weaknesses theme, so keep it about business and find ways to highlight your skills that are relevant to the job, such as being a good communicator or being organized, and avoid stories of not being able to get out of bed after you were dumped at prom.

The second type of questions consists of situational questions. These are questions that pose a hypothetical issue you may encounter on the job and ask how you would handle it. For example, "How would you handle an angry customer?" or "What would you do if you knew your boss was wrong?" The best way to answer these questions is to use an example from your past. You might not have encountered an angry customer, but perhaps an example from school or church could be applicable.

Some career coaches suggest using the STAR method when responding to situational interview questions. Begin with a Situation, and then describe the Tasks that were necessary, the Actions you took to deal with the situation, and the Results. A good place to start preparing a few STAR stories to have ready for the interview is to review the accomplishments you listed on your résumé or mentioned in your cover letter.

Speaking of résumés and cover letters, be sure to take freshly printed copies with you. Don't assume that each interviewer (and there may be two or three) has a copy at hand. Additionally, you want a copy for yourself and do *not* pull out your phone or iPad. Print off four copies of each and carry in a clean file folder or notepad carrier with paper and a dark blue or black ink pen.

Before your interview, reread the job description and revisit your research on the company or organization. Read through its website, list its accomplishments, and summarize any press releases. Stay with positive information as you don't want to bring up problems in your interview unless you are specifically applying for a job as a "fixer" such as a publicist.

Map out the location of the interview and, if at all possible, do a test drive to be aware of traffic issues or difficulty with parking. Online maps can give you an estimate of drive time but aren't always up-to-date on construction. Add at least fifteen to twenty minutes to that drive time so you know how early you'll need to leave. If you are taking public transportation or getting a ride with a friend, have a back-up plan in case you miss the bus or your friend bails on you.

When you arrive, *turn off your phone.* Don't just set it to vibrate as that isn't "silent." Better yet, leave your phone (and all electronic devices) in your car. If you didn't drive there, turn everything off and place them in a bag or deep in your pocket. Don't have it visible as it sends a message of distraction.

When you arrive, be sure to introduce yourself to the receptionist by saying, "Good morning/afternoon. My name is _____ and I have an appointment at [time] to interview for the position of _____." Be sure to make eye contact, smile, and speak clearly. If you know the name of the person you'll be interviewing with, be sure to add "I believe my interview is with _____." Then follow the directions you are given.

It is likely you'll sit for a few minutes but do *not* get on your phone or put on headphones. You need to take those few minutes to breathe deeply, review your STAR situations and familiarize yourself with your surroundings. Get an idea as to how the current employees behave. Do they look happy? Are they friendly? You may be working with them soon so pay attention. Be listening for your name so you can respond as soon as you are called. When the receptionist (or another representative) calls your name or walks up to you to collect you, stand up, smile, say "Yes, I am [name]" and shake the person's hand. Follow their directions, which should mean literally following them into the office or conference room for your interview. The person leading you should motion to a seat for you to take. Thank them and turn to the person or people sitting behind the desk or table.

While you are still standing, introduce yourself and shake each person's hand, paying attention to the names they give you. Open your folder and hand each person a copy of your résumé and cover letter. If one or more says they have one, smile and offer it to the next person. Don't let it throw you, just tuck any extras back into the folder and take your seat.

The interviewer will explain how he or she will proceed. If it is just one person, he or she will ask questions and you'll answer them. If there is more than one interviewer, each will take turns. Be sure to begin your answer by directing it to the person asking, but make eye contact with each as you respond, ending with the person who asked.

Typically at the end of the interview, you'll be asked if you have any questions. One of the biggest mistakes is to not have a question. Your level of enthusiasm and obvious interest will go a long way to selling yourself. However, this is tricky because you don't want to ask any yes/no questions or low-information questions that can easily be answered by a website search. Asking questions such as "What do you think are the most important qualities for an employee to be successful in this position?" or "Describe the culture of the company" allows you to learn more about the position while turning the interview into more of a conversation. Be aware of the time allotted for your interview so that you aren't risking interfering with the next interviewee (mostly, this is to respect the interviewer's time constraints) but end by asking "What are the next steps in the interview process?" or "What is your expected timeline to make a decision?" so that you have an idea as to how long you may need to wait before you hear anything.

Wait for the interviewer's lead to leave. One person will usually stand and walk you to the door. When that person stands, you should stand, thank each person with another handshake (hopefully, you'll remember their names and you can use them correctly but if you aren't 100 percent sure, just say "Thank you for your time" or "Thank you for interviewing me"), gather your things, and walk to the door. If you're feeling brave, you can add "I look forward to hearing from you soon." Be sure to thank the receptionist on your way out and wait until you are out of the building to turn your phone back on. There's a good chance that someone will be watching you so remain professional until you are out of the parking lot.

Before the end of the work day, email the people who interviewed you (at least the team leader) and thank them for interviewing you. The email shouldn't be long as the purpose is

1. To thank them for their time
2. To remind them of who you are

Writing a brief thank-you is the correct, grown-up thing to do.

Dear Mr./Ms./Mrs./Dr. (Last Name),

Thank you for taking the time to interview me today. I appreciate the opportunity to meet with you and learn more about (company/organization). I am excited for the possibility of working with you/your team.

Please feel free to contact me at (email address) or (phone number) if you would like any further clarification or information. I look forward to hearing from you.

Sincerely,

(your signature)

(your name)

Sample thank-you email. *Courtesy of the author*

ADA Concerns

If you need any accommodations for your interview such as needing to know the easiest access for a wheelchair or bringing a guide dog, be certain to contact the company (preferably the human resources department) well in advance of your interview. You do not need to include any needs in your résumé or cover letter as your disability should not make a difference in your getting an interview for a job you are qualified for.

Career Fairs

Colleges often host career fairs where employers come to campus so they can meet and interview many potential employees. You'll want to follow the same rules for conservative dress but take many copies of your résumé (a cover letter isn't as necessary unless you work ahead and know what companies will be there and make specific letters for various companies). Check with your campus host (probably career services) to determine whether you need to make appointments in advance.

Don't

- arrive late or be distracted/disorganized
- forget to turn off your phone
- appear desperate

- apologize for your background or lack of experience
- lie
- ask about salary, benefits, or vacation until *after* you have a solid job offer
- forget to send a thank you letter/email
- call every day asking for an update

Credit Cards

An inescapable fact is that you need credit. Even if you could save up enough cash to buy a car or home, you still need a good credit score. Much like your GPA, it is easy to ruin and difficult to rebuild your score.

Credit cards provide an opportunity for you to build up a good credit history but it is easy to make mistakes and credit regret is real. Credit and debit cards are not the same thing, although some debit cards can act as credit cards. A debit card is tied to your bank account (usually checking), and you must have the money in your account *before* you can use it.

A credit card allows you to spend money you don't already have. Essentially, using a credit card is like having a short-term loan as long as you pay it off within the billing cycle. (A billing cycle is usually a month.) If you pay off the used credit amount before a new billing cycle, you won't have to pay interest. If you don't pay it off within the billing cycle, you will begin accruing interest on the remaining balance.

When deciding which credit card to apply for, look at the rewards offers and the APR (annual percentage rate). Some credit cards offer cash back on all purchases. Others have purchase protection insurance that gives extended warranties or price protection (they'll refund part or all of the difference if a purchased item goes on sale within a limited period of time). The annual percentage rate sets the interest rate for your purchases. Don't let the word *annual* fool you, however. Interest will begin accruing as soon as the "grace period" ends and a new billing cycle begins.

APR doesn't mean that you get to charge stuff for a year before you begin paying it back or before purchases start accruing interest. Generally, a credit card with 10 percent APR is a good rate. There are ones lower but they are typically available to those who have already established a good credit history. It is likely that, as a college student with no credit history, you'll be offered an APR closer to 18–20 percent. Some credit cards offer zero percent APR for a limited time,

> ### Vocabulary Moment
> *Interest* is money paid at a particular rate for the use of borrowed money.

typically a few months to a year. This is a great deal but be sure to keep paying off your monthly balance or you risk coming to the end of your term and not having enough money to pay off the entire balance at once. At that point, interest will kick in and you'll owe quite a bit more *because interest is calculated from the time the purchase was made.* If you are close to the limit and the interest puts you over, you'll likely have to pay fees on top of the balance and interest. If you go over your limit, your credit card may be declined, you may have your interest rate raised, or your credit card may be canceled. (If your credit card is canceled you still have to pay back the money.)

Let's do a little math to discover just how tricky interest can be.

If your APR is 20 percent then your periodic interest rate is 0.0548 percent (APR divided by 365 days). Multiply your average daily balance and the number of days in the month to get the monthly accrued interest. That's easy. It's figuring out your average daily balance that's tricky.

Let's pretend you have a credit card balance of $1,000 (because you didn't listen to me about watching your limit) and a twenty-five-day billing cycle. On day one, you start with a $1,000 balance. On day five of your billing cycle, you make a $300 payment. On day ten, you charge $50. On day twenty-one, you make another $200 payment. To calculate your average daily balance, you total each day even if your balance didn't change, then divide by the number of days in your billing cycle.

Days one through four are $1,000 each.
Days five through nine are $700 each.
Days ten through twenty are $750 each.
Days twenty-one through twenty-five are $550 each.
(Day one balance + Day two balance + Day three balance . . .)/twenty-five (or the number of days in your billing cycle) = daily average balance.

Now you can calculate your interest owed by multiplying your daily average balance by the APR by the number of days in your billing cycle divided by the periodic interest rate. And *all* of that is added to your balance as soon as that billing cycle ends.

It doesn't take long for the debt to add up and overwhelm you. Too many people then get extra credit cards because they've filled up the first one and, before long, they can't even keep up with the minimum payments.

A minimum payment is the lowest amount that you can pay to avoid late charges. Some credit card companies base this on a percentage of your balance (such as 2 percent) and others add the interest and fees to the percentage. If your balance is low enough, you may just be charged a flat rate (such as $25, especially if 2 percent of your balance is less than that amount). You should still pay off

VantageScore is another organization developed by three major credit bureaus (Equifax, Experian, and TransUnion) and uses a different algorithm than FICO. When you apply for credit, you don't get to choose which scores are used. © iStock / almagami

your entire balance. Your credit card won't be canceled if you have a zero balance so don't feel as if you need to keep something charged to keep your card.

You have several different credit scores depending on which institution is determining it. The most common is your FICO score from the Fair Isaac Corporation. FICO looks at five factors when determining your score:

1. Payment history (35 percent)—make your payments on time
2. Credit utilization (30 percent)—pay off your balance each month
3. Length of credit history (15 percent)—keep older accounts open and active (minimally)
4. Types of accounts in use (10 percent)—having different types of loans helps but don't buy a new car just to accomplish this as you'll likely have student loans
5. New credit (10 percent)—don't apply for several new cards, especially close together

The folks at NerdWallet.com suggest college students follow these five steps for smart credit card use:[8]

1. Pay the bill on time. Thirty-five percent of your credit score comes from paying your bills on time.
2. Don't charge more than you can pay off in a month. Don't assume that you'll get such a great paying job upon graduation that you can easily pay off all of your racked-up debt. You can't predict the future so limit your purchases. Be careful not to let peer pressure or a desire for a more active social life tempt you into overspending.
3. Avoid getting too close to your limit. Credit bureaus prefer you keep your balance below 30 percent of your credit limit.
4. Don't open too many cards. It may be tempting to open more lines of credit so that you can charge more and stay below the 30 percent. However, the more cards you have, the harder it is to keep track of payment dates and spending habits.
5. Avoid fees. There are many credit companies that offer cards to students that don't have an annual fee (this is different than the APR—an annual fee is the amount you pay every year just for the privilege of having the card) but offer rewards. Shop around for a good deal.

Essentially, to start building a good credit history, get one credit card with no annual fee, a low APR, a moderate credit limit amount, and a rewards program. Charge only what you can pay off each month and make that payment on time. If you keep this up, the credit card company will raise your limit amount, but stay with your healthy financial habits because it won't be long before you are at the point where you can consider purchasing a car or house or engagement ring and you don't want to sabotage your future dreams.

Bank Accounts

It is possible that your parents have already helped you establish a bank account before you begin college. If not, there are some things you need to know about opening an account.

Forbes states that what students need in a bank account is

1. no fees
2. easy access to their money[9]

You can achieve this through many major banks, but not all banks have branches near your chosen college. Do a bit of homework to see where the ATMs are in relation to your new home because you do *not* want to pay fees by using other banks' ATMs. Your school may have ATMs on campus but they'll likely be generic ones that will charge fees no matter where you bank. Additionally, your bank may charge an additional fee if you use an ATM that doesn't belong to it. You don't want to pay five dollars in fees just to pull twenty dollars out for lunch.

Speaking of fees, when you research local banks, make certain that they don't charge a monthly fee or ATM fee or any other type of fee just for having an account or accessing your money.

The bank may offer a student account but that doesn't necessarily mean that it is the best option for a college student. Additionally, your college may offer student bank accounts but that doesn't guarantee no fees or help with building a credit history.

When you open a bank account, you'll likely receive a debit card. This is not the same as a credit card because your debit limit is based on how much money you have in your account. If you overspend, you will incur a fee—which is a bit ironic in that your bank is taking more of your money, which they already know you don't have enough of. The bank won't care about the irony, however, and will continue to charge overdraft fees until you deposit enough money to pay off all the fees and put your account back in the black (accounting term for having money—if your account is in the red, you don't have money).

You will use your bank account to pay bills and setting up automatic bill payments is incredibly useful to making sure your payments are on time. You still need to keep track of your account and payments to make sure that you have enough money in your account so that you don't "bounce" a payment.

Taxes

Welcome to adulthood! As we discussed earlier, part of making money is having the government keep part of it. However, depending on how many deductions you claimed on your I-9 (a tax form used for verifying your identity before employment) and the income bracket you are in, there is a possibility that you have overpaid on your taxes and that you will be able to have some of money refunded.

Begin by talking with your parents to determine if they are still claiming you as a dependent on their taxes. If they are, you cannot claim the same deductions or credits, and you'll have to indicate on your tax returns that someone else is claiming you as a dependent.

You'll need several forms to complete your taxes. If you put your home/ parent address on any of your forms (work applications, I-9, student loans, etc.), the forms may be sent to that address so ask your parents to be on the lookout. Increasingly, forms are being sent electronically so don't be so hasty to delete emails from unfamiliar addresses and check your spam folders.

Filing taxes can be incredibly stressful but avoiding it and hoping it'll just work itself out is a very bad idea. Many colleges offer free help for students, often by professional tax accountants. © *iStock / alfexe*

Your employer will send you a W-2, which is a record of your income and all withheld deductions. If you worked for more than one employer, be sure you get a W-2 from each. You should have received these by January 31, so if it's February and you don't have it, contact your employer (even if it is an ex-employer).

The law states that a dependent earning less than $6,350 in a year (January 1–December 31) does not have to file taxes. However, not filing is a mistake as you forfeit a potential refund.[10]

Form 1098-T is your tuition statement, which your college provides. If your parents or legal guardians claim you as a dependent, it is likely that they will claim these education credits but they'll need the form. This form should list paid tuition and related expenses, scholarships and grants, and adjustments from the previous year.

Form 1098-E lets you deduct any paid interest on student loans. If you paid more than $600 in interest, your lender should send you the form.

Form 8863 lets you see if you qualify for additional education credits such as the American Opportunity Tax Credit or the Lifetime Learning Credit.[11] You can find this worksheet at IRS.gov.

For more details on what can and cannot be deducted, read Kristen Kuchar's article "Tax Guide for College Students" at TheSimpleDollar.com.[12]

Tipping

It is likely that you will be consuming most of your college meals in a cafeteria or fast-food joint. However, whether it is for a date or just out of desperation for a sit-down meal, you may find yourself at a "real" restaurant.

In America, the standard recommended tip for good service is 15 percent of the bill (excluding tax), 20 percent for very good service but no less than 10 percent, even for poor service. However, food service workers (waitstaff) aren't the only people you should tip on your night out.

According to CNN's money guide, you should also tip the sommelier (wine steward) 15 percent of the cost of the bottle. Bartenders should receive 15–20 percent of the tab with a minimum of fifty cents per soft drink and one dollar per alcoholic drink. Cloakroom attendants are tipped one dollar per coat; parking valets should get two dollars to bring your car back to you; and washroom attendants receive fifty cents to one dollar. If you take a taxi, you can assume that 15 percent will be enough but you should add a dollar or two per bag if you have luggage. This is if you are taking the taxi to the airport or for an overnight trip. Luggage is neither expected nor necessary on a date.

Date night isn't the only place you will encounter tipping. Hairdressers/barbers, manicurists, masseurs, and spa personnel are each tipped at 15–20 percent with an extra two dollars for shampoo or shave provider. If you have food provided (pizza, Jimmy Johns, etc.), you should tip 10 percent (two dollar minimum) in addition to the delivery charge, which is often included when you order but doesn't, necessarily, go to the driver. If you get take-out, you don't need to tip.

Traveling? In addition to the taxi, you'll need to tip the airport skycap one dollar per bag curbside or two dollars per bag if he takes them to the check-in counter for you. Once you are at the hotel, tip the doorman one dollar per bag for help with luggage and one dollar per person for hailing a taxi. If a bellhop takes your luggage to your room, tip one dollar per bag with a two dollar minimum if you only have one bag. Leave two to five dollars per night tip for housekeeping (leave tip each day as those who clean your room might not be the same crew each day) and, while you don't need to tip the concierge for directions, you will need to tip five dollars for getting you tickets or reservations—ten dollars if they're difficult to get.

While some of these places will allow you to add the tip amount to your credit/debit card, it is always preferred to tip in cash. You know—that green paper with pictures of dead presidents and Founding Fathers (and, in 2020, one of the most amazing women in American history!).

The amount of tipping that is expected in America (both the dollar figure and how many different people are tipped) comes as quite a shock for international students as tipping is cultural. Another surprise is that American businesses do not include tax in the cost of their products, and often price items at ninety-five or ninety-nine cents instead of rounding to the nearest dollar.

You do not need to tip a gas station attendant but if you are in Oregon or New Jersey, you are not allowed to pump your own gas. Some local places such as coffee shops will have tip jars on the counter; these are optional.

Etiquette dictates that you should have the tips (in cash) already in your hands ready to give to the person before you ask for the help. It is awkward and time-consuming to dig through your purse or wallet counting out cash while the person watches. When you hand them the tip, make eye contact and say thank you. While you should tip discretely, don't try to "slip it to them on the sly" like you see in movies. This isn't an illegal maneuver—it is good manners.

If you think it's complicated now, wait until after college when you get to deal with figuring out tips for babysitters and nannies, garbage collectors, mail carriers, gardeners, housekeepers, pet sitters and groomers, handymen, and newspaper delivery carriers—just to name a few.

Tips for tipping:

- If you use a coupon or gift certificate, you need to tip on the full cost.
- Tip above the expected average for exceptional service, if you have been difficult, or if you are a regular (it's like a pre-tip for better, future service).
- If you have taken up a table for an extended time, tip more.
- When leaving a tip for housekeeping, put the paper money (change is heavy) in an envelope marked "housekeeping" and leave it on the nightstand. Do not just leave cash lying around and assume they'll know it's for them. Hotel staff are typically cautious of taking loose money from a room.

EXTRACURRICULAR ACTIVITIES

Between work and school and family responsibilities and dating and . . . you might not think you have time for extracurricular activities. However, one of the best parts of higher education is the abundance of opportunities to explore a variety of interests. It is quite probable that there will be no better, easier, or cheaper time in your life to explore the world, meet new people, form lifelong friendships, or try new experiences.

Extracurricular activities in higher education provide a range of opportunities from single-attendance sporting events to pledging a fraternity or sorority. Colleges also provide dozens (if not hundreds) of clubs representing a plethora (a word here that means "Holy cow, how do people think of some of these things?") of interests.

> "What activities will I have time for?" —Ty, grade 12

Colleges provide opportunities to continue your studies globally through study abroad programs that may last a few days or an entire year. Even during your vacation time, you may have the opportunity to explore the world more cheaply simply by taking advantage of student discounts on travel and lodging.

No matter your interests or income, college is the perfect time to explore, experience, and expand your horizons. Get involved!

Fraternities and Sororities

Fraternities and sororities are part of Greek life. These club-like organizations are named by taking two or three Greek letters to form the title (such as Sigma Chi or Alpha Kappa Alpha). Fraternities are for males (from the Latin word *frater* meaning "brother") and sororities are for females (from the Latin word *soror* meaning "sister").

During the mid to late nineteenth century, college students were almost entirely male. Some students began to form groups to debate and discuss current events and literature. This "brotherhood" grew, particularly in colleges and by teachers who supported students thinking for themselves and exploring extracurricular areas of interest. These men formed deep and lasting bonds of friendship and, while the foundation for fraternities was intellectual exploration, of course they found time to organize social events (yep—parties).

Eventually, these students graduated and became alumni and donated money to their former schools to help current members of the fraternity afford to rent or purchase "chapter houses" so that members could live together off campus (although the houses tend to be as close to campus as possible). As any homeowner will tell you, the cost of mortgage, utilities, upkeep, and repairs can be extensive. As fraternity membership grew and the properties aged, many fraternities incorporated and formed supervisory boards and became more business-like due to economic concerns. However, living off campus also had the effect of moving the focus of many fraternities from learning to socializing.

Memberships not only grew at originating schools but "chapters" also began to spring up at other schools. Each society has only one national name but there is no limit on the number of chapters (individual colleges) the society can have. For example, Delta Sigma Theta sorority was originally founded in 1913 at Howard University by twenty-two African American college women as a service organi-

Vocabulary Moment

An *alumnus* (male) or *alumna* (female) is someone who has graduated from a particular school. The Latin origin meant "the nurtured" but is modernly translated as "pupil"—the student, not the eyeball. A group of alumnus (either all male or males and females) are called *alumni*, while a group of only female graduates are *alumnae*. You may hear graduates referred to as *alums* by people who are wrong.

zation. Their first public act was to participate in the Women's Suffrage March in Washington, DC. They currently have more than one thousand collegiate and alumnae chapters worldwide.

Not every fraternity or sorority has a chapter at every college. Membership is based on an invitation—you have to be invited to join. However, many recruit heavily during "rush week," which is a week near the beginning of the school year (some colleges hold one at the beginning of each term). Rush week allows the campus Greek life chapters to put out information regarding their organization. If you don't already belong to a fraternity or sorority (you can only belong to one), you can shop around to see if there is an organization that interests you. Not all organizations are the same so, if you are considering "going Greek," you should carefully investigate what each one values (e.g., leadership, philanthropy, or spirituality).

Not everyone pledges (the Greek life word for joins) and not all of those who pledge are accepted. There are many steps to choosing and joining a fraternity or sorority and none of it may be for you—and that's OK, too.

Every step, from rushing to pledging to initiation to being a member can be time-consuming and expensive. The responsibilities of being a Greek can take your time and focus away from your studies, work, or other responsibilities. Living in a chapter house isn't free. Participating in Greek life is time-consuming even beyond the pledging stages. You need to be aware of the pros and cons and make a wise, personal choice.

Honors Societies

Like fraternities and sororities, honor societies are named after a combination of Greek letters. Unlike fraternities and sororities, you can belong to more than one honors society and they don't have chapter houses. The focus of an honors society is academic, and different societies exist for different academic areas.

I highly suggest that you join the honors society for your major. Hopefully, your college will have a chapter. Come to think of it, if you know your major before choosing a college, add "Do they have an appropriate honors society?" to your Q&A search list.

Did You Know?

John Heath founded the first Greek student society, Phi Beta Kappa ("Love of learning is the guide of life"), in 1776 at the College of William and Mary. Greek letters were chosen because Heath was the best Greek scholar on campus.[b]

Vocabulary Moment

You don't have to be in "honors" to join an honors society. However, most honors societies do have GPA requirements.

If your college doesn't have the right honor society, many will let you join at the national level. It should have a website so it will be fairly easy to check the requirements. There is also the possibility of starting a chapter on your college campus and the faculty members within your major department can help you with that. Perhaps they've just been waiting for an intelligent, outgoing leader such as yourself!

Assuming that your college does have a chapter of your major's honors society, it is possible that you will only be able to join by invitation. However, most chapters will do a search for all students in that major who meet the requirements and send out invitations. If or when you receive yours, take it seriously.

While most fraternities/sororities take pledges from only freshmen (or, in rare cases, sophomores), honors societies often require you to be at least a sophomore, have declared your major, have taken a minimum number of courses in that major, and have a minimum GPA. You'll likely need to pay a joining fee and annual dues. These will vary depending on the society and chapter. If the costs and responsibilities aren't delineated in the invitation, contact the person who sent the letter—or just show up to the information meeting and ask.

If you have a double major (or a declared minor), consider joining both societies. There is no rule against it and as long as you can manage the costs and commitments, it's worth it. For example, I encourage my English education majors to join both Kappa Delta Pi (international honors society for educators) and Sigma Tau Delta (international honors society for English majors). Many honors societies have scholarships, research and publication opportunities, and internship connections. The purpose of honors societies is to help you during school and throughout your career. You can remain a member after graduation and continue to make professional contacts (think LinkedIn but with a vetting process).

Most honors societies have service requirements. They are likely to have a particular societal issue they volunteer/donate to such as homelessness, abuse victims, or literacy. Odds are you'll need to participate in one or two annual events dedicated to that issue. There will be opportunities to run for office, recruit new members, solicit donations, and participate in community outreach or service learning projects. All of these look great on a résumé for an in-school internship, graduate school application, or career position.

Clubs

The most common and varied extracurricular opportunities in college are through clubs. There may be a dozen fraternities/sororities, a few dozen honors societies, but hundreds of clubs. There is no limit to the number of clubs you can join, rarely any minimum requirements, and participation can be up to you. Many clubs don't even have a membership fee.

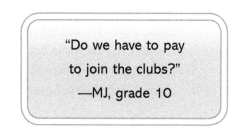

"Do we have to pay to join the clubs?"
—MJ, grade 10

The clubs you join will depend on your interests. There are clubs associated with sports/leisure (such as a skiing or chess), book- or movie-based clubs (such as a muggle quidditch team or cosplay), special interest clubs (such as LGBTQIA or abuse awareness), political clubs (such as young Democrats or Republicans), cultural clubs (such as African American students or Asian students), language clubs (such as—well, various languages so you can keep your skills up), academic clubs (such as pre-law or math—especially if there aren't honors society chapters), arts clubs (such as photography or painting), and hundreds more.

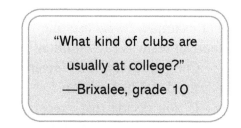

"What kind of clubs are usually at college?"
—Brixalee, grade 10

Starting a campus club isn't difficult so if there isn't already a club for something you are interested in (such as the Michigan Squirrel Club, the MIT Assassins Guild, or the Society for Creative Anachronism—yep, these are all real college clubs; in fact, the Michigan Squirrel Club has over four hundred members), get a couple of friends and a sympathetic faculty advisor and start your own club!

Each college has a student association—an elected group of students who represent the student body to the administration. Part of the responsibility of the student association is to oversee campus clubs. Visit them (I'm sure they'll also have a web page) and get the 411 on club requirements.

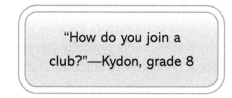

"How do you join a club?"—Kydon, grade 8

Athletics

School athletics come in various forms. If you wish to participate officially on the lacrosse team, for example (if you do not play lacrosse, substitute "lacrosse" with your sport of choice), you'll need to

1. make sure the school has a lacrosse team
2. contact the lacrosse coach
3. try out for the lacrosse team
4. discuss lacrosse scholarships

Overseen by the NCAA (National Collegiate Athletic Association), the number and types of official sports teams will depend on the individual school. According to NCAA statistics from 2016, almost 31 million people attended a college game and just under half of US citizens follow college sports.[1]

In regard to making money, men's football and men's basketball are the two most popular collegiate sports and some colleges take their sports *very* seriously. For example, *Forbes* lists the "value" of the 2017 University of Texas Longhorns football team as $129 million![2]

Comparatively, the University of Louisville Cardinals men's basketball team is valued at $36.1 million.[3]

If you decide that "most popular" has more to do with how many schools have an intercollegiate team, basketball is the clear winner with 2,197 men's and women's teams in the country. The second most common is cross-country at 2,065 teams. Cross-country programs are much less expensive to support but lack the glitz of many other sports. There are only 672 college football teams (that should tell you something about how expensive football programs are considering how popular the sport is and how much money can be made with a football team), making football the twelfth most common college sport (beaten out by some fairly obvious sports such as baseball/softball and soccer, as well as a couple of not-so-obvious competitors such as tennis and, yes, you guessed it, lacrosse).[4]

State schools typically have more athletics options than private schools, and bigger schools (more students) typically have more sports teams than smaller schools.

Did You Know?

Carleton College in Northfield, Minnesota, plays an annual softball game that adds an additional inning for each year the school has been in existence. The school was founded in 1866, so in 2019 their game will be up to 153 innings.

> ### Did You Know?
>
> ● Fourteen of the largest twenty-five sports stadiums in the world belong to US college football teams.[c]

Schools are designated into divisions and conferences and the number of schools within a division or conference varies widely across the country. Additionally, not all sports within the same school are given equal priority. It is possible to have a well-funded and popular soccer team but a small and fairly ignored basketball team at the same school.

Despite Title IX requirements, it is still usual to see male-participant sports receive more attention—most notably in fan attendance but sometimes in funding—than female-participant sports. Additional funding for male-participant sports often comes from more active boosters, as individuals are welcome to financially support whatever they like.

In an effort to encourage more students to attend female-participant sports, many schools offer cheaper (or free) tickets to these games. It is not true that male-participant sports are more exciting than female-participant sports. Much of your spectator enjoyment comes from your personal preference for a particular sport as well as the heightened competition of two well-matched teams (of either gender) playing their best.

No matter your preference—or if you don't like sports—if your school has at least one team that participates in divisional sports, *go to a game*. Attending a college sporting event is a huge part of the college experience. The best part, even during a dramatic overtime game of your favorite sport, is attending with a group of friends and getting caught up in the fandamonium of the event. So put on your school colors and scream yourself hoarse.

Each school will have its own ticket costs and may offer season passes for an individual sport, annual passes to all games, or, possibly, allow free admission with your student ID. If the games are free, you should go to many of them as they make great study breaks and socializing opportunities.

Intramural Sports

Schools also offer intramural opportunities. Intramural sports are played within a school so there are several school "teams" that play each other but no official team that plays another school's official team. Because you'll be playing with and against other students from your school, joining (or attending) intramural sports is a great way to meet others and show off for the hottie from your math class.

Intramural sports are easier to join (few have tryouts—you just join and play no matter your ability) and offer a wider variety of sports options as they don't require the extensive funding that some official sports do.

Even if your school has an official team, it is probable that there will be intramurals in the same sport. You may not want to (or not have been good enough to) play baseball for the school team, but you can keep up with your powerhouse skills through intramurals. Some intramurals are coed (boys and girls playing together), which is another perk for some college students.

Many colleges have standard intramural teams such as volleyball and racquetball but may also have less mainstream ones such as quidditch or dodgeball. Even less common intramurals include octopush (underwater hockey), battleship (based on the table game; picture canoes, swimming pools, and trying to drench enemies with buckets of water), and Segway polo (yep, members ride Segways instead of horses). If your school doesn't have a team, start one! (Well, start at least two because you really need at least two teams for any of these to work.)

Intramural sports are so popular and such an important part of the college experience for most students that the Best Colleges guide allows you to search for your perfect college through an intramural filter! Drexel University (a 125-year-old private university in Philadelphia, Pennsylvania) is ranked as number one, Gannon University (a private, coed Catholic university in Erie, Pennsylvania) is ranked number two, and Houston Baptist University (a private, coed Baptist university in Houston, Texas) rounds out the top three.

If you aren't interested in a private university, don't despair, two of the top ten best intramural colleges are public (one on each coast). But you'll have to check out the Best Colleges site to see which ones.[5]

The Arts

Whether it is an art exhibit, a musical concert, or a play, college provides abundant opportunities to expand your horizons, support your peers, and combat stress. The arts—fine and performing—are crucial to humanity. People are designed to be creative and need to find ways to unleash that creativity. Just as it is an important part of the college experience to catch an athletic event, you need to take advantage of the opportunities your school provides to gaze at the paintings, drawings, photos, and sculptures at student art exhibits. Dance and theater majors stage performances throughout the year and the music department will host everything from individual student recitals to orchestral concerts. If your English department doesn't host poetry readings (I'm pretty sure they do), head for a local coffee shop.

If you don't think of yourself as a patron of the arts, you might not have had the opportunity to catch audience fever. Many of these performances are free to students (grab your ID card), which means they make very convenient dates. Being able to sit in the audience and lose yourself in another world of sight and sound provides a break from studies and will lower your stress level. Don't make the mistake of thinking of student productions as lesser quality. Many of the participants are headed for a profession in their artistic areas and catching their colleges performances will give you an opportunity to say "I remember her" when she accepts her Oscar or "I saw him" when he grabs his Grammy.

Study Abroad

If at all possible, take the opportunity to study abroad. There are thousands of opportunities to spend a few weeks, a semester, a summer, or an entire year attending college in a foreign country. There are also opportunities to "study away"—which is spending time at another college while staying in America. It is likely that your college will have an office for study abroad (possibly called global engagement or international programs), but if you choose a college that doesn't have its own office, there are unaffiliated study abroad programs.

Why should you study abroad? The benefits are numerous.

1. You get to travel, and not just to the country you are studying in. Use your passport, backpack, student rail discounts, and long weekends to see the world. Remember to take your English-to-whatever-language-is-spoken-in-the-country-you-visit guide and memorize the appropriate translations for "Where is the nearest restroom?" and "Please take me to the American Embassy."

   Study abroad provides an opportunity for travel you may not have again, or for a long time. As you age and collect people (e.g., spouse and children), traveling becomes more complicated and expensive. Even if you have a well-paying job and a great vacation package, it is unlikely that you will be able to spend months completely embedded in a foreign country.

2. You get to explore a new culture. History, language, food, customs, traditions, food, and did I mention food? No book, movie, or restaurant can replicate being there. Climb Machu Picchu. Swim the shores of Sarakiniko. Ski Cortina d'Ampezzo. Safari in Namibia and Botswana. Sail up the Amazon River during Semester at Sea. Wherever you want to go, whatever you want to do, don't forget your camera!

3. Hone your language skills. Remember when we discussed the difference between a BA and a BS and I explained that you have to take several terms of a foreign language for a BA? (Well, maybe you don't remember my saying that as there is no rule that says you have to read this book in

order so if you haven't read chapter 1, *spoiler alert—a BA requires foreign language study!*) Studying abroad, especially for at least a year, provides an opportunity to immerse yourself in the language and will count for foreign language course credits. Your school may advise you to take one or two semesters of language and *then* complete a study abroad so you have some knowledge of the language before you live where it is the primary language.

4. Try new experiences. New places and new people mean new opportunities to explore new interests, engage in new activities, and discover new talents. You will also make new friends who are likely to be lifelong friends and members of your growing professional network. Many study abroad programs have the option for you to live with a host family to experience the "real" culture of the area.

5. Personal development. There is nothing like a study abroad to help you discover yourself and mature into an independent and self-assured adult. Being in a new place, away from your comfort zone and support group, tests your ability to adapt and problem solve. You learn to consider a variety of opinions and question your own beliefs and ideas.

6. Educational development. Education is not the same around the world. From teaching styles to class schedules, seeing your major from another perspective will help you better understand the career you desire to spend the rest of your life with. In addition, being able to list study abroad on your graduate school application will impress admissions boards with your commitment to your education and willingness to be challenged.

If you're worried about financing your study abroad, you can utilize your financial aid (you will still be in school) and there are scholarships specifically designed to use for international education. So make an appointment with your college's study abroad office and explore your options!

Vacations

In chapter 9, we talked about homesickness; combined with your personal finances, these two factors most often determine whether you'll head home, stay at school, or travel during your breaks.

The third factor is homework, but that doesn't seem to be as "important" in the decision making as the other two for some students.

Anyway, staying busy (as we discussed) is important to fighting off homesickness and, whenever possible, you should use vacation time for an actual vacation. Even if it turns out to be a "staycation" (with family or in your own school abode), do something besides eat, sleep, and study. Colleges provide breaks to support your overall mental, emotional, and physical well-being. When you use vacation time to continue to build stress and lose sleep, you are actually working against yourself. Tired, malnourished, and stressed brains do not think well.

CHANGES

You'll recall from memorizing that glorious introduction I wrote that my sister told me I would change more in the four years of college than I did in the four years I spent in high school. She was right. Everyone who matriculates (a college word for being enrolled) changes just about every aspect of themselves. Some changes are obvious and common while others will be quite unique to your situation; at least these changes will feel unique, but you won't go through anything that other college students haven't experienced. These changes are at the heart of *why* you go to college, and while some are scary, being aware and prepared will impact the whole college experience.

In 1969, Arthur Chickering developed a theory of psychosocial development that outlined seven areas of development that college students experience. While it may be difficult to believe that anything from 1969 is still relevant, his theory holds up.[1]

1. *Developing competence.* In addition to intellectual competence, this is a time in your life to develop physical and interpersonal competence. Don't be surprised when you find yourself leaving some friendships behind and cultivating others as your own interests and goals change.
2. *Managing emotions.* This doesn't mean ignoring them because ignoring your emotions just causes them to build up pressure and explode when you least expect them to. Managing your emotions means learning to process them in a healthy way. Understand that you can control your temper and sexual desire, that no one can "make you feel" a certain way, and that you are responsible for your actions and reactions.
3. *Becoming autonomous.* This is another way of describing independence. You learn to take care of yourself physically, mentally, emotionally, financially, and in everyday ways (such as feeding and cleaning up after yourself).
4. *Establishing your identity.* Who are you? Better yet, who do you want to become? Make a list of the characteristics you want to exhibit and work to cultivate those positives such as kindness, honesty, and dependability.

5. *Experiencing freeing interpersonal relationships.* Throughout childhood, your relationships were based heavily on dependence. As you mature, your relationships should become less about what others can do for you, and more about what you can do for them. Don't allow others to abuse you; look for mutually satisfying and uplifting relationships.

6. *Clarifying purposes.* Identify your career and personal life goals and make decisions based on whether it will help or hinder your achieving those goals (and establishing the positive identity you desire).

7. *Developing integrity or wholeness.* This is one of the more difficult aspects of maturity—learning to accept the uncertainties and unfairness that exists in the world while adapting society's rules to be personally meaningful.

Recently, cultural psychologists have added two areas to this framework that have found particular relevance in this consumer-heavy time.

8. *Interacting with the dominant culture.* "Dominant" changes with location so it isn't always referring to gender or race. For example, the dominant culture on a college campus is a "highly educated" culture. In large part, this is the point of this book—my helping you learn to interact (successfully) with the dominant culture by understanding how that culture works.

9. *Developing spirituality.* Whether you were raised inside or outside of any particular religion, this is the time in your life when you question what you've been told and discover what you believe because of what you've studied and experienced, not just because someone else told you to believe it. This is the same process you go through with politics, relationships, and every other aspect of your life. College really is about *questioning everything* and is a necessary part of establishing your identity.

The college section of *USA Today*[2] lists fifteen specific ways you'll change during college. Your family is likely to notice these first, then friends, and then you, so don't overreact if someone else points out one of these changes before you notice.

1. Spending a Saturday night watching TV with your friends or family sounds great.
2. You start making your bed every day.
3. You literally *need* coffee.
4. You read long books or articles for fun.
5. You see seniors posting about promposals—and are glad that's behind you.
6. You schedule and respect naps.
7. You don't have to be asked to do the dishes (or other chores).

8. You're passionate about something nobody else understands and you're OK with that.
9. You feel OK being alone in public.
10. You realize that something your professor said applies to your life.
11. You have a falling out with your first college friend.
12. You become opinionated about world issues.
13. You call your parents to tell them everything.
14. You realize there are only a few friends you really want to spend summer with.
15. Someone who knows you really well says you've changed (and you agree with them).

Some of you may have already discovered the joys of spending the weekend in your pajamas or spending time by yourself. If so, don't be surprised if college exacerbates these traits.

My college students want me to warn you that growing up can be quite scary and to encourage you to realize that everyone around you is going through the same things. You are not alone even though it may feel like you are. And those members of the higher education dominant culture? The faculty, staff, and administration? They've all been through it and have helped countless others navigate the complicated yet rewarding path to adulthood. So reach out to them. Despite their content area, degrees, or job description, they are all experts at helping you achieve your goals—professional and personal.

It may come as a surprise that your relationships with friends and family will change. Hopefully, they will change for the better as you begin a new level of friendship with your parents because you are all independent adults now. However, it is probable that there will be some growing pains on both sides.

If you are a first-generation student, you will be exposed to a lot of different ideas and experiences that your family might not understand. If they haven't read some of the literature you are working your way through, it might be difficult to pull family members into a discussion about themes or ideals. They may not be as excited about the new formula you memorized or the experiment you successfully recreated in the lab. It doesn't mean they aren't proud of you or interested in your successes. It just means that different people have different interests and you may need to work a little harder to find a topic for mutual discussion.

If you are from a particular background, it may be more difficult to find common ground. For example, you may be from a blue-collar family and are now working toward a white-collar career. You may have friends or family members who denigrate your devotion to higher education as thinking you are "better" than they are. If you are experiencing this cultural divide, I recommend Alfred Lubrano's *Limbo: Blue-Collar Roots, White-Collar Dreams*.

My grandparents were blue collar but had no problem supporting white-collar dreams—unless those dreams were from a female. However, my parents, particularly my mother, worked hard to give their daughters (they only had girls) opportunities Mom had been denied. My grandparents believed that educating a female past high school was a waste. Everything she needed to know about being a wife and mother was either learned by eighteen or would be her husband's place to teach her (I could never get a straight answer regarding what a husband knew about being a wife and mother that would require a woman to accept it unquestioningly). If she could cook, clean, and mind the babies, she knew everything that was worth a girl knowing.

My mother understood that education was the way to raise people out of poverty. She knew that having an educated mother was the best hope for her children—sons and daughters. This knowledge has been supported by recent research.[3] She sacrificed so that her daughters could have a future that she could only dream about—and it worked. Although she dropped out of high school (got her General Education Development diploma) and got married at sixteen, she kept educating herself. She loved to read and instilled a passion for education in her children. All three of her daughters graduated from college and two of us have terminal degrees in our fields. She protected us from a lot of the gender bias of her extended family, so I didn't realize how blatant it was until the summer after I got married.

I had finished my bachelor's and had started my master's program when I got married. My mother was very clear with her daughters that we could get married *after* we finished our college degrees. Where we went to college and what we majored in wasn't as important as our going and graduating. A few months after the wedding, my husband and I took a trip with my mother and sister back to the town my mother's relatives still lived in. One afternoon, my grandmother pulled me aside to apologize for what a bad mother I had (for the record, my mother was amazing!). I was stunned. Why did she think her daughter had turned into a bad mother? Because Mom had encouraged us to waste money on an education we didn't need. Seriously. My grandmother explained that it was good we had finished high school and even going to college was an acceptable strategy for "landing" a college boy with a better financial future, but to finish? And then go on to graduate school? What was the point? I had a husband who had a job. What more could I possibly want except to start making babies?

I was horrified. Not because being a stay-at-home wife and mother is a bad thing. My mom was and I had friends who were. I believe it is an amazing choice if it is the right choice for your situation. But education is all about giving us choices. Personally, I would not make a good stay-at-home mom. I am a much better mother because I leave during the day and teach and research and talk

"The most beautiful discovery true friends make is that they can grow separately without growing apart."—Elizabeth Foley. © *iStock / Deagreez*

to adults. Conversely, my husband is an amazing stay-at-home father. (Bet my grandmother didn't see that switch coming!)

The reason I tell you this story is to remind you that your decision to attend college at all—much less a particular college, major in a certain field, live on or off campus, work full or part time or not at all, and all other decisions you make—are likely to be questioned. You will choose to do things differently than your friends or family believe you should. And that's OK. You are you. You have to live your life and pay for your own mistakes. Just as it is impossible to be happy all of the time, it is impossible to make everyone else happy all of the time. Don't tie yourself into knots trying to please everyone. Always be kind and considerate; but know that you have one life, and just as they made their choices, you need to make yours. So choose wisely and bravely.

APPENDIX A

....

Q&A Tour Form

Make several copies of these questions and take notes for each campus.

School: _____ Tour Dates: _____

Academics (ask the tour guide or admissions officer)

1. How many hours per week do first-year students typically spend on homework?
2. What percentage of classes are taught by teaching assistants?
3. What is the average class size of introductory/first-year classes?
4. What is the average class size of upper-division courses?
5. What is the student-to-teacher ratio in my major?
6. What's the freshman-to-sophomore retention rate?
7. Do classes tend to be more lecture based, project learning, discussion based, or other?
8. What opportunities are there for undergraduate research?
9. What financial support is there for undergraduate research?
10. Is there a culminating senior year experience? Is it required or optional?
11. Do you have an honors college? If so, what are the requirements? Benefits?
12. Do you have a learning community or other freshman experience?
13. What is your four-year graduation rate?
14. What is your five-year graduation rate?
15. What does it take to graduate in four years?
16. What types of tutoring services are available?
17. What is the tutor-to-student ratio?
18. Is tutoring limited to a certain number of visits?
19. How involved are academic advisors?
20. Do the academic advisors contact us each term or are we expected to take the initiative?
21. What kinds of learning disability resources do you have?

22. What is the average wait time to get an appointment for the disability resource center?
23. What counseling services are available on campus?
24. What is the average wait time to get an appointment for counseling services?
25. What medical services are available on campus?
26. What is the average wait time to get an appointment for medical services?
27. What type of career services do you have?
28. What percentage of students study abroad? Where do they typically go? Average cost? Available financial help?

Student Life (ask the admissions officer or tour guide)

29. What types of dormitories are available?
30. What percentage of students live on campus?
31. Are first-year students required to live on campus?
32. Is there a separate first-year dormitory?
33. How long are dorm accommodations guaranteed?
34. Do most on-campus students go home on the weekend?
35. What sororities/fraternities are available on campus?
36. Which sororities/fraternities have "houses"?
37. What academic honors societies are available on campus? (Ask about your major.)
38. What social activities are offered to students?
39. What clubs are available on campus?
40. Are there available art/music practice spaces for nonmajors?
41. What is the number of library holdings? What special collections? Are there any agreements with other university libraries?
42. What are the crime rates on campus? (They are required to publish these annually but they may be a bit difficult to find on the website.)
43. Is there a late-night shuttle or escort service by campus security?

Financial Aid (ask the financial aid officer)

44. What is your average financial aid package?
45. What is the typical breakdown of loans versus grants?
46. What percentage of financial need does the school typically meet?
47. What is the average merit award?
48. What percentage of students receive grants?
49. What is the average college debt that students leave with?
50. What work-study opportunities are there?
51. How many students at the college get internships?

Questions for Current Students (tour guide and students in your major, athletics, clubs)

52. Why did *you* choose this college?
53. Are you happy with that choice or do you regret it?
54. Did you transfer here from another college? If so, why?
55. What are your favorite and least favorite things about this school?
56. Are the students friendly and welcoming?
57. Are the professors welcoming?
58. How hard do you have to work to get good grades?
59. Are there shops within walking distance or do you need a car?
60. What is the best place and worst place to eat on campus?
61. What is the best place and worst place to eat locally?
62. Does the dining hall cater to special dietary needs? Gluten free? Vegetarian?
63. Are weekends on campus active or does everyone disappear?
64. What do students do for fun on and off campus?
65. What's Greek life like, and how do students feel about it?
66. How good is the Wi-Fi on campus?

APPENDIX B

....

Campus Tour Record

Campus Tour Record for _____ [school]

Tour date(s): _____ Tour Guide: _____

	Agree	Neutral	Disagree
Academics			
The program for my chosen major (or general studies) is balanced in breadth (variety of offerings) and depth (higher-level classes of substance).			
The people in the major department made me feel welcome.			
The class I observed was interesting and informative.			
The student-to-teacher ratio supports personal interest.			
Fellow students made me feel welcome.			
A degree from here would prepare me for my future career/graduate school.			
I can see myself happily spending four to six years learning here.			

	Agree	Neutral	Disagree
Financial Aid			
I would graduate with little debt.			
My financial aid package would not decrease after the first year.			
My financial options were explained clearly and honestly.			
Tuition, fees, housing, food, and so on, are within my budget.			
I could easily get a job that will give me experience for my future career as well as earn money.			
Housing			
The dormitories were quiet.			
I felt safe and comfortable in the dormitories.			
The on-campus food was delicious.			
The Wi-Fi in the dorms was fast.			
Overall			
I felt "at home" on campus.			
The faculty/staff and students had positive and friendly interactions.			

	Agree	Neutral	Disagree
Everyone seemed to be genuinely happy to be a part of the school.			
There are many on-campus activities that I am interested in.			
There are many off-campus activities that I am interested in.			

APPENDIX C

Moving List

Room Needs/Storage

- Additional seating—Get a beanbag, folding chair, comfy chair, or other. Just assume you'll have friends over.
- Adhesive hooks and strips—Get ones that come off cleanly as many dorms have rules against putting holes in the walls.
- Alarm clock/clock radio—Something you won't sleep through; even if attendance isn't taken, you should go to class.
- Bed risers—Making your bed taller allows for more room for storage bins underneath.
- Bedside/desk lamp—Your roommate won't want the overhead florescent lights on at 2 a.m. when you are finally desperate enough to write that term paper.
- Bulletin board and/or dry erase board with pushpins and markers/eraser— If you intend to put it outside of your dorm door so your friends can leave you notes, remember that means *anyone* can leave you a note—and swipe your marker.
- Closet organizer—Dorm closets are small and you may have to share the space with your roomie.
- Fan—In addition to white noise, a fan provides airflow; your room may be stuffy.
- Framed pictures or a digital frame for many pictures.
- Hangers—The ones with removable clips for pants/skirts make great chip clips. The clips, not the hanger part.
- Mini toolkit—Include a screwdriver, hammer, wrench, duct tape.
- Mini trash can—Or larger trash can, depending on how trashy you intend to be. If you have a kitchen(ette) you'll want a larger one for fridge cleanouts. Tip: if you drill three or four small holes in the side of your trash can about one inch from the base, it will help lessen the suction created when you try to pull the bag out.

- Plants—Unless you don't have a green thumb, in which case you should get plastic plants. Or pictures of plants.
- Posters/Wall art—You only get to decorate *your half* of the room, so think about shared space when you plan what you want to put up on the walls.
- Small safe for valuables and documents—Trust but verify.
- Shoe rack—Choose one that fits under your bed or in your closet.
- Storage bins—The ones that slide under your bed are best.
- Wall mirror/full-length mirror—There may be one in your suite bathroom so check with the school.

Linens/Laundry Supplies

- Bedbug protecting mattress cover—Check with college for size needed; some college twin beds are extra long.
- Blankets/comforter/bedspread—You'll want two of them plus a throw/lap blanket. Make sure they are machine washable. The dorm laundry room may not have an extra-large capacity machine but a local laundromat will.
- Bleach—In addition to making your whites their whitest, bleach helps unclog and clean toilets; helps flowers last longer, which decreases the gross stuff from growing in the vase; disinfects cutting boards; and sanitizes your Legos and other plastic toys. Follow the cautions as bleach is a strong chemical.
- Color catchers—These look like dryer sheets but go in the washer to catch the dyes that come off your clothes during washing. *Note:* this miracle product does not mean you should just dump all of your clothes in the washer together. Sort your laundry and do separate loads. Remember, we talked about this in chapter 6.
- Dryer sheets—The thin layer of lubricant on a dryer sheet reduces static electricity and softens your clothes. Additionally, dryer sheets can be used to freshen clothes (put one in each drawer and in your closet, as well as shoes, and luggage), clean pots and pans, wipe soap scum from a shower door, buff chrome, repel mosquitos, remove rings from toilets, repel dust from electronics, and keep dust off blinds—along with many other uses.
- Drying rack—Some clothes are not intended for a dryer. If the tag says line dry, don't put it in the dryer. They aren't joking.
- Fabric softener—Add this miracle liquid to the appropriate wash cycle to make your clothes softer. You can still use a dryer sheet for the static cling. In addition, fabric softener can remove hair spray residue, keep paintbrushes pliable, remove hard water stains, clean windows, and refresh carpets.
- Foam mattress topper—Put it on your mattress to add more support and comfort.

- Iron and ironing board—Limited drawer and closet space makes for wrinkled clothes. Pro tip: be sure to get an iron that has automatic shutoff, and never iron your clothes if you are already wearing them.
- Laundry bag/basket—You may have a long haul between your room and the laundry room so get something with comfy handles.
- Laundry detergent—Detergent is soap. However, you cannot just use any kind of soap in a washing machine. Detergent can also be used to clean spots on carpets and upholstery, unclog drains, and clean oil spills on a driveway or garage floor.
- Lingerie bag—When you wash delicates (bras, nylons, and other hand-wash fabrics) or a sweater you don't want to pill (those little lint balls that show up like the pox), put them in a lingerie bag before putting in the washer. Then dry them on your rack or hang dry.
- Lint brush/roller—Scotch tape works but not as well.
- Mini sewing kit—Learn to sew a small tear, replace a button, and other little fixes.
- Pillows—You'll want two unless you are a girl—then you'll likely want six: two for sleeping, a bolster for under your knees or lower back support, two throws for decoration, and one body pillow.
- Quarters—Some residence hall laundry rooms have change makers or allow you to use a card to pay for a load of laundry, but many still use quarters. Banks will let you "buy" rolls of quarters.
- Sheets and pillowcases (two sets)—Yes, two. You'll want to be able to put clean sheets on your bed while you wash the other set and you don't want to be stuck with dirty sheets and no quarters.
- Storage tub with lid to store and transport laundry products safely—A paint bucket with lid and handle works well and it is stackable.
- Towels (three each of bath, hand, and face)—Write your name on the tags; buying similar colors will let you wash them all in the same load.
- Waterproof mattress pad—This goes over your mattress topper and under your sheets to add comfort and protect against staining the mattress.

Desk/School Supplies

- 3 × 5 index cards—Excellent for notes, flashcards, or giving your number to the hottie in the second row.
- Backpack/laptop case—Make sure you write your name inside.
- Three-ring binders—Get either a ½- to 1-inch binder for each class you are taking *or* a larger (2½-inch) binder and one pocket folder for each class if you wish to keep all your materials together.
- Calculator—Depending on your required classes, you may need something beyond a phone app.

- Calendar/planner—Get paper or electronic, depending on which works better for you.
- Cards/notes to send home—Remind your family you're thinking of them and accepting care packages; note cards can be created from scratch or ordered through Amazon.
- Desk chair—Check with school as some include one with a desk but the comfort rating is probably less than stellar.
- Desk organizer—At least *begin* the semester on top of things.
- Electronic storage media—Buy memory cards and flash drives *and* create a Google Drive account.
- Envelopes—An envelope is a folded and glued piece of paper that you send old-fashioned letters in. There are tutorials on YouTube. Honest.
- Erasers—You'll make a lot of mistakes in college.
- File folder for important documents—Then put it in your safe.
- Folders with pockets—Get one for each class you are taking.
- Glue—It's for sticking, not sniffing.
- Highlighter pens—Get multiple colors made especially for textbooks to avoid bleed-through.
- Lap desk with fan—Despite the research against studying in bed, you'll do it so get a good lap desk that won't let your laptop overheat.
- Laptop—A printer is optional as there are usually computer labs where you can print and many schools charge you nonrefundable print fees so you might as well use them.
- Lunchbox—Whether you live on or off campus, you'll want to pack healthy meals to take with you. Plus, it's cheaper than always eating out.
- Notebook paper—Get the loose-leaf kind for your three-ring binders. The spiral ones are loud and messy.
- Paper clips and binder clips
- Pencil holder and sharpener
- Pens and pencils
- Permanent marker
- Printer paper and ink
- Rubber bands
- Ruler
- Scissors
- Stamps—They go on the envelope. Watch the tutorial.
- Stapler, staples, and staple remover
- Sticky notes
- Tape (scotch, duct, electrical)
- Textbooks

Technology/Electronics

- Adapters (HDMI, ethernet, etc.)
- Batteries—Make a list of your battery needs: remotes, flashlight, and so on.
- Cell phone—If your phone doesn't have a high-quality camera, consider getting a separate one for all those memories you'll be making.
- Chargers (phone, laptop, camera, etc.)
- Cord organizer—You'll have limited space and will want to also limit the possibility of tripping.
- E-reader/tablet
- Extension cord/surge protector
- External hard drive—Your computer *will* crash. It's a college tradition.
- Headphones—Don't expect your roomie or neighbors to share your taste in music.
- MP3 player—While these are great for listening to while studying and walking around campus, don't listen during class. You're paying a lot of money for those classes so pay attention.
- Portable phone charger—An external battery pack/power bank that you can keep in your backpack for emergency charges.
- Two-prong adapters (3)—Check with residence halls to see if this is necessary.

Shared Items—Check with Roommate(s)

- Area rug—If your room is carpeted, this may be less necessary. However, a splash of color can add personality to your room.
- Audio equipment—Keep limited space in mind while looking at those stereo systems and settle for MP3 player docking speakers.
- Coffeemaker/microwave, if allowed—If a coffee pot is allowed, it's for more than just coffee. Place pasta—macaroni noodles and ramen noodles work best—in the pot and have the water boil over it (don't put in coffee grounds). Let noodles sit until done then drain water (except for ramen), add sauce/seasonings, and eat. The best part is you only have to wash the pot and fork!
- Small refrigerator—If one isn't provided but is allowed.
- TV and DVD player—Remember that your residence hall likely has rules against hanging things on the wall and the primary purpose of your desk is for studying.

Bathroom

- Air freshener—Most dorms have a ban on open flame so stick with the spray kind. If you like the wax warmers, check with the residence hall on its policy.
- Bathroom cleaning supplies—Bring them if needed for your dorm (e.g., drain cleaner, glass cleaner, rubber gloves, shower cleaner, sponges, toilet brush, toilet cleaner).
- Bathroom rug—It goes outside the shower so you don't slip.
- Shower caddy—You may have a shared bathroom that requires you to carry your toiletries back and forth.
- Shower curtain and rings—If needed; shower may have doors.
- Shower mat—It goes inside the shower so you don't slip.
- Shower shoes—A Google search of infections you can catch from a shower— especially MRSA—will convince you to invest in nonslip flip-flops.
- Upgraded showerhead—If your school allows it and you have a private or semi-private bathroom.

Toiletries

- Personal items such as shampoo, makeup, deodorant, toothbrush, razors, shaving cream

Clothes

- Remember you're leaving for at least three seasons so plan for rain, cold, and heat while keeping space limitations in mind. However, long weekends and other home trips are useful for seasonal closet changes.

Medical

- Acne medicine/cream
- Allergy medicine
- Aloe Vera lotion/gel
- Birth control pills
- Cold and flu medicine
- Condoms
- Cortisone cream
- Decongestant
- Eye drops
- First aid kit with bandages, antiseptic wipes, burn ointment
- Hot and cold packs
- Humidifier
- Insect repellent
- Menstrual pain medication
- Multivitamins
- Over-the-counter pain medication
- Prescription medicine
- Prescription refill information
- Retainer/mouth guard
- Rubbing alcohol

- Sunscreen
- Thermometer with covers
- Throat drops/lozenges/spray
- Upset stomach medication
- Vaseline

Household and Kitchen Items

- All-purpose cleaner
- Bowl, plate, and cup—Unbreakable is best and a set of four can be pretty cheap.
- Can/bottle opener
- Coffee mug—Get one or two for staying in and a travel one for class.
- Dish soap and a refillable dish wand
- Food-storage containers—Something you can write a date on is best so you know if you're still in the safe zone for leftovers. Remember: when in doubt, throw it out.
- Paper towels—You don't want to use up or ruin your cloth towels.
- Plastic storage bags (sandwich and freezer)
- Silverware—Again, a set of four is likely sufficient and inexpensive.
- Sponge and Magic Eraser—They really are magic. Also, get sponges without metal in them so you can sterilize them in the microwave at least once each week and replace them at least once each month.
- Tissues—No, *you're* crying!
- Trash bags—Get bags for your trash can and bigger ones that are sturdy enough to haul to the dumpster. The ones with odor shield are worth it.
- Water bottle—Schools are upgrading drinking fountains to ones that include bottle refilling stations, and drinking plenty of water is key to staying healthy.
- Wet wipes—Not just for babies, wet wipes can be used to clean up excess nail polish, remove eye makeup, remove hair dye stains, substitute for toilet paper, wipe up dust, even off of plants, remove stains, sanitize—especially light switches, door knobs, handles, and keyboards, wipe down trash cans, remove makeup and deodorant stains from clothing. And if you add a few drops of witch hazel to the ones with aloe in them, they can be used as an alternative to hemorrhoid cream.

Miscellaneous

- Art supplies
- Beach/swimming pool towel
- Bike—Check with the school to see if bikes are required to be registered.

- Bike helmet
- Bike lock
- Board games/playing cards
- Books to read for fun—Better yet, see how many of the school library's you can get through before graduation.
- DVDs
- Earplugs—Your roomie may snore.
- Flashlight
- Luggage tags
- Musical instruments
- Pepper spray (if legal in your state)
- Religious materials
- Safety pins
- Safety whistle
- Sleep mask
- Sports equipment
- Suitcase/duffel bag (including a weekend-sized one)
- Travel organizer for toiletries
- Umbrella
- Vacuum—The dorm might have full-sized ones but consider a hand-held one.
- Video game console and games
- Yoga mat—PS: wet wipes are great for sanitizing your yoga mat and you can keep a travel pack of them in your workout bag.

Documents—Keep in Your Safe

- AAA card—You should also know how to change your own tire and put gas in your car, as well as what all those warning lights mean and how to find a trustworthy mechanic in the area. You may be able to share your parent's membership. Your auto insurance carrier may have AAA-like benefits so price shop.
- Bank documents—Get a checking account if you don't already have one. Most jobs require direct deposit and you'll have bills that will need to be paid with a debit/credit card.
- Car registration and insurance information—When you register for campus parking, it is likely you'll also need the license plate numbers.
- Checks—If you don't know how to fill out a check, ask your grandmother.
- Copy of birth certificate
- Copy of Social Security card—Although you should have the number memorized, your job may require you to give them a copy of the front and back of your card.

- Create and carry an emergency contact card—The tech alternative is to have an ICE (In Case of Emergency) entry in your cell phone. EMTs will look for the ICE entry.
- Credit/debit card—In addition to your bank account, you may have a separate credit account and/or one linked to your parents. Please read the chapter on finances before you get terribly excited about all the credit card companies recruiting on campus.
- Driver's license or other official identification card
- Emergency contact list—In addition to the ICE contact on your phone, write down your contact list and leave it in your dorm room where your roommate and resident assistant can access it in case of an emergency.
- Financial aid documents—Much of this is now online. However, having a folder with printed copies, organized by semester/year is useful for reapplying each year.
- Health/dental insurance cards—It is likely that you will be on your parents/guardians' insurance but you'll still need your own cards. If you have a separate prescription and/or HSA (Health Savings Account) card(s), get a copy of those, too.
- Lease (if you have an apartment) or dormitory agreement (if you live on campus)
- Passport—If you don't have one but would like to study abroad, get a passport. It takes a while to process but lasts for several years so you might as well get one while you are still photogenic.
- Product warranties—This is mostly for your tech/electronics. Don't rely on the company's records or your scanned copy as it is likely that your computer will be the most important product you'll need repaired/replaced.
- Renters insurance—If you are under twenty-six and living in the dorm, your possessions *may* be covered under your parents' home owner/renter's insurance. However, you'll want to check with that insurance company to see the limits of what is covered and to what extent. You may be able to add scheduled personal property coverage—sometimes called a "floater"—to their insurance. AAA and other insurance companies offer renter's insurance so do a bit of price checking.
- Student ID—You won't believe the discounts you can get with a student ID! Additionally, you may need it to get into sporting events, concerts, plays, and the library. Some schools require you to get a sticker each semester to prove your ID is current. You may be able to get a new ID each year and some schools will charge you to replace the ID during the year.

Notes

Introduction

1. Richard Armour, *The Academic Bestiary* (New York: William Morrow, 1974), 3.
2. Cara Newlon, "College Students Still Often Find Spouses on Campus," *USA Today*, October 15, 2013, www.usatoday.com/story/news/nation/2013/10/15/college-marriage-facebook/2989039/, accessed November 14, 2017.
3. Maura Kelly, "How We Meet Our Spouses," *Wall Street Journal*, March 27, 2014, www.wsj.com/articles/SB10001424052702303325204579463272000371990, accessed November 14, 2017.
4. Philip Cohen, "Let's Not Panic over Women with More Education Having Fewer Kids," *Atlantic*, February 12, 2013, www.theatlantic.com/sexes/archive/2013/02/lets-not-panic-over-women-with-more-education-having-fewer-kids/273070/, accessed November 14, 2017.
5. CDC Newsroom, "Higher Education and Income Levels Keys to Better Health, According to Annual Report on Nation's Health," Centers for Disease Control and Prevention, May 15, 2012, www.cdc.gov/media/releases/2012/p0516_higher_education.html, accessed February 23, 2018.
6. Bureau of Labor Statistics, "Education Still Pays," United States Department of Labor, September 2014, www.bls.gov/careeroutlook/2014/data-on-display/education-still-pays.htm, accessed October 24, 2017.
7. Bureau of Labor Statistics, "Education Still Pays."

Chapter 1

1. ckoppenhaver92, "Vocational Education," *Teen Ink*, December 17, 2009, www.teenink.com/opinion/school_college/article/157657/Vocational-Education/, accessed May 2, 2017.
2. Joshua Wright, "America's Skilled Trades Dilemma: Shortages Loom as Most-In-Demand Group of Workers Ages," *Forbes*, March 7, 2013, www.forbes.com/sites/emsi/2013/03/07/americas-skilled-trades-dilemma-shortages-loom-as-most-in-demand-group-of-workers-ages/#55f6783c6397, accessed May 2, 2017.
3. Patrick Gillespie, "America Has Near Record 5.6 Million Job Openings," CNN Money, February 9, 2016, money.cnn.com/2016/02/09/news/economy/america-5-6-million-record-job-openings/index.html, accessed May 2, 2017.
4. Michael Zimm, "If You Want Your Child to Succeed, Don't Sell Liberal Arts Short," *Wall Street Journal*, March 2, 2018, www.wsj.com/articles/if-you-want-your-child-to-succeed-dont-sell-liberal-arts-short-1520030546, accessed March 2, 2018.
5. Emily Moore, "A STEM Degree Does NOT Guarantee a Higher Salary—Here's Why," Glassdoor, May 12, 2017, www.glassdoor.com/blog/stem-degree-higher-salary/, accessed July 9, 2017.

6. "College Personality Quiz," *U.S. News and World Report*, August 21, 2008, www.usnews.com/education/articles/2008/08/21/college-personality-quiz-part-1-enthusiasm, accessed March 16, 2017.

a. Diana B. Turk, *Bound by a Mighty Vow: Sisterhood and Women's Fraternities 1870–1920* (New York: NYU Press, 2004).
b. Fitness, "Heavy College Students Must Pass Fitness Class," NBC News, November 23, 2009, www.nbcnews.com/id/34068877/ns/health-fitness/t/heavy-college-students-must-pass-fitness-class/#.WqW8Kejwa00, accessed March 11, 2018.

Chapter 2

a. Jerome Karabel, *The Chosen: The Hidden History of Admission and Exclusion at Harvard, Yale, and Princeton* (New York: Houghton Mifflin, 2005).

Chapter 3

1. Rob Franek, "Get the Most Out of Your College Visits," *Princeton Review*, www.princetonreview.com/college-advice/college-visits, accessed April 22, 2017.

Chapter 4

1. Tyler Kingkade, "One Chart That Makes It Clear College Tuition Is Becoming Unaffordable," *Huffington Post*, June 18, 2014, www.huffingtonpost.com/2014/06/18/college-tuition-unaffordable-growth-median-income_n_5505653.html, accessed November 12, 2017.
2. "Median Incomes v. Average College Tuition Rates, 1971–2015," ProCon.org, April 20, 2017, college-education.procon.org/view.resource.php?resourceID=005532, accessed November 12, 2017.
3. Rebecca Joseph, "A Spoonful of Sugar for Waiting College Applicants," *Huffington Post*, updated May 17, 2014, www.huffingtonpost.com/rebecca-joseph/a-spoonful-of-sugar-for-waiting-college-applicants_b_4979468.html, accessed March 11, 2018.
4. Susannah Snider, "10 Questions College Financial Aid Advisers Wish Parents Would Ask," *US News and World Report*, April 2015, www.usnews.com/education/best-colleges/paying-for-college/slideshows/10-questions-college-financial-aid-advisers-wish-parents-would-ask, accessed November 17, 2017.

a. "National Merit Scholarship Qualifications," Study Point, www.studypoint.com/ed/national-merit-scholarship-qualifications/, accessed March 11, 2018.

Chapter 5

1. The College Board, "Compare Your Aid Awards," Big Future, bigfuture.collegeboard.org/pay-for-college/financial-aid-awards/compare-aid-calculator, accessed November 17, 2017.

2. Rebecca Kern, "7 Questions to Ask When Considering a Gap Year," *U.S. News and World Report*, May 19, 2010, www.usnews.com/education/best-colleges/right-school/timeline/articles/2010/05/19/7-questions-to-ask-when-considering-a-gap-year, accessed March 2, 2018.

3. Vicki Nelson, "Should My Student Consider Deferring Enrollment to College?" College Parents of America, www.mycollegeoptions.org/Core/SiteContent/Students/Advice/College-Resource-Center/For-Parents/College-Admissions/Deferring-College-Enrollment.aspx, accessed March 2, 2018.

4. Rob Franek, "Is Taking a Gap Year Right for You?" *Princeton Review*, https://www.princetonreview.com/college-advice/deferred-admission, accessed March 2, 2018.

Chapter 6

1. Ruth N. Lopez Turley and Geoffrey Wodtke, "College Residence and Academic Performance: Who Benefits from Living on Campus?" *Urban Education* 45, no. 4 (2010): 506–532, accessed July 8, 2018, doi:10.1177/0042085910372351.; Study.com "The Benefits of Living on Campus," *Educator Insider News Blog*, July 28, 2011, study.com/articles/The_Benefits_of_Living_On_Campus.html, accessed July 8, 2018; Kasha Patel; "10 Reasons to Live in a Dorm for 4 Years," *USA Today College*, August 21, 2012, accessed July 8, 2018, college.usatoday.com/2012/08/21/10-reasons-to-live-in-a-dorm-for-four-years/, accessed July 8, 2018.

a. "The Real Value of College," Best Value Schools, www.bestvalueschools.com/real-value-college/, accessed March 11, 2018.

Chapter 7

1. "Family Educational Rights and Privacy Act (FERPA)," US Department of Education, www2.ed.gov/policy/gen/guid/fpco/ferpa/index.html, accessed March 11, 2018.

2. "Peer Tutoring Facts," National Tutoring Association, www.ntatutor.com/peer-tutoring-facts.html, accessed December 9, 2017.

3. Karen Fisher, "The Employment Mismatch," *Chronicle of Higher Education*, March 4, 2013, www.chronicle.com/article/the-employment-mismatch/137625#id=overview, accessed March 2, 2018.

4. Tyler Kingkade, "College Textbook Prices Increasing Faster Than Tuition and Inflation," *Huffington Post*, updated December 6, 2017, www.huffingtonpost.com/2013/01/04/college-textbook-prices-increase_n_2409153.html, accessed March 2, 2018.

5. Pam A. Mueller and Daniel M. Oppenheimer, "The Pen Is Mightier Than the Keyboard: Advantages of Longhand over Laptop Note Taking," *Psychological Science* 25, no. 6 (April 2014): 1159–1168.

6. The Learning Strategies Center, "The Cornell Note-Taking System," Cornell University, http://lsc.cornell.edu/notes.html, accessed December 9, 2017.

7. Anne Hennegar, "Make Your Cornell Notes Template with Word," Time Atlas, updated July 24, 2017, www.timeatlas.com/cornell-note-template/, accessed December 9, 2017.

8. Diego Santos, "5 Popular Note Taking Strategies," *GoConqr* (blog), October 3, 2014, www.goconqr.com/en/examtime/blog/4-note-taking-strategies/, accessed December 9, 2017.

a. Lynn O'Shaughnessy, "20 Surprising Higher Education Facts," *US News and World Report*, September 6, 2011, www.usnews.com/education/blogs/the-college-solution/2011/09/06/20-surprising-higher-education-facts, accessed March 11, 2018.

Chapter 9

1. Anya Kamenetz, "How College Students Are Sleeping . . . or Not," nprEd, May 2, 2016, www.npr.org/sections/ed/2016/05/02/475581810/how-college-students-are-sleeping-or-not, accessed February 25, 2018.
2. William Dement, "Sleepless at Stanford: What All Undergraduates Should Know about How Their Sleeping Lives Affect Their Waking Lives," Stanford University Center of Excellence for the Diagnosis and Treatment of Sleep Disorders, September 1997, web.stanford.edu/~dement/sleepless.html, accessed February 25, 2018.
3. Victoria Knight, "Study Links College Students' Grades to Sleep Schedules," CNN, June 12, 2017, www.cnn.com/2017/06/12/health/student-sleep-grades-study/index.html, accessed February 25, 2018.
4. MNT Editorial Team, "How Much Should I Weigh for My Height & Age?" Healthline Media, January 5, 2016, www.medicalnewstoday.com/info/obesity/how-much-should-i-weigh.php, accessed February 25, 2018.
5. "Body Mass Index Table," National Institute of Health, US Department of Health and Human Services, www.nhlbi.nih.gov/health/educational/lose_wt/BMI/bmi_tbl.pdf, accessed February 25, 2018.
6. MNT Editorial Team, "How Much Should I Weigh for My Height & Age?"
7. Margaret Ashwell, 19th Congress on Obesity in Lyon, France, cited in MNT Editorial Team, "How Much Should I Weigh: Other Measurements," May 12, 2012, www.medicalnewstoday.com/info/obesity/waist-to-hip-height.php, accessed February 25, 2018.
8. MNT Editorial Team, "How Much Should I Weigh for My Height & Age?"
9. Caroline Kee, "33 Healthy Eating Habits Lazy College Students Will Appreciate." BuzzFeed, September 19, 2015, www.buzzfeed.com/carolinekee/calm-down-ramen-is-allowed?utm_term=.mw3PkarqQ#.soPK1YQJN, accessed February 25, 2018.
10. Anisha Jhaveri, "22 Healthy College Recipes You Can Make in Your Dorm Room," Greatist, August 2, 2016, greatist.com/eat/healthy-dorm-room-recipes, accessed February 25, 2018.
11. Valerie, "40+ Easy Recipes for College Students," Valerie's Kitchen, August 22, 2015, www.fromvalerieskitchen.com/40-easy-recipes-for-college-students/, accessed February 25, 2018.
12. Deena Shanker, "Buying Organic Vegetables at the Supermarket Is a Waste of Money," Quartz, August 28, 2015, qz.com/488851/buying-organic-veggies-at-the-supermarket-is-basically-a-waste-of-money/, accessed February 25, 2018; Rob Waugh. "Organic Food Is Pretty Much a Waste of Money, According to Science," Metro News, October 17, 2016, metro.co.uk/2016/10/17/actually-organic-food-is-pretty-much-a-waste-of-money-according-to-science-6196186/, accessed February 25, 2018; Alyssa Fiorentino and Rheanna O'Neil Bellomo. "Confirmed: Paying Extra for Organic Is a Waste of Money," Delish, September 1, 2015, www.delish.com/food-news/a43717/organic-produce-waste-of-money/, accessed February 25, 2018.
13. Gregg Henriques, "The College Student Mental Health Crisis," *Psychology Today*, February 15, 2014, www.psychologytoday.com/blog/theory-knowledge/201402/the-college-student-mental-health-crisis, accessed March 9, 2018.

14. National Alliance on Mental Illness, www.nami.org, accessed March 9, 2018.

15. Centers for Disease Control and Prevention, "Leading Causes of Death Reports, 1981–2016," CDC, webappa.cdc.gov/sasweb/ncipc/leadcause.html, accessed March 9, 2018.

16. David J. Drum, Chris Brownson, Adryon Burton Denmark, and Shanna E. Smith, "New Data on the Nature of Suicidal Crises in College Students: Shifting the Paradigm," *Professional Psychology: Research and Practice* 40, no. 3 (2009): 213–222, doi: 10.1037/a0014465, accessed March 9, 2018.

17. QPR Institute, www.qprinstitute.com, accessed March 9, 2018.

18. National Association of Mental Illness, "Getting the Right Start: Student Guide to Mental Health," NAMI, www.nami.org/NAMI/media/NAMI-Media/Infographics/NAMI-Getting -the-Right-Start.pdf, accessed March 9, 2018.

19. Judy Dodge Cummings. *Self-Injury: The Ultimate Teen Guide* (Lanham, MD: Rowman & Littlefield, 2017).

20. Shannon E. Ross, Bradley C. Niebling, and Teresa M. Heckert, "Sources of Stress among College Students," *College Student Journal* 33, no. 2: 312. SPORTDiscus with Full Text, EBSCO host, accessed March 6, 2018.

21. Jennifer Acosta Scott, "College Life: 10 Ways to Reduce Stress," Everyday Health, updated March 17, 2010, www.everydayhealth.com/college-health/college-life-10-ways-to-reduce -stress.aspx, accessed March 6, 2018.

22. Melissa Cohen, "Surviving Stress and Anxiety in College & Beyond," Learn Psychology, www.learnpsychology.org/student-stress-anxiety-guide/, accessed March 6, 2018.

23. Scott, "College Life."

24. Lea Winerman, "By the Numbers: Stress on Campus," Monitor on Psychology, September 2017, www.apa.org/monitor/2017/09/numbers.aspx, accessed March 6, 2018.

25. David R. Reetz, Carolyn Bershad, Peter LeViness, and Monica Whitlock, *The Association for University and College Counseling Center Directors Annual Survey* (Richmond, VA: AUCCCD, 2017), www.aucccd.org/assets/documents/aucccd%202016%20monograph%20-%20pub lic.pdf, accessed March 6, 2018.

26. Diana Rodriguez, "How to Handle Panic Attacks," Everyday Health, updated June 2, 2009, www.everydayhealth.com/anxiety/how-to-handle-panic-attacks.aspx, accessed March 6, 2018.

27. "Depression and College Students," National Institute of Mental Health, www.nimh.nih .gov/health/publications/depression-and-college-students/index.shtml#footnote1back, accessed March 6, 2018.

28. Tina P. Schwartz, *Depression: The Ultimate Teen Guide* (Lanham, MD: Rowman & Littlefield, 2017).

29. Lola Kolade, "How to Deal with Homesickness Freshman Year," Her Campus, August 5, 2017, www.hercampus.com/high-school/how-deal-homesickness-freshman-year, accessed March 6, 2018; Kelci Lynn Lucier, "3 Ways for Parents to Support a Homesick College Student," *U.S. News and World Report*, September 21, 2011, www.usnews.com/education/blogs/ the-college-experience/2011/09/21/3-ways-for-parents-to-support-a-homesick-college-stu dent, accessed March 6, 2018.

Chapter 10

1. "The Real Value of College," Best Value Schools, https://www.bestvalueschools.com/real -value-college/, accessed March 11, 2018.

2. Marissa B. Esser, Heather Clayton, Zewditu Demissie, Dafna Kanny, and Robert D. Brewer, "Current and Binge Drinking Among High School Students—United States, 1991–2015," *MMWR: Morbidity & Mortality Weekly Report* 66, no. 18 (May 12, 2017): 474–478. CINAHL, EBSCOhost, accessed March 11, 2018.

3. Staff, "17% of US Adults Engage in Binge Drinking," LiveScience, January 10, 2012, www.livescience.com/17830-binge-drinking-adults-united-states.html, accessed February 25, 2018.

4. Lauren Cahoon Roberts, "9 Ways Going to College Affects Your Health," *LiveScience*, September 3, 2013, www.livescience.com/39366-how-college-affects-health.html, accessed February 25, 2018.

5. Rachael Rettner, "Why We Get Dumb Drunk," LiveScience, July 6, 2011, www.livescience.com/14927-dumb-drunk.html, accessed February 25, 2018.

6. Dafna Kanny, Robert D. Brewer, Jessica B. Mesnick, Leonard J. Paulozzi, Timothy S. Naimi, and Hua Lu. "Vital Signs: Alcohol Poisoning Deaths—United States, 2010–2012," *MMWR: Morbidity and Mortality Report* 63, no. 53 (January 9, 2015): 1238–1242. MEDLINE, EBSCOhost, accessed February 25, 2018.

7. Kanny et al., "Vital Signs."

8. Amanda Chan, "After the Buzz: Binge Drinking Linked with Learning Trouble," LiveScience, May 16, 2011, www.livescience.com/35691-binge-drinking-verbal-learning.html, accessed February 25, 2018.

9. Roberts, "9 Ways Going to College Affects Your Health."

10. Mark Theoharis, "Supplying Alcohol to Minors," NOLO, www.criminaldefenselawyer.com/resources/criminal-defense/crime-penalties/supplying-alcohol-minors-and-legal-penalties.htm, accessed February 25, 2018.

11. "Warning Signs of Alcoholism," Alcohol Rehab Guide, www.alcoholrehabguide.org/alcohol/warning-signs/, accessed February 25, 2018.

12. Josh Hafner, "Juuling Is a Trend Popular with Kids. What Does It Mean to Juul?" *USA Today*, February 19, 2018, www.usatoday.com/story/money/nation-now/2017/10/31/juul-e-cigs-controversial-vaping-device-popular-school-campuses/818325001/, accessed March 14, 2018.

13. Office on Smoking and Health, "Current Cigarette Smoking Among Adults in the United States," Centers for Disease Control and Prevention, www.cdc.gov/tobacco/data_statistics/fact_sheets/adult_data/cig_smoking/, accessed March 14, 2018.

14. Gabby Schwartz, "As Vaping Increases for College Students, Health Risks Don't Go Up in Smoke," *Daily Cardinal*, December 5, 2017, www.dailycardinal.com/article/2017/12/as-vaping-increases-for-college-students-health-risks-dont-go-up-in-smoke, accessed March 14, 2018.

15. Student Health, "Benefits of Quitting," Oregon State University, http://studenthealth.oregonstate.edu/did-you-know/dyk-quit-tobacco, accessed March 14, 2018.

16. Student Health, "Benefits of Quitting."

17. "Addiction to Adderall," Addiction Center, updated February 2, 2018, www.addictioncenter.com/stimulants/adderall/, accessed March 14, 2018.

18. "Marijuana Symptoms and Warning Signs," Addiction Center, updated September 12, 2017, www.addictioncenter.com/drugs/marijuana/symptoms-signs/, accessed March 14, 2018.

19. "Marijuana Symptoms and Warning Signs."

20. "Ecstasy Addiction and Abuse," Addiction Center, edited February 14, 2018, www.addictioncenter.com/drugs/ecstasy/, accessed March 14, 2018.

21. Integrated Treatment of Substance Abuse & Mental Illness, "Drugs Commonly Abused by College Students," Dual Diagnosis, www.dualdiagnosis.org/drug-addiction/college-drug-abuse/, accessed March 14, 2018.

22. Sheri Mabry Bestor, *Substance Abuse: The Ultimate Teen Guide* (Lanham, MD: Rowman & Littlefield, 2015).
23. Kate E. Lechner, Carolyn M. Garcia, Ellen A. Frerich, Katherine Lust, and Marla E. Eisenberg, "College Students' Sexual Health: Personal Responsibility or the Responsibility of the College?" *Journal of American College Health*, November 27, 2012, p. 28, doi.org/10.1080/07448481.2012.750608, accessed March 4, 2018.
24. Lechner et al., "College Students' Sexual Health," 28.
25. Lechner et al., "College Students' Sexual Health," 28.
26. Health Guides, "Making Healthy Sexual Decisions," Center for Young Women's Health, updated May 17, 2017, youngwomenshealth.org/2013/05/23/making-healthy-sexual-decisions/, accessed March 4, 2018.
27. Staff, "Starting the Conversation," American Sexual Health Association, www.ashasexualhealth.org/sexual-health/talking-about-sex/starting-the-conversation/, accessed March 4, 2018.
28. L. Kris Gowen, *Sexual Decisions: The Ultimate Teen Guide* (Lanham, MD: Rowman & Littlefield, 2017).
29. Bea Hanson, "National Campus Safety Awareness Month: Changing the Institutional Response to Change the Statistics," United States Department of Justice Archives, September 22, 2016, www.justice.gov/archives/ovw/blog/national-campus-safety-awareness-month-changing-institutional-response-change-statistics, accessed March 4, 2018.
30. Olivia Ghafoerkhan, *Sexual Assault: The Ultimate Teen Guide* (Lanham, MD: Rowman & Littlefield, 2016).
31. Staff, "What Are Eating Disorders?" National Eating Disorders Association, www.nationaleatingdisorders.org/what-are-eating-disorders, accessed February 25, 2018.
32. "Eating Disorders on the College Campus: A National Survey of Programs and Resources," National Eating Disorders Association, February 2013, www.nationaleatingdisorders.org/sites/default/files/CollegeSurvey/CollegiateSurveyProject.pdf, accessed February 25, 2018.
33. Jessica R. Greene, *Eating Disorders: The Ultimate Teen Guide* (Lanham, MD: Rowman & Littlefield, 2014).
34. Sara Goldrick-Rab, Jed Richardson, and Anthony Hernandez, *Hungry and Homeless in College: Results from a National Study of Basic Needs Insecurity in Higher Education* (Madison: Wisconsin Hope Lab, 2017), wihopelab.com/publications/hungry-and-homeless-in-college-report.pdf, accessed March 18, 2018.
35. Marilyn S. Townsend, Janet Peerson, Bradley Love, Cheryl Achterberg, and Suzanne P. Murphy, "Food Insecurity Is Positively Related to Overweight in Women," *Journal of Nutrition* 131, no. 6 (2001): 1738–1745.
36. James Dubick, Brandon Mathews, and Clare Cady, *Hunger on Campus: The Challenge of Food Insecurity for College Students.* Creative Commons, 2016, studentsagainsthunger.org/wp-content/uploads/2016/10/Hunger_On_Campus.pdf, accessed March 18, 2018.
37. Lexy Gross, "College Campuses See Rise in Homeless Students," *USA Today College*, October 21, 2013, www.usatoday.com/story/news/nation/2013/10/21/homeless-students-american-colleges/3144383/, accessed March 18, 2018.
38. Anthony Abraham Jack, "It's Hard to Be Hungry on Spring Break," *New York Times*, March 17, 2018, www.nytimes.com/2018/03/17/opinion/sunday/spring-break-colleges-poor-students.html, accessed March 18, 2018.
39. Dubick, Mathews, and Cady, *Hunger on Campus.*

a. Nate C. Hindman, "Condom Ambulance: New Service Delivers Rubbers to New Jersey College Co-Eds," *Huffington Post*, updated February 14, 2013, www.huffingtonpost.com/2012/12/06/condom-ambulance-service-_n_2250898.html, accessed March 11, 2018.

Chapter 11

1. "The Real Value of College," Best Value Schools, www.bestvalueschools.com/real-value-college/, accessed March 11, 2018.
2. Bernardo J. Carducci and Lisa Kaiser. *Shyness: The Ultimate Teen Guide* (Lanham, MD: Rowman & Littlefield, 2017.
3. Melanie Greenberg, "The Science of Love and Attachment," *Psychology Today*, March 30, 2016, www.psychologytoday.com/blog/the-mindful-self-express/201603/the-science-love-and-attachment, accessed March 18, 2018.
4. Maralee McKee, "Thank you Notes: When to Send a Handwritten One, When It's OK to Email or Text & When One's Not Required," Manners Mentor, www.mannersmentor.com/social-situations/savvy-thank-yous, accessed February 14, 2018.
5. "Social Media," Snelling, www.snelling.com/job_seekers-employment-opportunities/job-seeker-resources/social-media/, accessed March 21, 2018.
6. Jason Tomaszewski, "Tweets Get Student Expelled: A Cautionary Tale," Education World, 2012, www.educationworld.com/a_admin/tweets-get-student-expelled.shtml, accessed March 4, 2018.
7. Rob Price, "Billionaire ex-Facebook President Sean Parker Unloads on Mark Zuckerberg and Admits He Helped Build a Monster," *Business Insider*, November 9, 2017, www.businessinsider.com/ex-facebook-president-sean-parker-social-network-human-vulnerability-2017-11, accessed March 4, 2018.
8. Gail Hand, "10 Smart Social Media Tips for Students." CollegeXpress, www.collegexpress.com/articles-and-advice/student-life/articles/college-health-safety/10-smart-social-networking-tips-students/, accessed March 4, 2018.
9. Juan De La Cruz, "Social Media Impacts Students Socially, Academically," North Iowa Area Community College, www.niacc.edu/logoslite/2016/11/10/social-media-impacts-students-socially-academically/, accessed March 4, 2018.

a. Judy Gould, "What Happens When Three Young Men Find Out They're Triplets? It's Not as Simple as 1-2-3," *People*, October 13, 1980, people.com/archive/what-happens-when-three-young-men-find-out-theyre-triplets-its-not-as-simple-as-1-2-3-vol-14-no-15/, accessed March 11, 2018.

Chapter 12

1. "Budgeting for College Students," Wells Fargo, www.wellsfargo.com/goals-going-to-college/student-budget/, accessed January 22, 2018.
2. "The Hidden Costs of College," Affordable Schools, affordableschools.net/hidden-costs-college/, accessed January 22, 2018.

3. Stacy Rapacon, "More College Students Are Working While Studying," CNBC, October 29, 2015, www.cnbc.com/2015/10/29/more-college-students-are-working-while-studying.html, accessed January 22, 2018.

4. Staff, "Your Paycheck," Pay Check City, September 17, 2014, www.paycheckcity.com/pages/article.php?page=Paycheck-101, accessed January 22, 2018.

5. Karen Fischer, "The Employment Mismatch," *Chronicle of Higher Education*, March 4, 2013, www.chronicle.com/article/the-employment-mismatch/137625#id=overview, accessed January 22, 2018.

6. Sally Herships, "The Difference between a Paid and Unpaid Internship? A Job Later," Marketplace, May 20, 2013, www.marketplace.org/2013/05/30/business/difference-between -paid-and-unpaid-internship-job-later, accessed January 22, 2018.

7. Career Services, "Dressing for Interviews," Michigan State University, careernetwork.msu .edu/jobs-internships/appearance-and-attire/dressing-for-interviews.html, accessed January 15, 2018.

8. Lindsay Konsko, "Top Five Credit Card Tips for Students," *NerdWallet* (blog), January 18, 2014, www.nerdwallet.com/blog/credit-cards/top-credit-card-tips-students/, accessed January 17, 2018.

9. Rob Berger, "The Best Bank Accounts for College Students," *Forbes*, August 20, 2016, www.forbes.com/sites/robertberger/2016/08/20/the-best-bank-accounts-for-college -students/#538570f5267e, accessed January 22, 2018.

10. Gianna Sen-Gupta, "9 Tips for Students and Others Filing Taxes for the First Time," *NerdWallet* (blog), January 29, 2018, www.nerdwallet.com/blog/loans/student-loans/expert -advice-students-filing-taxes/, accessed February 13, 2019.

11. Andrew Josuweit, "4 Valuable Tax Breaks for College Students," *Forbes*, February 16, 2018, www.forbes.com/sites/andrewjosuweit/2017/02/16/4-valuable-tax-breaks-for-col lege-students/#529b3539281e, accessed January 29, 2018.

12. Kristen Kucher, "Tax Guide for College Students," The Simple Dollar, February 13, 2018, www.thesimpledollar.com/tax-guide-for-college-students/, accessed February 26, 2018.

Chapter 13

1. "College Sports (NCAA)—Statistics and Facts," Statistics Portal, www.statista.com/top ics/1436/college-sports-ncaa/, accessed February 28, 2018.

2. Sports Money, "College Football's Most Valuable Teams," *Forbes*, www.forbes.com/pictures/ emdm45el/1-university-of-texas-longhorns/#353066eb30ed, accessed February 2, 2018.

3. Sports Money, "College Basketball's Most Valuable Teams," *Forbes*, www.forbes.com/pic tures/emdm45efll/1-louisville-cardinals/#ad47e587f79e, accessed February 2, 2018.

4. Cork Gaines and Mike Nudelman, "The 2 Most Common College Sports Are Basketball and Cross Country," *Business Insider*, August 22, 2017, www.businessinsider.com/most-popular -college-sports-2017-8, accessed February 2, 2018.

5. Staff, "Best Colleges for Intramural Sports," Best Colleges, www.bestcolleges.com/features/ best-colleges-for-intramural-sports/, accessed February 2, 2018.

a. "Most Students in Sororities," *US News and World Report*, updated 2016, www.usnews.com/ best-colleges/rankings/most-sororities, accessed March 11, 2018,.

b. Diana B. Turk, *Bound by a Mighty Vow: Sisterhood and Women's Fraternities 1870–1920* (New York: NYU Press, 2004).

c. *Wikipedia*, s.v. "List of Stadiums by Capacity," updated March 3, 2018, en.wikipedia.org/wiki/List_of_stadiums_by_capacity, accessed March 11, 2018.

Chapter 14

1. Rita Landino, "Growth and Change through the College Years," Psych Central, 2016, psychcentral.com/lib/growth-and-change-through-the-college-years, accessed March 4, 2018.

2. Surviving College, "15 Moments When You Realize College Really Has Changed You," *USA Today College*, October 6, 2014, college.usatoday.com/2014/10/06/15-moments-when-you-realize-college-really-has-changed-you/, accessed March 4, 2018.

3. Jessica F. Harding, Pamela A. Morris, and Diane Hughes, "The Relationship between Maternal Education and Children's Academic Outcomes: A Theoretical Framework," *Journal of Marriage and Family*, January 14, 2015, DOI: 10.1111/jomf.12156, accessed March 5, 2018.

Resources for Teens

Carducci, Bernardo J., and Lisa Kaiser. *Shyness: The Ultimate Teen Guide.* Lanham, MD: Rowman & Littlefield, 2017.

Cummings, Judy Dodge. *Self-Injury: The Ultimate Teen Guide.* Lanham, MD: Rowman & Littlefield, 2017.

Ghafoerkhan, Olivia. *Sexual Assault: The Ultimate Teen Guide.* Lanham, MD: Rowman & Littlefield, 2016.

Gowen, L. Kris. *Sexual Decisions: The Ultimate Teen Guide.* Lanham, MD: Rowman & Littlefield, 2017.

Greene, Jessica R. *Eating Disorders: The Ultimate Teen Guide.* Lanham, MD: Rowman & Littlefield, 2014.

Karabel, Jerome. *The Chosen: The Hidden History of Admission and Exclusion at Harvard, Yale, and Princeton.* New York: Houghton Mifflin, 2005.

Mabry Bestor, Sheri. *Substance Abuse: The Ultimate Teen Guide.* Lanham, MD: Rowman & Littlefield, 2015.

Schwartz, Tina P. *Depression: The Ultimate Teen Guide.* Lanham, MD: Rowman & Littlefield, 2017.

Wissner-Gore, Elizabeth. *What Colleges Don't Tell You (and Other Parents Won't Tell You).* New York: Hudson Street Press, 2006.

Index

Note: Page references for figures are italicized.

academic integrity, 59, 77–78; honor code, 77; plagiarism, 77–78
academic year. *See* academics
academics: academic year, 50, 91; credit hour, 9, 49, 55–59, 64–65, 67, 70, 74, 76, 91–92, 178; dropping a class, 65–67; general education class (gen ed), 6, 9–10, 15–17, 51, 53, 55, 57–58, 69, 108; hybrid class, 64–65; online education, 63–65; quarter, 50, 57, 104; registration, 38, 50–55, 58–59, 65–66, 74, 79, 146; semester, 46, 49–50, 56–57, 66, 70, 75, 85, 177–78; summer school, 50, 76; term (academic), 30, 50–51, 54, 57–58, 65–69, *74*, 76, 79, 83, 91, 108, 133–34, 152, 171; trimester, 50, 57
admission, *21*, 23, 25, 33–34, 38–39, 58, 87
advisor: academic,16, 18, 36, 50–55, 86, 108, 125, 134; faculty, 173; financial aid, 31, 104
alcohol, 12, 46, 95, 103, 106, 109–12, 114–16, 118–19, 130, 132, 166
art school. *See* specialty college
arts, participation in. *See* extracurricular activities
athletics. *See* extracurricular activities
attendance, 14, 43, 52–53, 59–60, 147–51

bank account. *See* finances

campus visit, 23–26, 33, 37, 53
career school. *See* vocational college
career services, 16–18, 108, 154–59

certificate, xiii, 7, 54
club. *See* extracurricular activities
communication: cover letter, 16, 152, 154–59; résumé, 11, 16, 21, 150–59, 172; thank-you note, 21, *25*, 136–37, *159*
community college, xiii, 5, 9, 50, *128*
counseling, 38, 45, 103–4, 107; career, 16, 20–21; therapy, 100, 104, 107, *121*, 123, 125
counselor. *See* counseling
cover letter. *See* communication
credit card. *See* finances
credit hour. *See* academics

dating, 48, 94, 128–30, 169
deferment, 38–39, 57, 142
depression, ix, 100–107, 114–17, 122, 128
disability services. *See* student support services
dormitory. *See* housing
dropping a class. *See* academics
drug use, 103, 106, 111–12, 114–16, 118, 120, 132

eating disorder, 95, 100–105, 114, 120–24
endorsement, 14, 54–55
exercise, 95, 99–100, 103, 106 122–23, 145
extracurricular activities, 15, 18–19, 23, 33–35, 54, 93, 153, 169–79; arts, participation in, 173, 176; athletics, 21, 142, 174–75; club, 87, 93, 119, 153, 169, 173; fraternity, 169–173; honor

society, 16, 67, 87, 171–73; intramural sport, 99, 175–76; sorority, 169–73

FAFSA. *See* financial aid
federal student aid (FSA). *See* financial aid
fees, 18, 20, 24, 35, 43, 61, 65, 68, 79, 141–42, 161, 163–64, 172–73
FERPA, 38, 52–53
finances, 34, 38, 43–44, 55, 131, 141–67, 178; bank account, 44, 163–64; credit card, 141–42, 160–64; paycheck, 141, 148–52; personal budget, 18, 43, 71, 141–44; taxes, 14, 28–29, 32, 148–52, 164–67; tipping, 166–67
financial aid, xiii, 23–24, 27–32, 35, 39, 44, 49–50, 52, 57, 65, 76, *88*, 152, 178; FAFSA, 28–32, 124, 152; federal student aid (FSA), 28–30, 39, 152; student aid report (SAR), 30
food insecurity, 93, 123–24
fraternity. *See* extracurricular activities

gap year. *See* deferment
general education classes (gen ed). *See* academics
graduation map, 16, 54

homesickness, 108, 178–79
honor code. *See* academic integrity
honor society. *See* extracurricular activities
housing, 4, 9, 14, 34–38, 43–48, 132, 142; dormitory, 24, 43–45, 79, *97*, 104, 124, 129, 142, 145; roommate, 38, 44–46, 104, 131–32, 145, 155
hybrid class. *See* academics

identification card (IDs), 79, 146
Instant Decision (ID) Day, 25
internship. *See* job
interview. *See* job
intramural sport. *See* extracurricular activities

job, 147–48; internship, 16, 23, 150–51, 172; interview, 16, 154–59; work study, 28, 148, 150–53
junior college. *See* community college

laundry, 43, 48
liberal arts, 4, 9–11, 57
loneliness. *See* homesickness

major: changing, *15*, 16–18, 35, 51, 54, 67, 107–8; declaring, 15–18, 50–51, 53–54, 172

National Decision Day, 26, 33–34, 36
note taking, 37, 60, 63, 71–73

on-campus housing. *See* housing
online education. *See* academics
organization, 63, 72–76, 105, 153, 156
orientation days, 36–38, 46, 52

panic attack, 102, 105–6, 115
paycheck. *See* finances
personal budget. *See* finances
plagiarism. *See* academic integrity

quarter. *See* academics

recommendation letters, 20–21, 134, 151
recruitment, 24, 87
registration. *See* academics
religious school. *See* specialty college
resident assistant (RA), 38, 43, 45, 100, 104, 107, 132
résumé. *See* communication
roommate. *See* housing

safety, *9*, 61, 78–79, 105, 109–10, 113, 119–21, 130, 139
same-sex school. *See* specialty college
schedule, 25, 39, 50–51, 53–54, 56, 58, 60, 64–65, 69–71, 74–75, 91–93, 95, 99, 137, 147–48
semester. *See* academics

sexual decisions, 104, 110, 117–20, 130–31, 181

smoking, 112–13, 131, 155

social media, 128, 132, 137–40, *150*

sorority. *See* extracurricular activities

specialized-mission school. *See* specialty college

specialty college, 11–12; arts school, 12; religious school, 11–12; same-sex school, 12; specialized-mission school, 12

stress, 93, 95, 99–106, 111, 114, 121, 127, 176–77, 179

student aid report (SAR). *See* financial aid

student support services, 62–63; disability support, 159; tutoring, 45, 59–63, 76, 104, 152–53

study abroad, 177–78

studying, 54, 60–63, 67, 71–73, 94–95, 100, *103*, 114–15, 131, 140

suicide, 100–101, 106–7

summer school. *See* academics

syllabus, 58–60, 75, 85–86, 132–34, 147

taxes. *See* finances

teaching assistant (TA), 10, 55, 63, 82

technical college. *See* vocational college

term, academic. *See* academics

textbook, 38, 67–71, 73, 75

thank-you note. *See* communication

therapy. *See* counseling

tipping. *See* finances

trade school. *See* vocational college

transcript. *See* academics

trimester. *See* academics

tuition, 7, 9, 14, 24, 27–28, 32, 35, 43, 49, 65–66, 68, 76, 141–42, 152, 165

tutoring. *See* student support services

two-year college. *See* community college

US Department of Education, 28, *88*

vocational college, xiii, 6–9

wait-list, 34

work study. *See* job

About the Author

Lisa Maxwell Arter is an assistant professor of English and the coordinator of the English Education program at Southern Utah University in Cedar City, Utah. Her research interests include children's and young adult literature, gender studies, literacy advocacy, preservice teacher preparation, and historical nonfiction K–12 integration.

Before Southern Utah University, Dr. Arter taught at Arizona State University, where she earned her PhD in Curriculum and Instruction: English Education. She chose to focus on preservice teacher education after teaching English and literacy intervention for seven years in a Title 1 middle school. Dr. Arter has worked as a K–12 teacher, coach, literacy trainer, and peer mentor. She has taught a range of composition, literature, and education courses at the undergraduate and graduate levels.

A lifetime member of both the History Channel Club and Sarcastics Anonymous (motto: Like We Need Your Support), Dr. Arter prefers reading to writing, cake decorating to cleaning, crocheting to knitting, and the Tenth Doctor to all others. If she weren't a teacher, she would like to have her own talk show (which, let's face it, is quite a lot like teaching). An avid Pinner, she finds clowns terrifying and likes the sound of fingernails on a chalkboard. Her favorite form of exercise is jumping to conclusions. If she could live inside of anyone's head for a month, it would be Terry Pratchett.

She lives in Cedar City, Utah, with her husband, children, and dogs.